King Arthur's Death

The Middle English
Stanzaic Morte Arthur
and
Alliterative Morte Arthure

The Middle English Texts Series is designed for classroom use. Its goal is to make available to teachers and students texts which occupy an important place in the literary and cultural canon but which have not been readily available in student editions. The series does not include those authors such as Chaucer, Langland, or Malory, whose English works are normally in print in good student editions. The focus is, instead, upon Middle English literature adjacent to those authors that teachers need in compiling the syllabuses they wish to teach. The editions maintain the linguistic integrity of the original work but within the parameters of modern reading conventions. The texts are printed in the modern alphabet and follow the practices of modern capitalization and punctuation. Manuscript abbreviations are expanded, and *u/v* and *j/i* spellings are regularized according to modern orthography. Hard words, difficult phrases, and unusual idioms are glossed on the page, either in the right margin or at the foot of the page. Textual notes appear at the end of the text, along with a glossary. The editions include short introductions on the history of the work, its merits and points of topical interest, and also include briefly annotated bibliographies.

King Arthur's Death

The Middle English
Stanzaic Morte Arthur
and
Alliterative Morte Arthure

Edited by
Larry D. Benson

Revised by
Edward E. Foster

Published for TEAMS
(The Consortium for the Teaching of the Middle Ages)
in Association with the University of Rochester

by

Medieval Institute Publications

WESTERN MICHIGAN UNIVERSITY

Kalamazoo, Michigan — 1994

Original edition © 1974 by the Bobbs-Merrill Company, Inc.

Library of Congress Cataloging-in-Publication Data

King Arthur's death : stanzaic Morte Arthur and alliterative Morte
   Arthure / edited by Larry D. Benson ; revised by Edward E. Foster. -
- Rev. ed.
     p. cm. -- (Middle English texts)
  Includes bibliographical references (p.).
  ISBN 1-879288-38-9
  1. Arthurian romances. 2. Romances, English. I. Benson, Larry
Dean, 1929- . II. Foster, Edward E. III. Morte Arthur. 1994.
IV. Morte Arthure. 1994. V. Series: Middle English texts
(Kalamazoo, Mich.)
PR2064.B4   1994
821'.108--dc20   94-26544
                                           CIP

ISBN 1-879288-38-9

Revised edition © 1994 by the Board of The Medieval Institute
Second Printing 1996
Third Printing 2000
Fourth Printing 2002
Fifth Printing 2005

Printed in the United States of America

Cover design by Elizabeth King

Contents

Preface to the Revised Edition

This volume differs substantially in editorial practice from other volumes in the TEAMS Series, because it is a revision of Larry D. Benson's *King Arthur's Death* (Indianapolis: Bobbs-Merrill, 1974) in the Library of Literature Series. Professor Benson goes further in regularization of spellings and forms than is characteristic of TEAMS editions. I have retained most features of his system, especially since the texts he established are highly readable and authentic in all material respects. The one oddity, which Benson notes, is that the texts may appear more "Midlands" than the manuscripts are, but the manuscript history is such that the matter of dialectal variation is problematic anyway.

Benson's edition incorporates many corrections from earlier editors without comment. I have followed his example since to be more detailed in attribution would be more of a distraction than an aid to readers. Thus, many obvious errors in the manuscripts are silently corrected. The "alliterative scribe," Robert Thornton, was particularly given to dittography, the accidental repetition of a letter or letters. The manuscript of the stanzaic poem, though freer of obvious errors, has many corrections within it which Benson and I have both accepted without tedious notation.

In the stanzaic poem, Benson has made nine changes from Bruce's edition (EETS e.s. 88), which is the basis for his text; I have accepted all of them and have so indicated in notes. The situation with the alliterative poem is more complex. Here Benson made many emendations based both on earlier commentators and on his own judgment. Where I have accepted Benson's changes, I have indicated my reliance on Benson, his sources, and subsequent editors such as Valerie Krishna (1976) and Mary Hamel (1984). Where I have disagreed, I have cited the sources of my readings.

I have also rearranged marginal glosses and foot-glosses to fit the TEAMS format and I have added and modified glossarial material as I saw fit. For example, Benson has generally glossed unfamiliar but frequently used words for their first five appearances; I have continued to gloss words when I thought it useful for the reader, especially in the case of words like *bydene* and *dight*, which have many shadings of meaning. In general, I have glossed more liberally to avoid, where possible, the necessity of distracting reliance on the Glossary. Suffice it to say that, despite my noble explanatory intentions, any confusions introduced are my responsibility.

Most of Benson's textual and explanatory notes have been reproduced largely verbatim. Many new or radically revised notes have also been added by myself and the editorial board at the University of Rochester, often with reference to the excellent notes in the recent editions by Krishna (K) and Hamel (H). Finally, I have updated the Bibliography and simplified the Glossary, mostly by removing etymological information.

Benson's Introduction has been retained and his section on Versification and Style has been incorporated into the Introduction. More recent commentaries, cited in the revised Bibliography, have not impaired the appropriateness of Benson's observations. I have made only minor editorial changes to the Preface and Introduction, and brought the bibliographical references up to date. I have omitted Benson's extensive sections on Pronunciation and Grammar and on Vocabulary. In general, I have tried to preserve the integrity of Benson's edition while including some more recent editorial judgments and exercising my own discretion about what might or might not be helpful to the reader. That is, after all, what is most important: to make these works, two of the finest poems of the fourteenth century, available and accessible to readers without attenuating their linguistic integrity.

I would like to thank Professor Benson for his willingness to have his edition tampered with, and for his permission to reprint in this revision some portions of the original volume. I would like to thank Matt Melendy and Greg Matthews, students of mine who patiently explained to me what was hard and what was not in these poems. I would also like to thank Cynthia Schelmerdine (Classicist), Walter Broman (Medievalist), and Jan Foster (wife and smart person) for their vision, literally and figuratively, in discovering errors and insufficiencies. And, finally, thanks to Alan Lupack, Russell Peck, Karen Saupe, and Tom Seiler, of the TEAMS project, for their assistance with the formatting, glossing, and annotating of this edition.

The Consortium for the Teaching of the Middle Ages is grateful to the National Endowment for the Humanities for its continued support of the Middle English Texts Series.

Whitman College   Edward E. Foster

Preface

The texts in this volume have been edited for readers who have had little or no training in Middle English. The two romances in this volume have never been easily accessible to students who are not specializing in Middle English. The *Stanzaic Morte Arthur*, linguistically a relatively easy work, is available only in a diplomatic scholarly edition that presents formidable difficulties to the beginning student or casual reader. The *Alliterative Morte Arthure*, a more difficult poem, is available only in scholarly editions that make so difficult a work almost impossible reading for all but advanced students. Yet these two romances are among the finest of our English medieval narrative poems; they deserve a wider readership simply for what they are, first-rate works of art. They are furthermore essential reading for the student of Malory, for the student of the Arthurian legend in England, and even for the reader who only wants a better understanding of medieval English narrative in the later Middle Ages.

The variety of Middle English in which these poems were written is not as difficult as may at first appear, and most of the initial difficulty is due to the reader's lack of familiarity with a relatively small number of words and a few syntactic peculiarities. The texts in this volume have been edited so that a beginning student can read them independently. The marginal glosses are designed to help with vocabulary, and the notes should clear up any syntactic difficulties. The student who reads these works with care should learn a good portion of the basic vocabulary necessary for further reading in Middle English texts. Consequently, when used as a first text in classes in Middle English, these poems can provide the student with an extensive body of Middle English, valuable in itself and intelligible even before beginning formal study of the language.

The texts of this volume have not been "simplified" in any significant way. The language itself remains about the same as it is in the manuscripts. However, the spelling has been regularized (in somewhat the same way editors of Chaucer have regularized his spelling), and this makes them much easier to read. Middle English itself is not very difficult, but Middle English spelling is nearly impossible, especially in texts such as these, which are both preserved in unique manuscripts well removed in time and place from their original authors. The *Stanzaic Morte Arthur* survives in a manuscript (British Museum MS Harley 2252) produced in the late fifteenth century by two different scribes who wrote in two different dialects, neither of which was that of the author, who apparently composed his work about a century before. The *Alliterative Morte Arthure* survives in a manuscript (Lincoln Cathedral MS

ix

Thornton A 1, 17, now called Lincoln Cathedral MS 91) that was written about 1440 by Robert Thornton; his copy was evidently a West Midlands text, though there is reason to believe our poem was written in the East Midlands.

It is no wonder that the language of the manuscripts is confused; each shows traces of at least two different dialects along with all the other difficulties that necessarily creep into vernacular texts in the process of transmission (the Winchester Manuscript of Malory's work, for example, shows that a number of lines were missing from Thornton's exemplar). Thus far, both poems have been edited only in more or less diplomatic editions that faithfully reproduce the confusion of the scribes, though Krishna, conservatively, and Hamel, more liberally, note the confusions and obvious errors. Such texts are essential for the advanced student, who must know and study the manuscript's representation of the language (and the editions in this volume are not intended as substitutes for such texts). However, for the beginning reader, and often even for the relatively advanced student, a faithful representation of the manuscript forms is frequently a misrepresentation of the language itself. Every teacher of Middle English is painfully aware of what happens when students are necessarily taught to pronounce what they see on the page and then inevitably do pronounce what they see, thus producing a strange and wildly varying language that has only a remote connection with Middle English. Long study and much practice are necessary before a student can easily distinguish between significant and insignificant spelling variations or can tell when a later scribe has foisted a fifteenth-century sound change off on a fourteenth-century poet.

In general, I have tried to use one spelling for each form, with the spellings selected on the basis of their existence in the manuscripts, their ease of recognition for a modern reader, and their faithfulness in representing the sound probably used by, or at least understandable to, the author. In few cases have all three criteria been met; where I have had to make a choice among the three, I have chosen ease in recognition, preferring a small error in sound or a slight deviation from the form the author may have used to a major difficulty in understanding. This has resulted in giving both texts a slightly more Midlands cast than they may have originally had.

I have regularized the plural pronoun forms in the *Stanzaic Morte Arthur*, but beyond that I have not changed the grammatical forms (retaining both the *-eth* and *-es* endings of the third person present tense of the verbs), since many of these variations probably represent competing forms rather than a confused dialect. I have chosen the spellings *shall* and *sholde* rather than *sal* and *suld* (the more numerous forms in the *Alliterative Morte Arthure*); I have usually preferred *o* to *a* in forms like *bold/bald*; I have used the modern spellings in most cases of variation of short vowels before *r*, such as *world/werld*, and in most cases of variation of short *e* and short *i* and short *u* and short *i*, and I have used the more modern forms in regularizing un-

x

stressed vowels (choosing *e* instead of *i* in inflectional endings and preferring *be-* to *bi-* in forms like *before/bifore*. I have generally used *-dg*, *-tch*, and *sh-* instead of the manuscript's *-gg-*, *-ch*, and *sch-*. The one case in which I have usually adopted a more archaic form is short French *a* plus an *n*, adopting the more common Modern English spelling of words like *giaunt* instead of the modern spelling *giant*. I have not aimed at complete consistency, since phonemes as well as grammatical forms were probably in competition. So were words; as the alliterations show, *Gawain* and *Wawain* were both acceptable forms of that knight's name, and so both forms have been retained. The idea is to produce a reasonably regular but not thoroughly anesthetized text.

Although the regularized spellings are intended as a guide to the pronunciation of these texts, I have not tried to use a phonemic alphabet of any sort, and in these texts, as in Modern English, the same sound may be represented in a variety of ways. I have retained five different spellings of /i/ and six different spellings of /e/. This obviously creates some initial difficulties in learning the correct pronunciation, a problem that would have been eliminated by a more purely phonemic alphabet, but I believe that these initial difficulties are more than compensated for by the ease in recognition this spelling allows and by the better preparation it provides for the student who intends to move from these texts to unregularized editions.

The occasional explanatory notes have been purposely kept to the minimum necessary for understanding the text, and the introduction has been kept as brief as possible. My hope is that the student will concentrate full attention on the texts themselves and thereby be led to further study.

The edition of the *Stanzaic Morte Arthur* is based mainly on Bruce's text (see Bibliography for this and other editions mentioned below), which was read against a microfilm of the manuscript. I have made a very few minor emendations (indicated in the Textual Notes). The edition of the *Alliterative Morte Arthure* is based mainly on Brock's text, which was also read against a microfilm of the manuscript. I have made a good many emendations (the most important are listed in the Textual Notes), and aside from the regularizing, which in both poems often involves new readings of the lines. The Textual Notes are very brief and, except for the important textual changes that they record, I have not been able to include a full discussion of the solutions I have adopted in the establishment and interpretation of the text. I hope it will be understood that I have omitted this information not out of any disrespect for the previous editors, including those whose work I have used to establish the readings, but because the considerable editorial apparatus this would require would have been out of place in an edition of this sort.

Several conjectured lines have been added to the *Alliterative Morte Arthure* and one to the stanzaic poem; they are indicated by brackets and are not counted in the numbering of lines.

King Arthur's Death

I owe thanks to Gavin R. Benson, who worked hard on the mimeographed trial texts on which this volume is based; to Cassandra Benson, who also helped on that job; to Dr. Edward Tucker, who supplied helpful suggestions about the first of the trial editions; to the members of my Middle English class at Arizona State University at Tempe during the summer of 1970, who put up with the first trial edition; and to the members of English 2100 at Harvard during the spring term of 1971, who supplied valuable suggestions about the second. Fee Whitehall labored above and beyond the ordinary call of editorial duty, and her sharp eye saved these texts from many more errors and inconsistencies than they now contain.

Lexington, Mass.   L. D. B.
1972

Introduction

The romances in this volume are two of the best and most important of our surviving Middle English romances. Each deals with the last years and death of King Arthur, and yet in tone, style, characterization, and especially in plot the two poems are sharply contrasting works. They reveal two quite different aspects of the medieval Arthurian legend, and they exemplify the best of two distinct romance traditions.

The *Alliterative Morte Arthure* ranks just after the works of the *Gawain*-poet among the finest products of that late medieval literary movement that we call the "Alliterative Revival." It lacks the delicacy and balance of *Sir Gawain and the Green Knight*, but the vigor of its narrative, the epic sweep of its action, and its coolly realistic presentation of fourteenth-century warfare lend the poem an interest of its own. The King Arthur of this poem is neither the "somewhat childish" romance king who appears in *Sir Gawain* nor the helpless cuckold he so often seems in French romance. He is a warrior king, shifting his troops about, sending out skirmishers, and ever ready to do battle himself.

This is primarily a poem of battles, and there are no better accounts of late medieval warfare than we find in this poem. Nor are there any more sobering reminders that all was not heroic and romantic in this age. The poet's account of the siege of Metz (lines 3032–43), with his description of the results of a medieval bombardment (from slings and catapults), reminds us all too sharply of more recent horrors. Yet our poet is finally more interested in the fates of men than of armies, and he has a keen eye for psychological facts. His description of Mordred's momentary repentance (lines 3886–96) is a marvelous touch, unprecedented in Arthurian tradition (in which Mordred is never treated with such sympathetic understanding) and worthy of a place alongside some of the best passages in Chaucer. Each reader will find his own favorite passages, for the *Alliterative Morte Arthure* well deserves the high reputation it has among specialists, who, because of the difficulties of the text, have thus far constituted almost its only modern audience.

The *Stanzaic Morte Arthur* is a very different narrative. It is a brilliant condensation of the French prose romance (*La Mort Artu*) which, along with the *Stanzaic Morte Arthur* itself, was the source of Malory's last two tales, "The Book of Sir Launcelot and Queen Guinevere" and "The Most Piteous Tale of the Morte Arthur." Writing a century before Sir Thomas Malory completed his own *Morte Darthur*, the unknown English romancer achieved many of the virtues that we associate

1

with Malory's later work and produced a relatively tight and fast-moving narrative. The French *Mort Artu* is a leisurely and complex narrative, characterized by an elaborate network of episodes and by a full treatment of the psychological and philosophical implications of the action. The author of the *Stanzaic Morte Arthur*, like most English romancers of his time, was less interested in psychological abstractions. He reduced the material he inherited from the French to about a fifth of its original length, producing a work that succeeds because of its lean and rapid narrative and that gains force because of its more obvious focus upon the actions themselves. Yet the author does not omit completely the psychologizing that characterized his French source. As any reader of Chaucer knows, the literature of the later fourteenth century, marked by a new interest in individual feelings, is often (as in The Second Nun's Tale or even parts of *Troilus*) what we might now call a sentimental literature ("Pitee runneth soon in gentle heart" is one of Chaucer's favorite sayings). Tears flow freely in this romance (as they do in the *Alliterative Morte Arthure*), but the compression of the narrative prevents the sentiment from becoming excessive. The poet's interest in the feelings of his characters humanizes them, just as his omission of the philosophical interest in Fortune, so important in the French, focuses the tragedy upon the real people caught in a real web of tragic circumstances.

Although these two romances deserve wider audiences primarily because of their literary value, they are also of great importance from the standpoint of literary history, because of the traditions they represent and because of their later influence. Most readers of English literature know the Arthurian legend only from the work (or works) of Sir Thomas Malory. Malory's great synthesis of earlier romances shaped the Arthurian legend for later English writers — for Spenser, for Milton, for Tennyson, for Mark Twain, for writers and readers of our own day; Malory's genius was such that almost all subsequent English treatments of Arthurian themes have been based on his work.

However, there was an English Arthurian tradition before Malory, and the two romances in this volume provide the best introduction to this tradition. One should say "traditions," for these two romances embody two distinct versions of the life and death of King Arthur. The *Alliterative Morte Arthure* is in the tradition of sober chronicle history, which stems ultimately from Geoffrey of Monmouth's twelfth-century *History of the Kings of Britain*. Our poet, of course, used other sources as well, but his fondness for precise dates, his use of real place names, and his comparative lack of interest in the supernatural lend his poem the air of chronicle rather than romance. So does his lack of interest in matters of love and courtly manners. Honor is more important than courtesy in his poem; Gawain is a great warrior, not a famous courtier, and Lancelot is only a young and fierce knight, with no hint of

2

interest in Guenevere (or Waynor, as she is called in this poem). Guenevere's desertion of Arthur seems more a political than an amatory act, and Arthur is infuriated rather than heartbroken at her betrayal.

The *Stanzaic Morte Arthur* represents a different tradition, more familiar to modern readers, one in which the emphasis is more romantic than historical. Arthur is the lord of the fictional Camelot (a place never mentioned in the alliterative poem), and his most important campaign is in Lancelot's legendary kingdom of Benwick rather than at Metz or Milan. When he goes to the Isle of Avalon, it is not because there are skilled surgeons there who try and fail to cure his wounds, as in the alliterative poem, but because the three strange ladies come to take him away in a magic boat. One can detect the skeleton of the historical tradition embedded in the plot of the *Stanzaic Morte Arthur*: while Arthur is engaged in a foreign war, Mordred, his steward, usurps his kingdom; Arthur returns, and in a final battle he and the traitor are both killed. This is the basic plot of both the stanzaic and alliterative poems. What the alliterative poet adds expands but does not essentially change the action. In the stanzaic poem, the tale of the love of Lancelot and Guenevere has been superimposed on the basic plot. The focus is shifted to the clash of loyalties and internal divisions within the Round Table itself; the significant foreign war is now that between Arthur's forces and Lancelot's, and Arthur's death is now due as much to the feud between Lancelot and Gawain as it is to Mordred's rebellion. Mordred is changed from the principal (and largely unmotivated) villain to simply one more element in the complex circumstances in which all the characters are trapped.

Sir Thomas Malory must have read a good many English romances before he turned to the French prose romances that were his main sources for the *Morte Darthur*. However, the only two English romances we can be sure he read are the two romances in this volume. Apparently Malory's first attempt to write an Arthurian romance of his own was what is now the second tale in the *Morte Darthur*, the "Tale of Arthur and the Emperor Lucius." This is a straightforward modernization, with relatively few changes, of the first half of the *Alliterative Morte Arthure*. As Vinaver has shown (in the introduction to his edition of Malory), Malory's adaptation of the alliterative poem had a profound influence on his style, and though he next turned to French sources, his experience with the alliterative rhythms of this romance is apparent throughout his later work.

The last romances Malory wrote were the last two tales in the *Morte Darthur*, "The Book of Sir Launcelot and Queen Guinevere" and "The Most Piteous Tale of the Morte Arthur." Though his principal source for these tales was the French *Mort Artu*, Malory again turned to English romance and drew on the *Stanzaic Morte Arthur*. When the English and French versions differed, he almost always preferred

3

the English version, and occasionally he carried over into his own work the exact wording of the stanzaic romance. Probably the influence of the stanzaic poem is even deeper than this, since Malory's handling of his other French sources — the way in which he condensed and modified the plots — shows that he seems to have been following the example of the *Stanzaic Morte Arthur.*

We cannot be sure exactly where or when the two romances in this volume were composed. Probably both were written in the North Midlands area of England in the fourteenth century, the *Stanzaic Morte Arthur* around the middle of the century, the *Alliterative Morte Arthure* toward the end, probably around 1400 or so (see note to line 3773). These, however, can be only guesses. All we can say for sure is that the unknown authors produced works of exceptional merit that have a unique importance for English literary history.

The two romances in this volume represent two distinct stylistic traditions. The *Alliterative Morte Arthure* belongs to the "Alliterative Revival," the literary movement that begins in the middle years of the fourteenth century and that includes such important writers as William Langland and the author of *Gawain and the Green Knight.* The *Stanzaic Morte Arthur* is written in the more common eight-syllable, four-beat line of English romance, a line that derives ultimately from French models. Despite its foreign source, this is a simpler, more popular style than that of the alliterative romance, and the author of the *Stanzaic Morte Arthur* probably intended his work for a somewhat wider and less sophisticated audience than the alliterative poet aimed for.

However, the author of the *Stanzaic Morte Arthur* selected an unusual and rather difficult stanza for his poem. It is an eight-line stanza riming *abababab.* There are variations from this, as there are from his normal eight-syllable line (the first stanza rimes *ababcbcb* and variant stanzas, such as lines 361–67, do appear), but in general the poet adheres to this rime scheme, which requires two sets of four riming words for each full stanza. Such a stanza is easy enough for a lyric poet to handle (and it appears in a number of relatively short Middle English poems) but it raises real difficulties in a long narrative poem, and it is not surprising that no other romancer attempted to use it.

Our poet was able to use it successfully because he adopted a number of traditional devices that eased his task of handling this stanza. He uses a relatively limited set of stock rimes, some of them several times over. *Launcelot du Lake,* for example, almost always rimes with *sake, take, make,* or *wake.* The relatively rare word *neven* ("to name") almost invariably rimes with *heven, steven* ("voice"), and *seven.* In addition to stock rimes such as these, the poet frequently uses imperfect rimes. In lines 528–35, for example, the word *life* rimes with *swithe, kithe,* and *blithe.* This is not due to carelessness, for the same group of rimes appears several

4

times in the poem. Nor does it seem to be due simply to including assonance within his definition of rime, since he also frequently rimes vowel sounds that are not exactly the same; he makes no clear distinction between open and closed vowel sounds and he is willing to rime words such as *dere* and *were*, as in the opening lines of the poem.

Such a use of rime has a definite advantage, not only for the poet but for the reader, since it helps to de-emphasize the rimes and to keep them from intruding too often upon the consciousness of the audience. As the reader will discover, the rimes remain well in the background and do not impede the narrative. That is not always the case in Middle English romance.

The sound texture of the *Stanzaic Morte Arthur* owes almost as much to alliteration as to rime. The earliest modern critic of this poem, the eighteenth-century bibliographer Humphrey Wanley, wrote that our poet "useth many Saxon or obsolete words, and very often delighted himself (as did the author of 'Piers Plowman') in the Chime of words beginning with the same letter as (that I may give one example) 'For well thee wist withouten ween.'" Examples of this delight in the chime of alliteration can be found in almost every stanza in the poem, beginning with the opening lines:

> *L*ordinges that are *l*ef and dere
> *L*isteneth, and I shall you tell. . . .

This fondness for alliteration and the frequent use of alliterative formulas (such as *wo and wele*) is not unusual among the authors of the riming romances, but the man who wrote the *Stanzaic Morte Arthur* seems particularly fond of the alliterative style, and one suspects that he could have cast his poem in the alliterative meter if he had so chosen.

In purely alliterative poems, such as the *Alliterative Morte Arthure*, there is no rime at the ends of the lines. Instead, each line falls into two half-lines which are united by alliteration — the identity (or near identity) of the initial sound of stressed syllables. In the first half-line most often two, but sometimes three, words will alliterate. In the second half-line usually only one word will alliterate. The alliteration always falls on a word that bears metrical stress; there are two (sometimes three) stressed words in the first half-line, and two (almost never three) in the second half-line. The number of unstressed syllables can vary considerably:

> Now *g*rete *g*lorious *G*od   through *g*race of Himselven
> And the *p*recious *p*rayer   of His *p*ris Moder
> *Sh*eld us fro *sh*amesdeede   and *s*inful workes,
> And *g*ive us *g*race to *g*uie   and *g*overn us here

> In this *w*retched *w*orld, through *v*irtuous living
> That we may *k*aire til his *c*ourt, the *k*ingdom of heven. . . . (lines 1–6)

The reader need not worry too much about the metrical pattern; if one reads the lines aloud deliberately (but not too slowly) with slight pauses at the ends of the half-lines and with attention to the sense, the stresses will fall where they should.

As shown by the lines above, the poet can take certain liberties with the alliterating sounds. *Sh-* can sometimes alliterate with *s-* and *w-* with *v-* (though these sounds may have been closer to one another than in Modern English). Moreover, it is a convention of this verse that any vowel sound can alliterate with any other vowel sound:

> Ye that *l*ust has to *l*ithe or *l*oves for to here
> Of *e*lders of *o*lde time and of their *a*wke deedes. . . . (lines 12–13)

Notice that only the important words (nouns, adjectives, verbs, and adverbs) bear the alliteration. The word "of" in the second line has no part in the alliterative scheme. Words like "of" (or "to" in the first line above) are not ordinarily stressed in speech, and such words are therefore not ordinarily stressed in alliterative poetry. That is why a reader can not go far wrong in getting the stress right by simply reading the lines with attention to the sense.

One characteristic of the alliteration of the *Alliterative Morte Arthure* is the author's fondness for carrying one alliterating sound through several lines in a kind of *tour de force*:

> But they fit them fair, these frek bernes,
> Fewters in freely on feraunt steedes,
> Foines full felly with flishand speres,
> Fretten off orfrayes fast upon sheldes;
> So fele fay is in fight upon the feld leved
> That ech a furth on the firth of red blood runnes. (lines 2139–2144)

The poet seems to have an endless stock of alliterating words, and if he stops at this point, it is probably not because he has run out of words beginning with *f*; only a couple of lines later he begins another series with *f*.

The alliterative style affects more than the meter. The poets of the Alliterative Revival used the traditional line of Anglo-Saxon poetry, which had disappeared from written records about two centuries before and was revived by a number of poets (mainly living in the West and North of England) in the fourteenth century. Evidently the style of alliterative poetry had been preserved by popular, unlettered

6

poets who continued to compose and transmit poems by oral, non-written means from Anglo-Saxon times until well into the fourteenth century. Verse composed in this manner depends on a heavily formulaic language and a fixed, archaic poetic vocabulary. Even the casual reader of the *Alliterative Morte Arthure* will soon recognize how much of this old, formulaic style is preserved in the poems of the Alliterative Revival. Half-lines (especially second half-lines) tend to be used over and over in identical (or nearly identical) forms, and the poet makes frequent use of the specialized vocabulary characteristic of alliterative poetry, with its many synonyms for "man" (*renk, bern, lede, freke, gome, shalk,* etc.) or for the verb "go" (*graith, boun, ferk,* etc.) Much of the difficulty in a first reading of an alliterative poem is its use of this special poetic diction, consisting largely of words that are seldom encountered outside alliterative verse.

Although the ultimate background of the alliterative style is a popular, non-literary tradition, poems such as the *Alliterative Morte Arthure* are sophisticated works that were probably addressed to rather limited audiences that prized the verbal dexterity these poems display. The language was difficult even for the average listener in Middle English times, and the poets tended to prefer description and analysis to rapidly moving plot such as we associate with more popular poetry. The *Stanzaic Morte Arthur*, with its emphasis on action, has a popular appeal quite different from that of the *Alliterative Morte Arthure*, in which the careful attention to the texture of events, to the description of armor and dress, to the niceties of feasting, to fine points of heraldry, and to the exact details of military campaigns reveals the interests of a leisured and aristocratic audience. The author expects his hearers to understand an occasional French phrase, to recognize his geographical references (at least the European ones), and to share with him an interest that goes beyond the action to the definition of the quality of the action and of the life it represents.

Stanzaic Morte Arthur

Select Bibliography

Manuscript

Harley 2252, fols. 86a–133b; late fourteenth century. (British Library)

Editions

Le Morte Arthur, The Adventures of Sir Launcelot du Lake. Ed. Thomas Ponton. London: William Bulmer and Company, 1819.

Le Morte Arthur. Ed. F. J. Furnivall. With prefatory essay by Herbert Coleridge. London and Cambridge: Macmillan and Company, 1864. [Dedicated to Alfred Tennyson. Not printed in stanzas.]

Le Morte Arthure. Ed. J. Douglas Bruce. EETS e.s. 88. London, New York, Toronto: Oxford University Press, 1903. Rpt. Millwood, N.Y.: Kraus, 1973. [This edition is the basis for most subsequent editions.]

Le Morte Arthur. Ed. S. B. Hemingway. New York: Riverside Press, 1912. [Differs little from Bruce; fuller notes.]

Le Morte Arthur: A Critical Edition. Ed. P. F. Hissiger. The Hague, Paris: Mouton, 1975. [The text differs little from Bruce and Hemingway; notes are scanty.]

Le Morte Arthur. Ed. Shunichi Noguchi. Centre for Mediaeval English Studies. Tokyo: University of Tokyo, 1990.

Translation

Kahn, Sharon. *The Stanzaic Morte: A Verse Translation of Le Morte Arthur*. Lanham: University Press of America, 1986.

Stanzaic Morte Arthur

Criticism

Alexander, Flora M. "'The Treason of Lancelote du Lake': Irony in the Stanzaic *Morte Arthur*." In *The Legend of Arthur in the Middle Ages*. Ed. P. B. Grout and others. Arthurian Studies 7. Cambridge: D. S. Brewer, 1983. Pp. 15–27, 227–28. [A discussion of the ironies that create detachment in preparation for the burial of Guinevere with Arthur at Glastonbury.]

Beston, John B., and Rose Marie Beston. "The Parting of Lancelot and Guinevere in the Stanzaic Le Morte Arthur." *Journal of the Australasaian Universities Language and Literature Association* 40 (1973), 249–59.

Edwards, A. S. G. "Stanzaic Morte Arthur, line 3651." *Notes and Queries* 41 (1994), 14–15.

Jaech, Sharon L. Jansen. "The Parting of Lancelot and Gaynor: The Effect of Repetition in the Stanzaic *Morte Arthur*." *Interpretations* 15 (1984), 59–69. [Examines the parting of Lancelot and Guinevere as a means of unifying themes in the poem primarily through repetition.]

Kennedy, Edward Donald. "The Stanzaic Morte Arthur: The Adaption of a French Romance for an English Audience." In *Culture and the King: The Social Implications of the Arthurian Legend*. Ed. Martin B. Schichtman and James P. Carley. Albany: State University of New York Press, 1994. Pp. 91–112.

Knopp, Sherron E. "Artistic Design in the Stanzaic *Morte Arthur*." *ELH* 45 (1978), 563–82. [Argues the structural coherence of the poem.]

Twomey, Michael. "A Note on Detachment in the Stanzaic 'Morte Arthur.'" *Bulletin Bibliographique de la Societe Internationale Arthurienne* 26 (1974), 206–07.

Wertime, Richard A. "The Theme and Structure of the Stanzaic *Morte Arthur*." *PMLA* 87 (1972), 1075–82. [Defends the poem's coherence and seriousness of purpose.]

Stanzaic Morte Arthur

Lordinges that are lef and dere   *beloved*
   Listeneth, and I shall you tell,   *Listen*
By olde dayes what aunters were   *adventures*
   Among our eldres that befell;
5 In Arthur dayes, that noble king,
   Befell aunters ferly fele,   *adventures wondrous many*
And I shall tell of their ending,
   That mikel wiste of wo and wele.   *much knew; joy*

The knightes of the Table Round,
10   The Sangrail when they had sought,   *Holy Grail*
Aunters they before them found   *Adventures*
   Finished and to ende brought;
Their enemies they bette and bound   *beat*
   For gold on life they left them nought.
15 Four yere they lived sound,   *in health*
   When they had these workes wrought.

Til on a time that it befell
   The king in bed lay by the queen;
Of aunters they began to tell,
20   Many that in that land had been:
"Sir, yif that it were your will,   *if*
   Of a wonder thing I wolde you mene,   *would; tell*
How that your court beginneth to spill   *become empty*
   Of doughty knightes all bydene;   *completely*

25 "Sir, your honour beginnes to fall,
   That wont was wide in world to sprede,   *spread*
Of Launcelot and other all,
   That ever so doughty were in deed."
"Dame, there to thy counsel I call:
30   What were best for such a need?"

11

"Yif ye your honour holde shall,   *If*
    A tournament were best to bede,   *announce*

"For-why that aunter shall begin   *Because; adventure*
    And be spoke of on every side,
35   That knightes shall there worship win   *honor*
    To deed of armes for to ride.   *by riding*
Sir, lettes thus your court no blinne,   *not cease*
    But live in honour and in pride."   *admiration*
"Certes, dame," the king said then,   *Certainly*
40   "This ne shall no lenger abide."   *shall no longer*

A tournament the king let bede;   *commanded to be announced*
    At Winchester sholde it be   *should*
Young Galehod was good in need;
    The cheftain of the cry was he,   *chieftain; company*
45   With knightes that were stiff on steed,   *strong on horses*
    That ladies and maidens might see
Who that beste were of deed,
    Through doughtiness to have the gree.   *feats of strength; prize*

Knightes arme them bydene   *at once*
50   To the tournament to ride,
With sheldes brode and helmes sheen   *shields broad; bright*
    To win grete honour and pride.   *great; admiration*
Launcelot left with the queen,   *remained*
    And seke he lay that ilke tide;   *sick; same time*
55   For love that was them between,
    He made enchesoun for to abide.   *occasion (excuse)*

The king sat upon his steed,
    And forth is went upon his way;   *has gone*
Sir Agravain for such a need,
60   At home beleft, for sooth to say,   *remained; truth*
For men told in many a thede   *nation*
    That Launcelot by the queen lay;
For to take them with the deed,   *in the act*
    He awaites both night and day.

65	Launcelot forth wendes he	*goes*
	Unto the chamber to the queen,	
	And set him down upon his knee	*himself*
	And salues there that lady sheen	*salutes; bright*
	"Launcelot, what dostou here with me?	*dost thou*
70	The king is went and the court bydene;	*as well*
	I drede we shall discovered be	*dread*
	Of the love is us between.	
	"Sir Agravain at home is he;	
	Night and day he waites us two."	
75	"Nay, " he said, "my lady free,	*noble*
	I ne think not it shall be so;	*do not think*
	I come to take my leve of thee,	*leave*
	Out of court ere that I go."	
	"Ya, swithe that thou armed be,	*Indeed, quickly*
80	For thy dwelling me is full wo."	*lingering to me; painful*
	Launcelot to his chamber yede	*went*
	There rich attire lay him before,	
	Armed him in noble weed,	*himself; material*
	Of that armour gentylly was shore.[1]	
85	Sword and sheld were good at need	*shield*
	In many batailes that he had bore,	*battles*
	And horsed him on a grey steed	
	King Arthur had him geve before.	*given*
	Holdes he none highe way,[2]	
90	The knight that was hardy and free,	*noble*
	But hastes both night and day	
	Fast toward that riche citee	*great city*
	(Winchester it hight, for sooth to say)	*is called; truth*
	There the tournament sholde be;	*Where; should*
95	King Arthur in a castle lay,	

---

[1] *From which his armor was nobly (gentylly) fashioned (shore)*

[2] *He does not keep to the high (main) road*

Full much there was of game and glee.   *pleasure*

For-why wolde men Launcelot behold,   *Because; desired to see*
  And he ne wolde not himselfe show   *did not want to*
With his shouldres gan he fold   *did turn away*
100   And down he hanged his hed full low,   *head*
As he ne might his limmes weld;   *As if; control his limbs*
  Keeped he no bugle blow;   *i.e., had no trumpeter*
Well he seemed as he were old,   *as if*
  For-thy ne couth him no man know.   *Therefore; could*

105 The king stood on a towr on hight;   *tower; on high*
  Sir Ewain clepes he that tide: *calls; time*
"Sir Ewain, knowestou any wight   *knowest thou in any way*
  This knight that rides here beside?"
Sir Ewain spekes wordes right   *speaks; directly*
110   (That ay is hende is not to hide):   *Whatever; genteel*
"Sir, it is some olde knight
  Is come to see the yonge knightes ride."   *young*

They beheld him both anon
  A stounde for the steedes sake;   *moment; horse's*
115 His horse stomeled at a stone   *stumbled*
  That all his body there-with gan shake;   *So that; did*
The knight then braundished ich a bone,   *shook; every*
  As he the bridle up gan take;   *did*
There-by wiste they both anon   *knew; immediately*
120   That it was Launcelot du Lake.

King Arthur then spekes he   *speaks*
  To Sir Ewain these wordes right: *directly*
"Well may Launcelot holden be   *considered*
  Of all the world the beste knight,
125 Of beautee and of bountee,   *beauty; generosity*
  And sithe is none so much of might,   *since there is no one*
At every deede best is he,

And sithe he nolde it wiste no wight, [1]

	"Sir Ewain, will we don him bide;	*make; wait*
130	He weenes that we know him nought."	*supposes*
	"Sir, it is better let him ride,	*to let*
	And let him don as he hath thought;	*do*
	He will be here ner beside,	*nearby*
	Sithe he thus fer hider hath sought;	*so far hither*
135	We shall know him by his deed	
	And by the horse that he hath brought."	

	An erl wonned there beside,	*earl dwelled*
	The Lord of Ascolot was hight;	*called*
	Launcelot gan thider ride,	*did; thither*
140	And said he will there dwell all night;	
	They received him with grete pride;	*great pomp*
	A riche soper there was dight;	*supper; prepared*
	His name gan he hele and hide.	*did; conceal*
	And said he was a strange knight.	*foreign*

145	Then had the erle sonnes two,	*earl*
	That were noble knightes maked new.	*newly made*
	In that time was the manner so, [2]	
	When yonge knightes sholde sheldes shew,	
	Til the first yere were ago	
150	To bere armes of one hew,	
	Red or white, yellow or blo;	*blue*
	There-by men yonge knightes knew.	*young*

	As they sat at their soper,	*supper*
	Launcelot to the erl spake there:	*earl*
155	"Sir, is here any bacheler	*young knight*
	That to the tournament will fare?"	

---

[1] *And since he wants no one to know it*

[2] *At that time it was the custom that, / When young knights were to show their shields for the first time, / They should bear arms all of one color (without any heraldic device) / Until the first year had passed*

"I have two sonnes that me is dere,   *dear*
   And now that one is seke full sore,   *sick*
So that in company he were,   *Providing that he had company*
160   Mine other son I wolde were there."   *would*

"Sir, and thy son will thider right,   *if; wants to go directly there*
   The lenger I will him abide,   *longer*
And help him there with all my might,
   That him none harme shall betide."
165   "Sir, thee seemes a noble knight,
   Courtais and hende, is not to hide;   *courteous; polite*
At morrow shall ye dine and dight,   *In the morning; prepare*
   Togeder I rede well that ye ride."   *Together I advise*

"Sir, of one thing I will you minne,   *put in mind*
170   And beseech you for to speed,   *succeed*
Yif here were any armour in   *If*
   That I might borrow it to this deed."   *for*
"Sir, my son lieth seke here-in;   *sick*
   Take his armour and his steed;
175   For my sonnes men shall you ken,   *know*
   Of red shall be your bothes weed."   *both your garments*

Th'erl had a doughter that was him dere;
   Mikel Launcelot she beheld;   *Intently (much)*
Her rode was red as blossom on brere   *cheek; briar*
180   Or flowr that springeth in the feld;   *flower; field*
Glad she was to sit him ner,   *near*
   The noble knight under sheld;   *shield*
Weeping was her moste cheer,[1]
   So mikel on him her herte gan helde.

185   Up then rose that maiden still,
   And to her chamber went she tho;   *then*
Down upon her bed she fell,
   That nigh her herte brast in two.   *nearly; heart broke*

---

[1] *She was most often seen weeping, / So firmly was her heart set*

16

Launcelot wiste what was her will,   *knew; desire*
190 Well he knew by other mo; [1]
Her brother cleped he him til,   *called; to him*
  And to her chamber gonne they go.   *did*

He sat him down for the maidens sake,
  Upon her bedde there she lay;   *bed where*
195 Courtaisly to her he spake,   *Courteously*
  For to comfort that faire may.   *maid*
In her armes she gan him take,   *did*
  And these wordes gan she say:
"Sir, but yif that ye it make,   *unless you do it (save my life)*
200 Save my life no leche may."   *physician; can*

"Lady," he said, "thou moste let;   *must stop*
  For me ne gif thee nothing ill; [2]
In another stede mine herte is set;   *place*
  It is not at mine owne will;
205 In erthe is nothing that shall me let   *earth; prevent*
  To be thy knight loud and still;   *ever (at any time)*
Another time we may be met
  When thou may better speke thy fill."   *speak*

"Sithe I of thee ne may have more,   *Since; may not*
210 As thou art hardy knight and free,   *bold; noble*
In the tournament that thou wolde bere   *would bear*
  Some sign of mine that men might see."
"Lady, thy sleve thou shalt of-shere;   *cut off*
  I will it take for the love of thee;
215 So did I never no ladies ere,   *for any; before*
  But one that most hath loved me."

On the morrow when it was day,   *In the morning*
  They dined and made them yare,   *ready*
And then they went forth on their way,

---

[1] *He knew well by other signs in addition to her weeping*

[2] *Do not make yourself sick for my sake*

220	Togeder as they brethern were.	*together as if*
	They met a squier by the way	*squire*
	That from the tournament gan fare,	*did travel*
	And asked him yif he couth them say	*if; could*
	Which party was the bigger there.	*i.e., more powerful*

225	"Sir Galahod hath folk the more,	
	For sooth, lordinges, as I you tell,	*lords*
	But Arthur is the bigger there;	*more powerful*
	He hath knightes stiff and fell;	*unwavering; fierce*
	They are bold and breme as bore,	*fierce as a boar*
230	Ewain, and Bors, and Lionel."	
	Th'erles son to him spake there:	
	"Sir, with them I rede we dwell."	*advise*

	Launcelot spake, as I you rede;	*tell*
	"Sithe they are men of grete valour,	*Since*
235	How might we among them speed,	*succeed*
	There all are stiff and strong in stour?	*Where; unwavering; battle*
	Help we them that hath most need;	*Let us help those*
	Again the best we shall well doure;	*Against; endure*
	And we might there do any deed,	*If*
240	It wolde us turn to more honour."	

	Launcelot spekes in that tide	*time*
	As knight that was hardy and free:	*noble*
	"Tonight without I rede we bide;	*outside; advise; remain*
	The press is grete in that citee."	*crowd*
245	"Sir, I have an aunt here beside,	
	A lady of swithe grete beautee;	*very great beauty*
	Were it your will thider to ride,	*thither*
	Glad of us then wolde she be."	

	Tho to the castle gonne they fare,	*Then; did*
250	To the lady fair and bright;	
	Blithe was the lady there	
	That they wolde dwell with her that night;	
	Hastely was their soper yare	*supper; ready*
	Of mete and drink richly dight.	*food; prepared*

18

255	On the morrow gonne they dine and fare,	*ate; set forth*
	Both Launcelot and that other knight.	

	When they come into the feld,	*field*
	Much there was of game and play;	*pleasure*
	A while they hoved and beheld	*paused*
260	How Arthurs knightes rode that day.	
	Galehodes party began to held,	*draw back*
	On foot his knightes are led away.	
	Launcelot — stiff was under sheld —	*stout*
	Thinkes to help, yif that he may.	*Intends; if; can*

265	Beside him come then Sir Ewain,	
	Breme as any wilde bore;	*Fierce; boar*
	Launcelot springes him again	*runs; against*
	In redde armes that he bore;	*red*
	A dint he gave with mikel main;	*blow; much force*
270	Sir Ewain was unhorsed there,	
	That all men wend he had been slain,	*supposed*
	So was he wounded wonder sore.	*very painfully*

	Sir Bors thought nothing good,	
	When Sir Ewain unhorsed was;	
275	Forth he springes as he were wode,	*as if; crazy*
	To Launcelot, withouten lees;	*without lies (I tell it)*
	Launcelot hit him on the hood,	*helmet*
	The nexte way to ground he chese;	*closest; went*
	Was none so stiff again him stood;	*resolute against*
280	Full thin he made the thickest press.	*crowd*

	Sir Lionel began to teen,	*mourn*
	And hastely he made him boune;	*ready*
	To Launcelot with herte keen,	*heart*
	He rode with helm and sworde brown;	*shining sword*
285	Launcelot hit him, as I ween,	*suppose*
	Through the helm into the crown,	*skull*
	That ever after it was seen	
	Both horse and man there yede adown.	*went*

	The knightes gadered togeder there	*gathered together*
290	And gonne with craft their counsel take;	*did; skill*
	Such a knight was never ere	
	But it were Launcelot du Lake;	
	But, for the sleeve on his crest was there,	*because*
	For Launcelot wolde they him not take,	
295	For he bore never none such before,	
	But it were for the queenes sake.	*Except*

	"Of Ascolot he never was	
	That thus well beres him today!"	*bears himself*
	Ector said, withouten lees,	*without lies*
300	What he was he wolde assay.	*test*
	A noble steed Ector him chese,	*chose for himself*
	And forthe rides glad and gay;	
	Launcelot he met amid the press,	*crowd*
	Between them was no childes play.	

	Ector smote with herte good	*heart*
305	To Launcelot that ilke tide;	*very time*
	Through helm into his hed it yode	*head; went*
	That nighe lost he all his pride.	*nearly*
	Launcelot hit him on the hood	*helmet*
310	That his horse fell and he beside.	
	Launcelot blindes in his blood;	*is blinded; his own*
	Out of the feld full fast gan ride.	*field*

	Out of the feld they riden tho	*ride then*
	To a forest high and hore.	*hoary*
315	When they come by them one two,[1]	
	Off his helm he takes there.	
	"Sir," he said, "me is full wo;	*(it) is very sad to me*
	I drede that ye be hurt full sore."	*dread; very painfully*
	"Nay," he said, "it is not so,	*i.e., Lancelot*
320	But fain I wolde at rest we were."	*eagerly*

---

[1] *When they came alone by themselves (those two alone)*

20

"Sir, mine aunt is here beside,
    There we bothe were all night;   *where*
Were it your will thider to ride,
    She will us help with all her might,
325 And send for leches this ilke tide,   *physicians; very time*
    Your woundes for to hele and dight;   *heal; prepare (dress)*
And I myself will with you abide,
    And be your servaunt and your knight."

To the castle they took the way,
330   To the lady fair and hende.   *courteous*
She sent for leches, as I you say,   *physicians*
    That wonned both fer and hende,   *lived; far; near*
But by the morrow that it was day,   *morning*
    In bed he might himself not wend;   *turn*
335 So sore wounded there he lay
    That well nigh had he sought his end.

Tho King Arthur with mikel pride   *Then; much pomp*
    Called his knightes all him by,
And said a month he wolde there bide,
340   And in Winchester lie.
Heraudes he did go and ride   *Heralds; caused to*
    Another tournament for to cry;   *announce*
"This knight will be here beside,
    For he is wounded bitterly."

345 When the lettres made were,   *letters*
    The heraudes forth with them yede,   *heralds; went*
Through Yngland for to fare,   *England*
    Another tournament for to bede;   *announce*
Bade them busk and make them yare,   *hasten; ready*
350   All that stiff were on steed.   *stout*
Thus these lettres sente were   *letters*
    To tho that doughty were of deed.   *those*

Til on a time that it befell
    An heraud comes by the way
355 And at the castle a night gan dwell

21

	There as Launcelot wounded lay,	*Where*
	And of the tournament gan tell	
	That sholde come on the Sunday;	*should*
	Launcelot sighes wonder still	
360	And said: "Alas and wele-away!	*woe is me*

	"When knightes win worship and pride,	*honor; admiration*
	Some aunter shall hold me away,	*chance*
	As a coward for to abide.	
	This tournament, for sooth to say,	
365	For me is made this ilke tide;	*very time*
	Though I sholde die this ilke day,	*very*
	Certes, I shall thider ride."	*Certainly*

	The leche answered also soon	*physician; immediately*
	And said: "Sir, what have ye thought?	*intended*
370	All the craft that I have done	
	I ween it will you help right nought.	*believe; not at all*
	There is no man under the moon,	
	By Him that all this world hath wrought,	*created*
	Might save your life to that time come	*if the time should come*
375	That ye upon your steed were brought!"	

	"Certes, though I die this day,	*Certainly*
	In my bed I will not lie;	
	Yet had I lever do what I may	*rather; can*
	Than here to die thus cowardly!"	
380	The leche anon then went his way	*physician immediately*
	And wolde no lenger dwell him by;	*longer*
	His woundes scrived and still he lay,	*broke open*
	And in his bed he swooned thrie.	*thrice*

	The lady wept as she were wode,	*crazy*
385	When she saw he dede wolde be;	*dead would be*
	Th'erles son with sorry mood	
	The leche again clepes he	*physician; calls*
	And said: "Thou shalt have yiftes good	*gifts*
	For-why that thou wilt dwell with me."	*Providing*
390	Craftily then staunched he his blood	*Skillfully*

And of good comfort bade him be.

	The heraud then went on his way	*herald*
	At morrow when the day was light,	*morning*
	Also swithe as ever he may,	*As quickly*
395	To Winchester that ilke night;	*same*
	He salued the king, for sooth to say	*saluted*
	(By him sat Sir Ewain the knight),	
	And sithe he told upon his play [1]	
	What he had herde and seen with sight:	*heard*

400	"Of all that I have seen with sight,	
	Wonder thought me never more [2]	
	Than me did of a fooled knight	*foolish*
	That in his bed lay wounded sore;	
	He might not heve his hed up-right	*lift*
405	For all the world have wonne there; [3]	
	For anguish that he ne ride might	*could not ride*
	All his woundes scrived there."	*broke open*

	Sir Ewain then spekes wordes free,	*noble*
	And to the kinge said he there:	
410	"Certes, no coward knight is he;	
	Alas, that he nere hole and fere!	*is not healthy and sound*
	Well I wot that it is he	*know*
	That we all of unhorsed were.	*By whom all of us were unhorsed*
	The tournament is best let be,	
415	Forsooth, that knight may not come there."	

	There tournament was then no more,	
	But thus departeth all the press;	*company*
	Knightes took their leve to fare;	*leave*
	Ichon his owne way him chese.	*Each one; took*
420	To Camelot the king went there,	

---

[1] *And then he told them about his amusements*

[2] *Never a greater wonder did it seem to me*

[3] *Even if by doing so he could have won the whole world*

There as Queen Gaynor was;	*Where; Guinevere*
He wend have found Launcelot there;	*expected to*
Away he was, withouten lees.	*without lies*

Launcelot sore wounded lay;	*painfully*
425 Knightes sought him full wide;	
Th'erles son night and day	
Was alway him beside.	*always*
Th'erl himself, when he ride may,	*can*
Brought him home with mikel pride	*much pomp*
430 And made him both game and play	*pleasure*
Til he might bothe go and ride.	*could; walk*

Bors and Lionel then swore,	
And at the king their leve took there,	*from; leave*
Again they wolde come never more,	
435 Til they wiste where Launcelot were.	*knew*
Ector went with them there	
To seech his broder that was him dere.	*seek; brother*
Many a land they gonne through fare	*did*
And sought him bothe fer and ner.	*far and near*

440 Til on a time that it befell	
That they come by that ilke way,	*same*
And at the castle at mete gonne dwell,	*food did*
There as Launcelot wounded lay.	*Where*
Launcelot they saw, as I you tell,	
445 Walk on the walles him to play;	*enjoy himself*
On knees for joy all they fell,	
So blithe men they were that day.	*Such glad*

When Launcelot saw tho ilke three	*those same*
That he in worlde loved best,	
450 A merrier meeting might no man see,	
And sithe he led them to rest.	*then*
Th'erl himself, glad was he	
That he had gotten such a guest;	
So was the maiden fair and free	
455 That all her love on him had cast.	

When they were to soper dight   *prepared*
    Bordes were set and clothes spredde;   *tablecloths*
Th'erles doughter and the knight
    Togeder was set, as he them bade;   *Together*
460   Th'erles sonnes that both were wight,   *strong*
    To serve them were never sad,
And th'erl himself with all his might,
    To make them both blithe and glad.   *happy*

But Bors ever in mind he thought
465   That Launcelot had been wounded sore:
"Sir, were it your will to hele it nought [1]
    But tell where ye thus hurte were?"
"By Him that all this world hath wrought,"
    Launcelot himselfe swore,
470   "The dint shall be full dere bought,   *blow; dearly*
    Yif ever we may meet us more!"   *If*

Ector ne liked that no wight,   *not a bit*
    The wordes that he herde there;   *heard*
For sorrow he lost both strength and might;
475   The colours changed in his lere.   *face*
Bors then said these wordes right: *directly*
    "Ector, thou may make ivel cheer;   *evil (sour) expression*
For sooth, it is no coward knight
    That thou art of ymanased here."   *menaced by*

480   "Ector," he said, "were thou it were   *was it you who*
    That wounded me thus wonder sore?"
Ector answered with simple cheer: *innocent expression*
    "Lord, I ne wiste that ye it were;   *didn't know*
A dint of you I had there;   *blow from*
485   Felled I never none so sore."
Sir Lionel by God then swore
    That "Mine will seen be ever more!" [2]

---

[1] *Sir, would it be your desire not to conceal it*

[2] *That "My (wound) will be seen forevermore!"*

Sir Bors then answerd as tite   *quickly*
    As knight that wise was under weed: *garment*
490 "I hope that none of us was quite;   *suppose; free (of wounds)*
    I had one that to ground I yede;   *went*
Sir, your broder shall ye not wite;   *brother; must; blame*
    Now knowes either others deed;
Now know ye how Ector can smite,
495   To help you when ye have need."

Launcelot lough with herte free   *laughed; noble*
    That Ector made so mikel site: *much lament*
"Brother, nothing drede thou thee,   *dread*
    For I shall be both hole and quite.   *healthy; free (of harm)*
500 Though thou have sore wounded me,
    There-of I shall thee never wite,   *blame*
But ever the better love I thee,
    Such a dint that thou can smite."

Then upon the thridde day,   *third*
505   They took their leve for to fare;   *leave*
To the court they will away,
    For he will dwell a while there:
"Greet well my lord, I you pray,
    And tell my lady how I fare,
510 And say I will come when I may,
    And biddeth her long nothing sore." [1]

They took their leve, withouten lees,   *without lies*
    And wightly went upon their way;   *stoutly*
To the court the way they chese,   *went*
515   There as the Queen Gaynor lay.   *Where; Guinevere*
The king to the forest is,
    With knightes him for to play;
Good space they had withouten press   *without a crowd*
    Their errand to the queen to say.   *message*

---

[1] *And tell her not to long sorely for me*

520 They kneeled down before the queen,
         The knightes that were wise of lore,   *learning*
     And said that they had Launcelot seen
         And three dayes with him were,
     And how that he had wounded been,
525   And seke he had lie full sore: *sick; lain*
     "Ere ought long ye shall him seen;   *Before much longer; see*
         He bade you longe nothing sore."   *languish not sorely*

     The queen lough with herte free,   *laughed; relieved*
         When she wiste he was on life: *knew; alive*
530 "O worthy God, what wele is me!   *joy*
         Why ne wiste my lord it also swithe!"[1]
     To the forest rode these knightes three,
         To the king it to kithe;   *make known*
     Jesu Crist then thankes he,
535   For was he never of word so blithe.   *Because; of a word so happy*

     He cleped Sir Gawain him ner,   *called; near*
         And said: "Certes, that was he
     That the red armes bore,
         But now he lives, wele is me!"   *joy*
540 Gawain answerd with milde cheer,   *expression*
         As he that ay was hende and free: *ever; courteous; noble*
     "Was never tithandes me so dere,   *tidings*
         But sore me longes Launcelot to see."   *I yearn*

     At the king and at the queen   *From*
545   Sir Gawain took his leve that tide,
     And sithe at all the court bydene,   *then; together*
         And buskes him with mikel pride,   *hastens; display*
     Til Ascolot, withouten ween,   *To; doubt*
         Also fast as he might ride;   *As*
550 Til that he have Launcelot seen,
         Night ne day ne will he bide.

---

[1] *If only my husband knew this quickly!*

By that was Launcelot hole and fere   *healthy; sound*
    Buskes him and makes all yare;   *Hastens; ready*
His leve hath he take there;
555   The maiden wept for sorrow and care:
"Sir, yif that your willes were,   *if it were your wish*
    Sithe I of thee ne may have more,
Some thing ye wolde beleve me here,   *leave*
    To look on when me longeth sore."   *I yearn*

560 Launcelot spake with herte free,   *noble*
    For to comfort that lady hende: *courteous*
"Mine armour shall I leve with thee,
    And in thy brothers will I wende;   *go*
Look thou ne longe not after me,
565   For here I may no lenger lende;   *longer remain*
Long time ne shall it nought be
    That I ne shall either come or sende."   *send word*

Launcelot is redy for to ride,   *ready*
    And on his way he went forth right;   *directly*
570 Sir Gawain come after on a tide,   *time*
    And askes after such a knight.
They received him with grete pride
    (A riche soper there was dight),   *prepared*
And said, in herte is nought to hide,
575   Away he was for fourtenight.   *a fortnight*

Sir Gawain gan that maiden take
    And sat him by that sweete wight,   *creature*
And spake of Launcelot du Lake;
    In all the world nas such a knight.   *was not*
580 The maiden there of Launcelot spake,
    Said all her love was on him lighte: *alighted*
"For his leman he hath me take;   *beloved*
    His armour I you shewe might."   *show*

"Now damesel," he said anon,   *immediately*
585   "And I am glad that it is so;
Such a leman as thou hast one,   *beloved*

In all this world ne be no mo.   *more (i.e., better)*
   There is no lady of flesh ne bone
      In this worlde so thrive or thro,   *excellent; strong*
590   Though her herte were steel or stone,
      That might her love holde him fro.   *withhold from him*

   "But damesel, I beseech thee,
      His shelde that ye wolde me shew;   *show*
   Launcelotes yif that it be
595   By the coloures I it knew."   *would know it*
   The maiden was both hende and free,   *courteous; noble*
      And led him to a chamber new;
   Launcelotes sheld she let him see,
      And all his armour forth she drew.

600   Hendely then Sir Gawain   *Courteously*
      To the maiden there he spake:
   "Lady," he said, "withouten laine,   *without concealment*
      This is Launcelotes sheld du Lake.   *Launcelot du Lake's shield*
   Damesel," he said, "I am full fain   *very pleased*
605   That he thee wolde to leman take   *as a beloved*
      And I with all my might and main   *force*
   Will be thy knight for his sake."

   Gawain thus spake with that sweete wight   *creature*
      What his will was for to say.
610   Til he was to bed ydight,   *prepared*
      About him was game and play.   *pleasure*
   He took his leve at erl and knight   *from*
      On the morrow when it was day,
   And sithen at the maiden bright,   *then*
615   And forth he went upon his way.

   He niste where that he might,   *did not know; could go*
      Ne where that Launcelot wolde lende,   *stay*
   For when he was out of sight,
      He was full ivel for to find.   *evil (i.e, difficult)*
620   He takes him the way right.   *directly*
      And to the courte gan he went;   *go*

Glad of him was king and knight,
    For he was both courtais and hende.   *courteous*

Then it befell upon a tide,
625   The king stood by the queen and spake:
Sir Gawain standes him beside;
    Ichon til other their mone gan make,   *Each to; complaint*
How long they might with bale abide   *suffering*
    The coming of Launcelot du Lake;
630   In the court was little pride,
    So sore they sighed for his sake.

"Certes, yif Launcelot were on life,   *alive*
    So long fro court he nolde not be."   *away from; would not*
Sir Gawain answerd also swithe: *quickly*
635   "There-of no wonder thinketh me;   *it seems to me*
The fairest lady that is on life
    Til his leman chosen hath he;   *As his beloved*
Is none of us but wolde be blithe
    Such a seemly for to see."   *seemly (i.e., lovely) one*

640   The King Arthur was full blithe   *glad*
    Of that tithinges for to lere,   *tidings; learn*
And asked Sir Gawain also swithe   *quickly*
    What maiden that it were.
"Th'erles doughter," he said as swithe,   *quickly*
645   Of Ascolot, as ye may here,   *hear*
There I was made glad and blithe;
    His sheld the maiden shewed me there."

The queen then said wordes no mo,   *more*
    But to her chamber soon she yede,   *immediately; went*
650   And down upon her bed fell so
    That nigh of wit she wolde wede.   *nearly; go mad*
"Alas, " she said, "and wele-a-wo,   *woe is me*
    That ever I ought life in lede! [1]

---

[1] *That I ever had life in this nation (was ever born)!*

The beste body is lost me fro
655   That ever in stour bestrode steed."   *battle*

Ladies that about her stood,
    That wiste of her privitee,   *private affairs*
Bade her be of comfort good;
    Let no man such semblaunt see.   *appearance*
660 A bed they made with sorry mood,
    Therein they brought that lady free;
Ever she wept as she were wode;   *crazy*
    Of her they had full grete pitee.   *pity*

So sore seke the queen lay,   *sorely sick*
665 Of sorrow might she never let,   *stop*
Til it fell upon a day
    Sir Lionel and Ector yede   *went*
Into the forest, them to play.
    That flowred was and braunched sweet,   *had sweet branches*
670 And as they wente by the way,
    With Launcelot gonne they meet.   *did*

What wonder was though they were blithe,
    When they their master saw with sight!
On knees they felle also swithe,   *quickly*
675 And all they thanked God all-might;
Joy it was to see and lithe   *hear*
    The meeting of the noble knight.
And sithe he frained also swith: *then he quickly asked*
    "How fares my lady bright?"

680 Then answered the knightes free,
    And said that she was seke full sore:
"Grete dole it is to here and see,   *hear*
    So mikel she is in sorrow and care;
The king a sorry man is he,
685 In court for that ye come no more;
Dede he weenes that ye be,   *Dead he supposes*
    And all the court, both less and more.

"Sir, were it your will with us to fare,
   For to speke with the queen,
690 Blithe I wot well that she were   *Glad; would be*
   Yif that she had you ones seen.   *but once*
The king is mikel in sorrow and care,
   And so is all the court bydene;   *as well*
Dede they ween well that ye are   *Dead; think*
695   From court for ye so long have been."

He grauntes them at that ilke sithe   *grants; time*
   Home that he will with them ride;
Therefore the knightes were full blithe
   And busked them with mikel pride   *hastened*
700 To the court also swithe;
   Night ne day they nolde abide;   *would not*
The king and all the court was blithe
   The tidandes when they herde that tide.   *tidings; heard*

The king stood in a towr on high,   *tower*
705   Besides him standes Sir Gawain;
Launcelot when that they sigh   *saw*
   Were never men on molde so fain.   *on earth so happy*
They ran as swithe as ever they might   *quickly*
   Out at the gates him again;   *against (i.e., toward)*
710 Was never tidandes to them so light;   *tidings; joyful*
   The king him kissed and knight and swain.   *young man*

To a chamber the king him led;
   Fair in armes they gonne him fold,   *embrace*
And set him on a riche bed,
715   That spredde was with a cloth of gold;   *spread*
To serve him there was no man sad,
   Ne dight him as himselfe wolde   *But served him whatever he wanted*
To make him both blithe and glad,
   And sithe aunters he them told.   *afterwards adventures*

720 Three dayes in court he dwelled there
   That he ne spake not with the queen,
So muche press was ay them ner;   *crowd*

The king him led and court bydene.   *as well*
The lady, bright as blossom on brere,   *briar*
725   Sore she longed him to sen;   *see*
Weeping was her moste cheer,   *most [frequent] expression*
   Though she ne durst her to no man mene.   *dared not speak to any man*

Then it fell upon a day
   The king gan on hunting ride,
730   Into the forest him to play,
   With his knightes by his side.
Launcelot long in bedde lay;
   With the queen he thought to bide.
To the chamber he took the way
735   And salues her with mikel pride.   *salutes; great honor*

First he kissed that lady sheen,   *beautiful*
   And salues her with herte free,   *salutes*
And sithe the ladies all bydene;
   For joy the teres ran on their blee.   *face(s)*
740   "Wele-away," then said the queen,
   "Launcelot, that I ever thee see!
The love that hath us be between,   *been*
   That it shall thus departed be!

"Alas, Launcelot du Lake,
745   Sithe thou hast all my herte in wold,   *in [your] possession*
Th'erles doughter that thou wolde take
   Of Ascolot, as men me told!
Now thou levest for her sake   *abandon*
   All thy deed of armes bold;
750   I may wofully weep and wake
   In clay til I be clongen cold! [1]

"But, Launcelot, I beseech thee here,
   Sithe it needelinges shall be so,   *of necessity*
That thou never more diskere   *reveal*

---

[1] *Until I am clasped in cold clay (dead and buried)*

755   The love that hath been betwix us two,
        Ne that she never be with thee so dere, [1]
            Deed of armes that thou be fro,
        That I may of thy body here,
            Sithe I shall thus beleve in wo."

760   Launcelot full still then stood:
            His herte was hevy as any stone;   *heavy*
        So sorry he wex in his mood,   *grew; mind*
            For rewth him thought it all to-torne.   *sorrow; was destroyed*
        "Madame," he said, "For Cross and Rood,   *Cross*
765   What betokeneth all this mone?   *means; moan*
        By Him that bought me with His blood,
            Of these tidandes know I none.   *tidings*

        "But by these wordes thinketh me   *it seems to me*
            Away ye wolde that I were;
770   Now have good day, my lady free,
            For sooth, thou seest me never more!"
        Out of the chamber then wendes he;
            Now whether his herte was full of wo!   *Now [consider]*
        The lady swoones sithes three;   *three times*
775   Almost she slew herselfe there.

        Launcelot to his chamber yede,   *went*
            There his own attire in lay,
        Armed him in an noble weed,
            Though in his herte were little play;
780   Forth he sprang as spark of glede,   *from a live coal*
            With sorry cheer, for sooth to say;
        Up he worthes upon his steed,   *gets*
            And to a forest he wendes away.

        Tithinges come into the hall   *tidings*
785   That Launcelot was upon his steed;

---

[1] *May she never be so dear to you / That you give up performing deeds of arms; / Since I must remain alone in sorrow, / I would at least like to hear of your deeds of prowess*

Out then ran the knightes all,
　　Of their wit as they wolde wede;　　　　　*would go mad*
Bors de Gawnes and Lionel
　　And Ector that doughty was of deed,
790　Followen him on horses snell,　　　　　　*swift*
　　Full loude gonne they blow and grede.　　*blow horns; cry*

There might no man him overtake;
　　He rode into a forest green;
Muche mone gonne they make,　　　　　　*moan*
795　　The knightes that were bold and keen.
"Alas," they said, "Launcelot du Lake,
　　That ever sholdestou see the queen!"　　*you should have seen*
And her they cursed for his sake,
　　That ever love was them between.

800　They ne wiste never where to fare,
　　　Ne to what land that he wolde;　　　　*would go*
Again they went with sighing sore,
　　The knightes that were keen and bold;
The queen they found in swooning there,
805　　Her comely tresses all unfold;
They were so full of sorrow and care,
　　There was none her comforte wolde.　　*who would comfort her*

The king then hastes him for his sake,
　　And home then come that ilke day,
810　And asked after Launcelot du Lake,
　　　And they said: "He is gone away."
The queen was in her bed all naked,
　　And sore seke in her chamber lay;
So muche mone the king gan make,
815　　There was no knight that lust to play.　　*wanted*

The king clepes Gawain that day,　　　　　*summons*
　　And all his sorrow told him til:　　　　*to him*
"Now is Launcelot gone away,
　　And come, I wot, he never will."　　　　*know*
820　He said: "Alas and wele-away,"

Sighed sore and gave him ill;　　　　　　　　　　*made himself sick*
"The lord that we have loved alway,
　　In court why nill he never dwell?"　　　　　　　*will not*

Gawain spekes in that tide,　　　　　　　　　　*time*
825　　And to the king said he there:
"Sir, in this castle shall ye bide,
　　Comfort you and make good cheer,
And we shall both go and ride,　　　　　　　　　*walk*
　　In alle landes fer and ner;　　　　　　　　　*far and near*
830　So prively he shall him not hide　　　　　　　*secretly*
　　Through hap that we ne shall of him here."　　*By chance; hear*

Knightes then sought him wide;
　　Of Launcelot might they not here,　　　　　　*hear*
Til it fell upon a tide,
835　　Queen Gaynor, bright as blossom on brere,　*Guinevere; briar*
To mete is set that ilke tide,　　　　　　　　　*supper*
　　And Sir Gawain sat her ner,
And upon that other side
　　A Scottish knight that was her dere.　　　　　*dear to her*

840　A squier in the court hath thought　　　　　　*squire; intended*
　　That ilke day, yif that he might,
With a poison that he hath wrought
　　To slay Gawain, yif that he might;
In frut he hath it forthe brought　　　　　　　　*fruit*
845　　And set before the queene bright;
An apple overest lay on loft,　　　　　　　　　　*uppermost; above*
　　There the poison was in dight.　　　　　　　　*prepared*

For he thought the lady bright
　　Wolde the best to Gawain bede;　　　　　　　*offer*
850　But she it gave to the Scottish knight,
　　For he was of an uncouthe stede.　　　　　　*foreign place*
There-of he ete a little wight;　　　　　　　　　*ate; bit*
　　Of tresoun took there no man heed;　　　　　*treason*
There he lost both main and might　　　　　　　*force*
855　　And died soon, as I you rede.　　　　　　　*immediately; tell*

36

They niste not what it might bemene,   *knew; mean*
 But up him stert Sir Gawain   *leaped*
And sithen all the court bydene,   *then; together*
 And over the borde they have him drayn. *table; drawn*
860 "Wele-away," then said the queen,
 "Jesu Crist, what may I sayn?   *say*
Certes, now will all men ween
 Myself that I the knight have slain."

Triacle there was anon forth brought;   *Medicine*
865 The queene wend to save his life;   *hoped*
But all that might help him nought,
 For there the knight is dede as swithe. *right away*
So grete sorrow the queen then wrought,
 Grete dole it was to see and lithe: *hear*
870 "Lord, such sites me have sought!   *misfortunes*
 Why ne may I never be blithe?"

Knightes don none other might   *could do nothing else*
 But buried him with dole ynow   *much sorrow*
At a chapel with riche light,   *i.e., expensive candles*
875 In a forest by a clough;   *ravine*
A riche tomb they did be dight,   *had prepared*
 A crafty clerk the lettres drow,   *drew*
How there lay the Scottish knight
 The queen Gaynor with poison slogh. *slew*

880 After this a time befell
 To the court there come a knight;
His broder he was, as I you tell,
 And Sir Mador for sooth he hight;   *was called*
He was an hardy man and snell   *fierce*
885 In tournament and eek in fight,
And mikel loved in court to dwell,   *greatly*
 For he was man of muche might.

Then it fell upon a day
 Sir Mador went with mikel pride

37

890   Into the forest, him for to play, [1]
      That flowred was and braunched wide;
    He fand a chapel in his way,   *found*
      As he came by the cloughes side,   *ravine's*
    There his owne broder lay,
895   And there at mass he thought to abide.   *to stay*

    A riche tomb he fand there dight   *found*
      With lettres that were fair ynow;   *very fair*
    A while he stood and redde it right;   *read*
      Grete sorrow then to his herte drow;   *drew*
900   He fand the name of the Scottish knight
      The Queen Gaynor with poison slogh.   *slew*
    There he lost both main and might,
      And over the tomb he fell in swough.   *swoon*

    Of swooning when he might awake,
905   His herte was hevy as any lede;   *heavy; lead*
    He sighed for his brothers sake;
      He ne wiste what was beste rede.   *counsel*
    The way to court gan he take,
      Of nothing ne stood he drede;   *in dread*
910   A loude cry on the queen gan make,
      In challenging of his brothers dede.   *death*

    The king full sore then gan him drede,
      For he might not be again the right;   *against*
    The queen of wit wolde nighe wede,   *nearly run mad*
915   Though that she aguilte had no wight. *of guilt; not a bit*
    She moste there beknow the deed   *must; confess*
      Or find a man for her to fight,
    For well she wiste to dethe she yede,   *would go*
      Yif she were on a quest of knightes.   *judged by*

920   Though Arthur were king the land to weld,   *rule*

---

[1] *To amuse himself [he went] into the forest, / Which was in flower and had wide branches overhead*

	He might not be again the right;	*against*
	A day he took with spere and sheld	*set; spear*
	To find a man for her to fight,	
	That she shall either to dethe her yeld	*yield*
925	Or put her on a quest of knightes;	*submit herself to judgment by*
	There-to both their handes upheld	*i.e., Mador and Gaynor*
	And trewly their trouthes plight.	*pledged their words*

When they in certain had set a day
And that quarrel undertake,
930   The word sprang soon through ech countree   *immediately; each*
What sorrow that Queen Gaynor gan make;
So at the last, shortly to say,
Word come to Launcelot du Lake,
There as he seke ywounded lay;
935   Men told him holly all the wrake,   *wholly; trouble*

How that Queen Gaynor the bright
Had slain with grete tresoun   *treason*
A swithe noble Scottish knight
At the mete with strong poisoun;   *poison*
940   Therefore a day was taken right
That she sholde find a knight full boun   *ready*
For her sake for to fight
Or elles be brent without ransoun.   *burnt; ransom*

When that Launcelot du Lake
945   Had herde holly all this fare,   *heard completely; affair*
Grete sorrow gan he to him take,
For the queen was in such care,
And swore to venge her of that wrake,   *for that trouble*
That day yif that he livand were;   *if he were living*
950   Then pained he him his sorrows to slake   *exerted himself*
And wex as breme as any bore.   *grew fierce; wild boar*

Now leve we Launcelot there he was,
With the ermite in the forest green   *hermit*
And tell we forth of the case
955   That toucheth Arthur, the king so keen.   *concerns*

39

Sir Gawain on the morn to counsel he tas,   *takes*
    And morned sore for the queen;   *mourned grievously*
Into a towr then he him has   *tower*
    And ordained the best there them between.

960 And as they in their talking stood
         To ordain how it best might be,
     A fair river under the towr yode,   *went*
         And soon there-in gonne they see
     A little bote of shape full good   *boat*
965   To them-ward with the streme gan te;   *current approached*
     There might none fairer sail on flood
         Ne better forged as of tree.   *made of wood*

     When King Arthur saw that sight,
         He wondred of the rich apparail   *furnishings*
970 That was about the bote ydight;   *boat arranged*
         So richly was it covered sanzfail,   *without fail*
     In manner of a vout with clothes ydight   *vault; fashioned*
         All shinand as gold as it gan sail.   *shining*
     Then said Sir Gawain the goode knight:
975   "This bote is of a rich entail."   *fashion*

     "For sooth, sir," said the king tho,
         "Such one saw I never ere;
     Thider I rede now that we go;
         Some adventures shall we see there,
980 And yif it be within dight so   *decorated*
         As without, or gayer more,
     I dare savely say there-to   *safely*
         Begin will aunters ere ought yare."[1]

     Out of the towr adown they went,   *tower*
985   The King Arthur and Sir Gawain;
     To the bote they yede withoute stint,   *went without delay*
         They two alone, for sooth to sayn;   *say*

---

[1] *Adventures will begin very soon*

And when they come there as it lente,   *remained*
    They beheld it fast, is not to laine;   *carefully; hide*
990 A cloth that over the bote was bent
    Sir Gawain lift up, and went in bain.   *readily*

When they were in, withouten lees,   *without lies (truly)*
    Full richly arrayed they it fand,   *found*
And in the middes a fair bed was
995   For any king of Cristen land.   *Christian*
Then as swithe, ere they wolde sese,   *cease*
    The coverlet lift they up with hand;
A dede woman they sigh there was,   *saw*
    The fairest maid that might be fand.

1000 To Sir Gawain then said the king:
    "For sooth, deth was too unhende,   *discourteous*
When he wolde thus fair a thing
    Thus yonge out of the world do wend;   *make go*
For her beautee, without leesing,   *beauty; lying*
1005   I wolde fain wite of her kind, [1]
What she was, this sweet derling,   *darling*
    And in her life where she gan lende."   *lived*

Sir Gawain his eyen then on her cast   *eyes*
    And beheld her fast with herte free,   *carefully*
1010 So that he knew well at the last,
    That the Maid of Ascolot was she,
Which he some time had wooed fast
    His owne leman for to be,   *beloved*
But she answerd him ay in haste
1015   To none but Launcelot wolde she te.   *draw*

To the king then said Sir Gawain tho:
    "Think ye not on this endres day,   *other day*
When my lady the queen and we two
    Stood togeder in your play,

---

[1] *I would like to know about her family lineage*

1020   Of a maid I told you tho,
         That Launcelot loved paramour ay?"   *as a lover forever*
     "Gawain, for sooth," the king said tho,
         "When thou it saidest well think I may."

     "For sooth, sir," then said Sir Gawain,
1025   "This is the maid that I of spake;
     Most in this world, is not to laine,   *hide*
         She loved Launcelot du Lake."
     "Forsooth," the king then gan to sayn,   *did say*
         "Me reweth the deth of her for his sake;   *I rue*
1030   The enchesoun wolde I wite full fain; [1]
         For sorrow I trow deth gan her take."   *believe*

     Then Sir Gawain, the goode knight,
         Sought about her withoute stint   *delay*
     And fand a purse full rich aright,   *richly arrayed*
1035   With gold and perles that was ybent;   *pearls; banded*
     All empty seemed it nought to sight;
         That purse full soon in hand he hent;   *seized*
     A letter there-of then out he twight;   *took*
         Then wite they wolde fain what it ment. [2]

1040   What was there writen wite they wolde,
         And Sir Gawain it took the king,   *gave it to the king*
     And bade him open it that he sholde.
         So did he soon, withoute leesing;   *lying*
     Then fand he when it was unfold
1045   Both the end and the beginning
     (Thus was it writen as men me told)
         Of that fair maidens dying:

     "To King Arthur and all his knightes
         That longe to the Round Table,   *belong*
1050   That courtais been and most of mightes   *who are courteous*

---

[1] *I would very much like to know the cause*
[2] *Then they wanted to know what it said*

     Doughty and noble, trew and stable,   *steadfast*
     And most worshipful in alle fightes,
       To the needful helping and profitable,
     The Maid of Ascolot to rightes   *by right (justly)*
1055   Sendeth greeting, withouten fable;   *without lying (truly)*

     "To you all my plaint I make
       Of the wrong that me is wrought,
     But nought in manner to undertake   *claim*
       That any of you sholde mend it ought,
1060   But only I say for this sake,
       That, though this world were through sought,   *searched through*
     Men sholde nowhere find your make,   *equal (match)*
       All noblesse to find that might be sought. [1]

     "Therefore to you to understand
1065   That for I trewly many a day   *truly*
     Have loved leliest in land,   *most loyally*
       Deth hath me fette of this world away;   *fetched me from*
     To wite for whom, yif ye will fonde,   *know; wish to discover*
       That I so long for in langour lay,
1070   To say the sooth will I not wonde,   *delay*
       For gaines it nought for to say nay.   *For denying it gains nothing*

     "To say you the soothe tale,   *true*
       For whom I have suffred this wo,
     I say deth hath me take with bale,   *suffering*
1075   For the noblest knight that may go;
     Is none so doughty dintes to dele,   *blows; deal out*
       So real ne so fair there-to;   *royal nor*
     But so churlish of manners in feld ne hall,
       Ne know I none of frend ne fo.   *friend nor foe*

1080   "Of fo ne frend, the sooth to say,
       So unhende of thewes is there none;   *discourteous in manners*
     His gentilness was all away,

---

[1] *Though they searched out all the nobleness in the world*

43

All churlish manners he had in wone;		*[his] possession*
For no thing that I coude pray,		*could*
1085	Kneeling ne weeping with rewful mone,	*pitiful moan*
To be my leman he said ever nay,		
And said shortly he wolde have none.		

"Forthy, lordes, for his sake   *Therefore*
    I took to herte grete sorrow and care,
1090 So at the last deth gan me take,
    So that I might live no more;
For trewe loving had I such wrake   *pain*
    And was of bliss ybrought all bare;   *made barren*
All was for Launcelot du Lake,
1095   To wite wisely for whom it were."

When that King Arthur, the noble king,
    Had redde the letter and ken the name,   *read; learned*
He said to Gawain, without leesing,
    That Launcelot was gretly to blame,
1100 And had him won a reproving,   *reproof*
    For ever, and a wicked fame;
Sithe she died for grete loving,
    That he her refused it may him shame.

To the king then said Sir Gawain:
1105   "I gabbed on him this ender day,   *lied about him; other*
That he longed, when I gan sayn,[1]
    With lady other with some other maye.
But sooth then said ye, is not to laine,   *hide*
    That he nolde not his love lay[2]
1110 In so low a place in vain,
    But on a pris lady and a gay."

"Sir Gawain," said the king tho,

---

[1] *When I said that he belonged / To a lady or to some other maid*

[2] *That he would not waste his love / In so low a place (a mere maiden) / But would rather love some noble and gay lady*

44

"What is now thy beste rede?   *advice*
How may we with this maiden do?"
1115   Sir Gawain said: "So God me speed,   *As God may save me*
Yif that ye will assent there-to,
Worshipfully we shull her lede   *Honorably; take*
Into the palais and bury her so   *palace*
As falles a dukes doughter in-deed."   *befits*

1120 There-to the king assented soon;
Sir Gawain did men soon be yare,   *commanded; ready*
And worshipfully, as fell to don,   *fitting to do*
Into the palais they her bore.   *palace*
The king then told, withoute lone,   *concealment*
1125   To all his barons, less and more,
How Launcelot nolde not graunt her boon, *would not grant her plea*
Therefore she died for sorrow and care.

To the queen then went Sir Gawain
And gan to tell her all the case:
1130 "For sooth, madame," he gan to sayn,   *say*
"I yeld me guilty of a trespas.   *confess myself*
I gabbed on Launcelot, is not to laine,   *lied about; hide*
Of that I told you in this place;   *Concerning what*
I said that his bidding bain   *lover ready at his bidding*
1135   The dukes doughter of Ascolot was.

"Of Ascolot that maiden free
I said you she was his leman;
That I so gabbed it reweth me,   *lied; pains me*
And all the sooth now tell I can;
1140 He nolde her not, we mowe well see; [1]
For-thy dede is that white as swan;
This letter there-of warrant will be;
She plaineth on Launcelot to eche man." *complains about; every*

---

[1] *He did not want her, as we can well see, / And therefore, that maiden, as white as a swan, is dead*

The queen was wroth as wind,   *angry*

1145   And to Sir Gawain said she then:

"For sooth, sir, thou were too unkind

    To gabbe so upon any man,   *lie so about*

But thou haddest wiste the sooth in mind,   *Unless you knew*

    Whether that it were sooth or none;

1150   Thy courtaisy was all behind   *gone*

    When thou tho sawes first began.   *those tales*

"Thy worship thou undidest gretlich,   *honor; damaged greatly*

    Such wrong to wite that goode knight;   *So wrongly to blame*

I trow that he ne aguilt thee never much [1]

1155   Why that thou oughtest with no right   *cause*

To gabbe on him so vilainlich,   *lie*

    Thus behind him, out of his sight.

And, sir, thou ne wost not right wiselich [2]

    What harm hath falle there-of and might.

1160   "I wend thou haddest be stable and trew

    And full of all courtaisy,

But now me think thy manners new;   *changed*

    They ben all turned to vilainy,   *are; churlishness*

Now thou on knightes makest thy glewe   *tricks*

1165   To lie upon them for envy;

Who that thee worshippeth, it may them rew;   *honors*

    Therefore, devoied my company!"   *leave*

Sir Gawain then slyly went away;   *wisely*

    He sigh the queen agreved sore;   *saw; sorely aggrieved*

1170   No more to her then wolde he say,

    But trowed her wrath have ever more.   *believed; would last forever*

The queen then, as she nigh wode were,   *crazy*

---

[1] *I believe he never wronged you so much / That you ought so unjustly / To lie about him so churlishly*

[2] *And, sir, you do not know right wisely (realize) / What harm has and could yet come from what you said*

Wringed her handes and said: "Wele-away!
 Alas! in world that I was bore!   *born*
1175 That I am wretched well say I may!"

"Herte, alas! Why were thou wode   *crazy*
 To trowe that Launcelot du Lake   *believe*
Were so false and fikel of mood   *fickle*
 Another leman than thee to take?
1180 Nay, certes, for all this worldes good,
 He nolde to me have wrought such wrake!"   *pain*

(At this point one leaf from the manuscript has been lost; evidently it
told of the burial of the Maid of Ascolot and of the queen's distress, the
material in chapters 74 and 78 of the French *Mort Artu*, our poet's source.
Probably not more than ninety lines are missing, but I follow the line-
numbering in Bruce's edition.)

To find a man for her to fight
 Or elles yeld her to be brent;   *surrender; burnt*
1320 If she were on a quest of knightes   *judgment*
 Well she wiste she sholde be shent;   *shamefully destroyed*
Though that she aguilt had no wight,   *of guilt; no trace*
 No lenger life might her be lent.   *to her; granted*

The king then sighed and gave him ill,   *made himself ill*
1325 And to Sir Gawain then he yede,
To Bors de Gawnes and Lionel,
 To Ector that doughty was in deed,
And asked if any were in will   *intended*
 To help him in that mikel need.
1330 The queen on knees before them fell,
 That nigh out of her wit she yede.

The knightes answerd with little pride —
 Their hertes was full of sorrow and wo —
Said: "All we saw and sat beside
1335 The knight when she with poison slogh,   *slew*
And sithe, in herte is not to hide,
 Sir Gawain over the borde him drow;   *table; drew*

47

Again the right we will not ride,   *Against*
    We saw the sooth verily ynow."   *very truly*

1340   The queene wept and sighed sore;
    To Bors de Gawnes went she tho,   *then*
On knees before him fell she there,
    That nigh her herte brast in two;   *burst*
"Lord Bors," she said, "thine ore!   *mercy*
1345   Today I shall to dethe go,
But yif thy worthy will were   *Unless*
    To bring my life out of this wo."

Bors de Gawnes stille stood,
    And wrothe away his eyen went;   *angrily; eyes turned*
1350   "Madame," he said, "By Cross on Rood,   *Body (?); Cross*
    Thou art well worthy to be brent!   *burned*
The noblest body of flesh and blood,
    That ever was yet in erthe lente,   *given*
For thy will and thy wicked mood,   *mind*
1355   Out of our company is went."   *has gone*

Then she wept and gave her ill,   *made herself sick*
    And to Sir Gawain then she yede;
On knees down before him fell,
    That nigh out of her wit she yede;
1360   "Mercy!" she cried loud and shrill,
    "Lord, as I no guilt have of this deed,
Yif it were thy worthy will   *[I ask] if it*
    Today to help me in this need?"

Gawain answerd with little pride;
1365   His herte was full of sorrow and wo:
"Dame, saw I not and sat beside
    The knight when thou with poison slogh?   *slew*
And sithe, in herte is not to hide,
    Myself over the borde him drow.   *drew*
1370   Again the right will I not ride;
    I saw the sooth very ynow."   *very truly*

Then she went to Lionel,
    That ever had been her owne knight;
On knees adown before him fell,
1375   That nigh she loste main and might.
"Mercy," she cried loud and shrill,
    "Lord, as I ne have aguilte no wight,   *harmed no one*
Yif it were thy worthy will   *[I ask] if it*
    For my life to take this fight?"

1380 "Madame, how may thou to us take [1]
    And wot thyself so witterly   *certainly*
That thou hast Launcelot du Lake
    Brought out of ower company?
We may sigh and moning make
1385   When we see knightes keen in cry;   *company*
By Him that me to man gan shape,   *create*
    We are glad that thou it abye!"   *suffer*

Then full sore she gan her drede;   *fear for herself*
    Well she wiste her life was lorn;   *lost*
1390 Loude gan she weep and grede,   *cry*
    And Ector kneeles she beforn:
"For Him that on the Rood gan sprede   *Cross; spread*
    And for us bore the crown of thorn,
Ector, help now in this need,
1395   Or, certes, today my life is lorn!"

"Madame, how may thou to us take,   *come to us*
    Or how sholde I for thee fight?
Take thee now Launcelot du Lake,   *Entrust yourself to*
    That ever has been thine owne knight.
1400 My dere brother, for thy sake
    I ne shall him never see with sight!
Cursed be he that the batail take   *battle*
    To save thy life again the right!"

---

[1] *Madame, how can you come to us / When you yourself know so well*

49

There wolde no man the batail take;
1405   The queen went to her chamber so;
So dolefully mone gan she make,   *moan*
    That nigh her herte brast in two;
For sorrow gan she shiver and quake,
    And said: "Alas and wele-a-wo!
1410   Why nadde I now Launcelot du Lake?   *do I not have*
    All the court nolde me not slo!   *would not be able to slay me*

"Ivel have I beset the deed,   *Evilly (i.e., uselessly); used*
    That I have worshipped so many a knight,   *honored*
[And I have no man in my need]
1415   For my love dare take a fight.
Lord, King of alle thede,   *nations*
    That all the world shall rede and right,   *advise; direct*
Launcelot Thou save and heed, [1]
    Sithe I ne shall never him see with sight."

The queene wept and gave her ill;   *made herself sick*
1420   When she saw the fire was yare,   *ready*
Then morned she full still.   *mourned*
    To Bors de Gawnes went she there,
Besought him, yif it were his will,
    To help her in her mikel care;
1425   In swooning she before him fell;
    The wordes might she speke no more.

When Bors saw the queen so bright,
    Of her he hadde grete pitee;
In his armes he held her up-right,
1430   Bade her of good comfort be:
"Madame, but there come a better knight   *unless*
    That wolde the batail take for thee,   *battle*
I shall myselfe for thee fight,
    While any life may last in me."

---

[1] *May You save and care for Launcelot*

1435	Then was the queene wonder blithe,	*glad*
	That Bors de Gawnes wolde for her fight,	
	That ner for joy she swooned swithe,	*nearly; promptly*
	But as that he her held up-right;	*Except that*
	To her chamber he led her blithe,	
1440	To ladies and to maidens bright,	
	And bade she sholde it no man kithe,	*tell no man of it*
	Til he were armed an redy dight.	*ready*

Bors, that was bold and keen,
    Cleped all his other knightes,
1445 And tooken counsel them between,
    The beste that they couthe and might,   *knew how; could do*
How that he hath hight the queen   *promised*
    That ilke day for her to fight
Against Sir Mador, full of teen,   *anger*
1450   To save her life, yif that he might.

The knightes answerd with wo and wrake   *pain*
    And said they wiste witterly   *certainly*
That "She hath Launcelot du Lake
    Brought out of ower company.   *our*
1455 Nis none that nolde this batail take [1]
    Ere she had any vilainy,
But we will not so glad her make,
    Before we ne suffer her to be sorry."   *allow; repent*

Bors and Lionel the knight,
1460   Ector, that doughty was of deed,
To the forest then went they right
    Their orisons at the chapel to bede   *prayers; offer*
To our Lord God, all full of might,
    That day sholde lene him well to speed, [2]
1465 A grace to vanquish the fight;
    Of Sir Mador they had grete drede.

---

[1] *There is not one who would have refused this battle / Before her behavior became criminal*

[2] *That he might grant him (Bors) success, / Give him the grace to win the battle*

As they came by the forest side,
   Their orisons for to make,   *prayers*
The noblest knight then saw they ride
1470   That ever was in erthe shape;   *created*
His loreme lemed all with pride;   *reins gleamed*
   Steed and armour all was blake;
His name is nought to hele and hide: *conceal*
   He hight Sir Launcelot du Lake!

1475 What wonder was though they were blithe,
   When they their master see with sight!
On knees fell they as swithe,
   And thanked all to God All-might.
Joy it was to here and lithe   *hear; listen to*
1480   The meeting of the noble knight;
And after he asked also swithe:
   "How now fares my lady bright?"

Bors then told him all the right,
   It was no lenger for to hide,
1485 How there died a Scottish knight,
   At the mete the queen beside: *meal*
"Today, sir, is her deth all dight,   *prepared*
   It may no lenger be to bide,   *wait*
And I for her have take the fight.

1490 "Sir Mador, strong though that he be,
   I hope he shall well prove his might."   *expect*
"To the court now wend ye three
   And recomfort my lady bright;   *comfort*
But look ye speke no word of me;
1495   I will come as a strange knight."   *foreign*

Launcelot, that was mikel of might,
   Abides in the forest green;
To the courte went these other knightes
   For to recomfort the queen.   *comfort*
1500 To make her glad with all their might
   Grete joy they made them between;
For-why she ne sholde drede no wight,   *So that; nothing*
   Of good comfort they bade her ben.   *be*

Bordes were set and clothes spredde;   *Tables*
1505   The king himself is gone to sit;

The queen is to the table led,
    With cheekes that were wan and wet;
Of sorrow were they never unsad;
    Might they neither drink ne ete;
1510 The queen of dethe was sore adredde,   *afraid*
    That grimly teres gan she let.

And as they were at the thridde mese,   *third course*
    The king and all the court bydene,   *as well*
Sir Mador all redy was,
1515 With helm and sheld and hauberk sheen;   *shining*
Among them all before the dese,   *dais (raised platform)*
    He bloweth out upon the queen   *raises an outcry against*
To have his right withouten lees,
    As were the covenantes them between.   *agreements*

1520 The king looked on all his knightes;
    Was he never yet so wo;
Saw he never on him dight   *anyone prepare himself*
    Against Sir Mador for to go.
Sir Mador swore by Goddes might,
1525 As he was man of herte thro,   *fierce*
But yif he hastely have his right
    Among them all he sholde her slo.   *slay*

Then spake the king of mikel might,
    That ay was courtais and hende:
1530 "Sir, let us ete and sithen us dight;   *afterwards prepare ourselves*
    This day nis not yet gone to the end.
Yet might there come such a knight,
    Yif Goddes will were him to send,
To finde thee thy fill of fight
1535 Ere the sun to grounde wend.

Bors then lough on Lionel;   *laughed*
    Wiste no man of their hertes word;
His chamber anon he wendes til,
    Withoute any other word,
1540 Armed him at all his will,
    With helm and hauberk, spere and sword;   *spear*
Again then comes he full still
    And set him down to the borde.

The teres ran on the kinges knee   *tears*

1545	For joy that he saw Bors adight;	*prepared*
	Up he rose with herte free	
	And Bors in armes clippes right,	*embraces*
	And said: "Bors, God foryeld it thee,	*reward you for it*
	In this need that thou wolde fight;	
1550	Well acquitest thou it me	*Well do you repay me for it*
	That I have worshipped any knight!"	*honored*

	Then as Sir Mador loudest spake	
	The queen of tresoun to becall,	*accuse*
	Comes Sir Launcelot du Lake,	
1555	Ridand right into the hall.	*Riding directly*
	His steed and armour all was blake,	
	His visor over his eyen fall;	*eyes; was lowered*
	Many a man began to quake;	
	Adrede of him nigh were they all.	*Afraid; nearly*

1560	Then spake the king, mikel of might,	
	That hende was in ich a sithe:	*every occasion*
	"Sir, is it your will to light,	*alight*
	Ete and drink and make you blithe?"	
	Launcelot spake as a strange knight:	*foreign*
1565	"Nay, sir," he said as swithe,	*quickly*
	"I herde tell here of a fight;	
	I come to save a ladyes life.	

	"Ivel hath the queen beset her deedes	*To no effect; employed*
	That she hath worshipped many a knight,	
1570	And she hath no man in her needes	
	That for her life dare take a fight.	
	Thou that her of tresoun gredes [1]	
	Hastely that thou be dight;	
	Out of thy wit though that thou wedes,	*run mad*
1575	Today thou shalt prove all thy might."	

	Then was Sir Mador also blithe	
	As fowl of day after the night;	*bird*
	To his steed he went that sithe,	
	As man that was of muche might.	
1580	To the feld then ride they swithe;	
	Them followes both king and knight,	

---

[1] *You who accuse her of treason, / Quickly see that you are ready to fight*

The batail for to see and lithe;   *hear*
   Saw never no man stronger fight!

     Unhorsed were bothe knightes keen,
1585   They metten with so muche main,   *met; force*
     And sithe they fought with swordes keen.
       Both on foot, the sooth to sayn.   *say*
     In all the batailes that Launcelot had been,
       With hard acountres him again,   *encounters; against*
1590   In pointe had he never been
       So nigh-hand for to have been slain.

     There was so wonder strong a fight,
       O foot nolde nouther flee ne found, [1]
     From lowe noon til late night,   *low noon (about ten a.m.)*
1595   But given many a woful wound.   *they give*
     Launcelot then gave a dint with might;
       Sir Mador falles at last to ground;
     "Mercy!" cries that noble knight,
       For he was seke and sore unsound.

1600   Though Launcelot were breme as bore,   *fierce*
       Full sternely he gan up stand;
     O dint wolde he smite no more;   *A blow*
       His sword he threw out of his hand.
     Sir Mador by God then swore:
1605   "I have fought in many a land,
     With knightes both less and more,
       And never yet ere my match I fand;

     "But, Sir, a prayer I wolde make,
       For thing that ye love most on life,
1610   And for Our Sweete Lady sake,   *Lady's (i.e., Virgin Mary's)*
       Your name that ye wolde me kithe."   *tell*
     Launcelot gan his visor up take,
       And hendely him shewed that sithe;
     When he saw Sir Launcelot du Lake,
1615   Was never man on molde so blithe.   *earth*

     "Lord," then said he, "Wele is me,
       Mine avauntement that I may make   *boast*

---

[1] *Neither would flee nor advance one foot*

That I have stande one dint of thee,   *stood; blow*
    And foughten with Launcelot du Lake;
1620 My brothers deth forgiven be
    To the queen for thy sake."
Launcelot him kist with herte free,   *kissed*
    And in his armes gan him up take.

King Arthur then loude spake
1625   Among his knightes to the queen:
"Ya, yonder is Launcelot du Lake,   *Yea*
    Yif I him ever with sight have seen!"
They riden and ronne then for his sake,   *run*
    The king and all his knightes keen;
1630 In his armes he gan him take;
    The king him kist and court bydene.   *kissed*

Then was the queene glad ynow,
    When she saw Launcelot du Lake,
That nigh for joy she fell in swough,   *swoon*
1635   But as the lordes her gan up take.   *Except that*
The knightes alle wept and loughe   *laughed*
    For joy as they togeder spake;
With Sir Mador, withouten wo,
    Full soon acordement gonne they make.   *reconcilement*

1640 It was no lenger for to abide
    But to the castle they rode as swithe,
With trompes and with mikel pride,   *trumpeters*
    That joy it was to here and lithe;   *listen to*
Though Sir Mador might not go ne ride,   *walk*
1645   To the court is he brought that sithe,   *time*
And knightes upon ich a side
    To make him both glad and blithe.

The squiers then were taken all,   *squires*
    And they are put in harde pain,   *i.e., tortured*
1650 Which that had served in the hall   *Those who*
    When the knight was with poisun slain.
There he graunted among them all [1]
    (It might no lenger be to laine)   *hide*
How in an apple he did the gall,   *put the poison*

---

[1] *One among all the squires there admitted*

56

1655	And had it thought to Sir Gawain.	*intended for*

When Sir Mador herde all the right,
    That no guilt had the lady sheen,   *bright*
For sorrow he lost main and might
    And on knees fell before the queen.
1660 Launcelot then him held up right,
    For love that was them between;
He kist both king and knight   *kissed*
    And sithen all the court bydene.   *then; as well*

The squier then was done to shende,   *squire; put to death*
1665   As it was bothe law and right,
Drawen and honged and for-brende,   *Drawn; hanged; burned*
    Before Sir Mador, the noble knight.
In the castel they gonne forth lende,   *castle; remain*
    The Joyous Gard then was it hight;   *called*
1670 Launcelot, that was so hende,   *courteous*
    They honoured him with all their might.

A time befell, sooth to sayn,   *say*
    The knightes stood in chamber and spake,
Both Gaheriet and Sir Gawain,
1675   And Mordred, that mikel couthe of wrake,   *knew much of trouble-making*
"Alas!" then said Sir Agravain,
    "How false men shall we us make?
How long shall we hele and laine   *conceal and hide*
    The tresoun of Launcelot du Lake?

1680 "Well we wote, withouten ween,   *know; without doubt*
    The king Arthur our eme sholde be,   *uncle*
And Launcelot lies by the queen;
    Again the king traitour is he,
And that wote all the court bydene,
1685   And iche day it here and see;
To the king we sholde it mene,   *tell*
    Yif ye will do by the counsel of me."

"Well wote we," said Sir Gawain,
    "That we are of the kinges kin,
1690 And Launcelot is so mikel of main   *great; power*
    That suche wordes were better blinne.   *stopped*
Well wot thou, brother Agravain,
    Thereof sholde we but harmes win;

Yet were it better to hele and laine   *hide; conceal*
1695   Than war and wrake thus to begin.

"Well wot thou, brother Agravain,
    Launcelot is hardy knight and thro;   *fierce*
King and court had oft been slain
    Nadde he been better than we mo,   *Had he not*
1700   And sithen might I never sayn
    The love that has been between us two;
Launcelot shall I never betrayn,   *betray*
    Behind his back to be his fo.

"Launcelot is kinges son full good,
1705   And thereto hardy knight and bold,
And sithen, and him need bestood,   *And, moreover, if he had need*
    Many a land wolde with him hold.   *i.e., be his ally*
Shed there sholde be mikel blood
    For this tale, yif it were told;
1710   Sir Agravain, he were full wode,   *insane*
    That such a thing beginne wolde."

Then thus-gates as the knightes stood,   *in this manner*
    Gawain and all the other press,
In come the king with milde mood;
1715   Gawain then said: "Fellowes, pees!"   *be still*
The king for wrath was nighe wode
    For to wite what it was;
Agravain swore by Cross and Rood: *cross*
    "I shall it you tell withoute lees."   *lies*

1720 Gawain to his chamber went;
    Of this tale nolde he nought here;   *would not hear any*
Gaheriet and Gaheries of his assent,
    With their brother went they there;
Well they wiste that all was shent,   *lost*
1725   And Sir Gawain by God then swere: *swore*
"Here now is made a comsement   *commencement*
    That beth not finished many a yere."   *will not be*

Agravain told all bydene
    To the king with simple cheer,   *innocent expression*
1730 How Launcelot ligges by the queen,   *lies*
    And so has done full many a yere,
And that wot all the court bydene

And iche day it see and here:
"And we have false and traitours been
1735 That we ne wolde never to you diskere."   *reveal*

"Alas!" then said the kinge there,
"Certes, that were grete pitee;
So as man nadde never yet more   *no man ever had more*
Of beautee ne of bountee,   *generosity*
1740 Ne man in world was never yet ere
Of so mikel nobilitee.
Alas, full grete dole it were
In him sholde any tresoun be!

"But sithe it is so, withouten fail,
1745 Sir Agravain, so God thee rede,
What were now thy best counsel,
For to take him with the deed?   *in the act*
He is man of such apparail,   *accomplishments*
Of him I have full mikel drede;
1750 All the court nolde him assail
Yif he were armed upon his steed."

"Sir, ye and all the court bydene
Wendeth tomorrow on hunting right,
And sithen send word to the queen
1755 That ye will dwell without all night,   *outside (the court)*
And I and other twelve knightes keen
Full prively we shall us dight;   *secretly*
We shall him have withouten ween   *doubtless*
Tomorrow ere any day be light."

1760 On the morrow with all the court bydene
The king gan on hunting ride,
And sithen he sent word to the queen
That he wolde all night out abide.
Agravain with twelve knightes keen
1765 Atte home beleft that ilke tide   *At home remained*
Of all the day they were not seen,
So privily they gonne them hide.   *secretly*

Tho was the queene wonder blithe
That the king wolde at the forest dwell;
1770 To Launcelot she sent as swithe
And bade that he sholde come her til.   *to her*

59

Sir Bors de Gawnes began to lithe,   *listen*
   Though his herte liked ill;   *it ill-pleased his heart*
"Sir," he said, "I wolde you kithe   *tell*
1775   A word, yif that it were your will.   *i.e., if you please*

"Sir, tonight I rede ye dwell;   *remain (here)*
   I drede there be some tresoun dight
With Agravain, that is so fell,   *By; fierce*
   That waites you both day and night.
1780 Of all that ye have gone her til,[1]
   Ne greved me never yet no wight,
Ne never yet gave mine herte to ill,
   So mikel as it doth tonight."

"Bors," he said, "holde still;
1785   Such wordes are not to kithe;   *make known*
I will wend my lady til,
   Some new tithandes for to lithe;
I ne shall nought but wite her will;   *know what she wants*
   Look ye make you glad and blithe;
1790 Certainly I nill not dwell,   *will not remain*
   But come again to you all swithe."

For-why he wend have comen soon   *Because; return immediately*
   For to dwell had he not thought,
None armour he did him upon   *put upon himself*
1795   But a robe all single wrought;   *uniquely made*
In his hand a sword he fone,   *grasped*
   Of tresoun dredde he him right nought;[2]
There was no man under the moon
   He wend with harm durst him have sought.

1800 When he come to the lady sheen
   He kist and clipped that sweete wight;   *kissed; embraced; creature*
For sooth, they never wolde ween   *expect*
   That any tresoun was there dight;
So mikel love was them between
1805   That they not departe might;

---

[1] *Of all the nights that you have gone to her, / None ever bothered me in any way / Or made my heart so sick / As this one does tonight*

[2] *He had absolutely no fear of treason (betrayal); / He supposed there was no man on earth / Who would dare attempt to do him harm*

To bed he goeth with the queen,
    And there he thought to dwell all night.

He was not busked in his bed,   *He had hardly gotten in his bed*
    Launcelot in the queenes bowr,   *bower (bedroom)*
1810 Come Agravain and Sir Mordred,
    With twelve knightes stiff in stour;   *bold in battle*
Launcelot of tresoun they begredde,   *accused*
    Calld him false and kinges traitour,
And he so strongly was bestedde,   *set upon*
1815   There-in he had none armour.

"Wele-away," then said the queen,
    "Launcelot, what shall worthe of us two?   *become*
The love that hath been us between,
    To such ending that it sholde go!
1820 With Agravain, that is so keen,
    That night and day hath been our foe,
Now I wot, withouten ween,
    That all our wele is turned to wo!"

"Lady," he said, "thou must blinne;   *stop*
1825   Wide I wot these wordes beth rife; [1]
But is here any armour in
    That I may have to save my life?"
"Certes, nay," she said then,
    "This aunter is so wonder strife   *circumstance; very bad*
1830 That I ne may to none armour win   *obtain*
    Helm ne hauberk, sword ne knife."   *(see note)*

Ever Agravain and Sir Mordred
    Calld him recreant false knight,   *perjured*
Bade him rise out of his bed,
1835   For he moste needes with them fight.   *must; by necessity*
In his robe then he him cledde,   *clad*
    Though he none armour gette might;
Wrothly out his sword he gredde;   *Fiercely; drew*
    The chamber door he set up right.   *stood close to*

1840 An armed knight before in went
    And wend Launcelot well to slo,   *thought; slay*

---

[1] *I know that this news will be widely told*

But Launcelot gave him such a dint,
    That to the grounde gan he go;
The other all again then stent;   *stopped*
1845   After him durste follow no mo;   *dared*
To the chamber door he sprent   *leaped*
    And clasped it with barres two.   *locked; two bars*

The knight that Launcelot has slain,
    His armour fand he fair and bright;
1850 Hastely he hath them off-drayn   *the armor drawn off*
    And there-in himselfe dight.
"Now know thou well, Sir Agravain,
    Thou prisouns me no more tonight!"
Out then sprang he with mikel main,
1855   Himself against them all to fight.

Launcelot then smote with herte good;
    Wite ye well, withouten lees,
Sir Agravain to dethe yode,   *went*
    And sithen all the other press;   *then the rest of the gang*
1860 Was none so strong that him withstood,
    By he had made a little rese,   *By the time; attack*
But Mordred fled as he were wode,
    To save his life full fain he was.   *eager*

Launcelot to his chamber yode,   *went*
1865   To Bors and to his other knightes;
Bors, armed, before him stood;
    To bedde yet was he not dight.   *bed*
The knightes for fere was nighe wode,   *fear*
    So were they dreched all that night;   *disturbed by dreams*
1870 But blithe wexed they in their mood
    When they their master saw with sight.

"Sir," said Bors, the hardy knight,
    "After you have we thought full long;
To bedde durst I me not dight,
1875   For drede ye had some aunter strong;   *fierce encounter*
Our knightes have be dreched tonight   *disturbed by dreams*
    That some naked out of bedde sprong,
For-thy we were full sore affright,
    Lest some tresoun were us among."

1880 "Ya, Bors, drede thee no wight,

But beth of herte good and bold,
And swithe awaken up all my knightes
And look which wille with us hold;
Look they be armed and redy dight,
1885   For it is sooth that thou me told;
We have begonne this ilke night   *begun*
    That shall bring many a man full cold."

Bors then spake with drery mood: *dreary*
    "Sir," he said, "sithe it is so,
1890 We shall be of hertes good,
    After the wele to take the wo."
The knightes sprent as they were wode,   *leaped*
    And to their harnes gonne they go;   *harness (equipment)*
At the morrow armed before him stood
1895   A hundreth knightes and squiers mo.   *hundred*

When they were armed and redy dight,
    A softe pas forth gonne they ride,   *At a gentle pace*
As men that were of mikel might,
    To a forest there beside.
1900 Launcelot arrayes all his knightes,   *arranges in formation*
    And there they lodgen them to bide.   *lodge*
Til they herde of the lady bright,
    What aunter of her sholde betide.   *chance*

Mordred then took a way full gain,   *direct*
1905   And to the forest went he right,
His aunters told, for sooth to sayn,   *adventures*
    That were befallen that ilke night.
"Mordred, have ye that traitour slain,
    Or how have ye with him dight?"
1910 "Nay, sir, but dede is Agravain,
    And so are all our other knightes."

When it herde Sir Gawain,
    That was so hardy knight and bold:
"Alas! Is my brother slain?"
1915   Sore his herte began to colde: *grow cold*
"I warned well Sir Agravain,
    Ere ever yet this tale was told,
Launcelot was so much of main
    Against him was strong to hold."   *i.e., difficult*

1920 It was no lenger for to bide;
   King and all his knightes keen
  Took their counsel in that tide,
   What was best do with the queen.   *to do*
  It was no lenger for to bide;
1925 That day forbrent sholde she ben.   *burned to death*

  The fire then made they in the feld;
   There-to they brought that lady free;
  All that ever might wepen weld   *weapon*
   About her armed for to be.
1930 Gawain, that stiff was under sheld,
   Gaheriet, ne Gaheries ne wolde not see;
  In their chamber they them held;
   Of her they hadde grete pitee.

  The king Arthur that ilke tide
1935 Gawain and Gaheries for sent;
  Their answers were not for to hide;
   They ne wolde not be of his assent;
  Gawain wolde never be ner beside
   There any woman sholde be brent;   *burned*
1940 Gaheriet and Gaheries with little pride,
   All unarmed thider they went.

  A squier gan tho tithandes lithe,   *heard the news*
   That Launcelot to court hath sent;   *Whom*
  To the forest he went as swithe,
1945 There Launcelot and his folk was lente, *stayed*
  Bade them come and haste blithe: *hasten quickly*
   "The queen is ledde to be brent!"
  And they to horse and armes swithe,
   And ich one before other sprent.   *leaped*

1950 The queen by the fire stood,
   And in her smok all redy was;   *(see note)*
  Lordinges was there many and good,
   And grete power, withouten lees;
  Launcelot sprent as he were wode;
1955 Full soone parted he the press;
  Was none so stiff before him stood
   By he had made a little rese.   *By the time; attack*

  There was no steel stood them again,

Though fought they but a little stound;   *time*
1960 Lordinges that were much of main,
 Many good were brought to ground;
Gaheriet and Gaheries both were slain
 With many a doleful dethes wound;
The queen they took withoute laine,   *without doubt*
1965   And to the forest gonne they found.   *go*

The tithinges is to the kinge brought,
 How Launcelot has tan away the queen: *taken*
"Such wo as there is wrought!
 Slain are all our knightes keen!"
1970 Down he fell and swooned oft;
 Grete dole it was to here and seen;   *see*
So ner his herte the sorrow sought,
 Almost his life wolde no man ween.   *Almost no one expected him to live*

"Jesu Crist! What may I sayn?
1975   In erthe was never man so wo;
Such knightes as there are slain,
 In all this world there is no mo.
Let no man telle Sir Gawain
 Gaheriet his brother is dede him fro,
1980 But wele-away, the rewful reyne,   *pitiful kingdom*
 That ever Launcelot was my fo!"

Gawain gan in his chamber him hold;
 Of all the day he nolde not out go;
A squier then the tithandes told;
1985   What wonder though his herte were wo?
"Alas," he said, "My brother bold,
 Were Gaheriet be dede me fro?" [1]
So sore his herte began to colde,   *grow cold*
 Almost he wolde himselfe slo.

1990 The squier spake with drery mood
 To recomfort Sir Gawain: *comfort*
"Gaheriet ailes nought but good; [2]
 He will soon come again."
Gawain sprent as he were wode

---

[1] *Can it be that Gahariet is dead and away from me?*

[2] *Nothing but good ails Gahariet (he is all right)*

65

1995	To the chamber there they lay slain;	
	The chamber floor all ran on blood	*with*
	And clothes of gold were over them drayn.	*drawn*

A cloth he heves then upon height;　　　　　　　　*lifts; up high*
　What wonder though his herte were sore,
2000　So dolefully to see them dight,
　　That ere so doughty knightes were!
When he his brother saw with sight,
　A word might he speke no more;
There he lost both main and might
2005　　And over him fell in swooning there.

Of swooning when he might awake,
　The hardy knight, Sir Gawain,
By God he swore and loude spake,
　As man that muche was of main:
2010　"Betwix me and Launcelot du Lake,
　　Nis man on erthe, for sooth to sayn,　　　　*There is no man*
Shall trewes set and pees make　　　　　　　　*truce*
　Ere either of us have other slain!"

A squier that Launcelot to court had sent
2015　　Of the tithandes gan he lithe;
To the forest is he went
　　And told Launcelot also swithe
How lordinges that were rich of rent,　　　　　*property*
　Fele good had lost their life,　　　　　　　　*Many*
2020　Gaheriet and Gaheries sought their end;
　　But then was Launcelot nothing blithe.

"Lord," he said, "What may this ben?"　　　　　*be*
　Jesu Crist! What may I sayn?
The love that hath betwixt us been!
2025　　That ever Gaheriet me was again!　　　　*was against me*
Now I wot for all bydene
　A sorry man is Sir Gawain;
Accordement thar me never ween　　*I may never expect reconciliation*
　Til either of us have other slain."

2030　Launcelot gan with his folk forth wend,
　With sorry herte and drery mood.
To queenes and countesses fele he send　　　　*many*
　And grete ladies of gentle blood,

66

That he had oft their landes defend
2035   And foughten when them need bestood.
Ichon her power him lend   *Each one; granted*
    And made his party stiff and good.

Queenes and countesses that riche were
    Send him erles with grete meyne;   *company*
2040 Other ladies that might no more   *could (send)*
    Sent him barons or knightes free.
So mikel folk to him gan fare
    Hidous it was his host to see;   *Hideous (frightening)*
To the Joyous Gard went he there
2045   And held him in that strong citee.

Launcelotes herte was full sore
    For the lady fair and bright;
A damesel he did be yare,   *commanded to be ready*
    In rich apparail was she dight,
2050 Hastely in message for to fare
    To the king of mikel might,
To prove it false — what might he more? —   *prove [the accusation] false*
    But proffers him therefore to fight.

The maiden is redy for to ride,
2055   In a full rich apparailment
Of samite green, with mikel pride,   *silk*
    That wrought was in the Orient;
A dwarf sholde wende by her side;   *travel*
    Such was Launcelotes commaundement;   *command*
2060 So were the manneres in that tide,   *customs; time*
    When a maid on message went.   *as a messenger*

To the castle when she come,
    In the palais gan she light;   *palace*
To the king her errand she saide soon   *message*
2065   (By him sat Sir Gawain the knight),
Said that lies were said him upon;
    Trew they were by day and night;   *they (Lancelot and Guinevere)*
To prove it as a knight sholde don   *do*
    Launcelot profferes him to fight.

2070 The king Arthur spekes there
    Wordes that were keen and thro: *bold*

"He ne might prove it never more, [1]
    But of my men that he wolde slo.
By Jesu Crist," the king swore
2075   And Sir Gawain then also,
"His deedes shall be bought full sore,   *dearly*
    But yif no steel nill in him go!" [2]

The maiden hath her answer;
    To the Joyous Gard gan she ride;
2080   Such as the kinges wordes were
    She told Launcelot in that tide.
Launcelot sighed wonder sore,
    Teres from his eyen gan glide.
Bors de Gawnes by God then swore:
2085   "In middes the feld we shall them bide!"

Arthur wolde no lenger abide,
    But hastes him with all his might.
Messengeres did he go and ride,   *commanded to walk and ride*
    That they ne sholde let for day ne night,   *stop*
2090   Throughout Yngland by ich a side,   *on every side*
    To erle, baron, and to knight,
Bade them come that ilke tide,
    With horse strong and armour bright.

Though the knight that were dede them fro, [3]
2095   Thereof was all their mikel care,
Three hundreth they made mo,
    Out of castle ere they wolde fare,
Of Yngland and Ireland also,
    Of Wales and Scottes that beste were,
2100   Launcelot and his folkes to slo
    With hertes breme as any bore.

When this host was all boun,   *ready*
    It was no lenger for to bide,
Raises spere and gonfanoun,   *banner*
2105   As men that were of mikel pride;

---

[1] *Even if he could not prove it, he would slay some of my men*

[2] *Unless no steel (sword) will go in him*

[3] *Although their great sorrow was for the knight that was dead and away from them*

With helm and sheld and hauberk brown,   *shining*
   Gawain himself before gan ride
To the Joyous Gard, that riche town,   *fortified place*
   And set a sege on ech a side.   *siege*

2110 About the Joyous Gard they lay
   Seventeen weekes and well more,
Til fell upon a day
   Launcelot home bade them fare:
   "Breke your sege! Wendes away!   *Break; Turn*
2115   You to slay grete pitee it were."
He said: "Alas and wele-away,
   That ever began this sorrow sore!"

Ever the king and Sir Gawain
   Calld him false recreant knight,   *perjured*
2120 And said he had his brethern slain,
   And traitour was by day and night,
Bade him come and prove his main
   In the feld with them to fight.
Launcelot sighed, for sooth to sayn;
2125   Grete dole it was to see with sight.

So loud they Launcelot gonne ascry,   *call at*
   With vois and hidous hornes bere, *braying of horns*
Bors de Gawnes standes him by,
   And Launcelot makes ivel cheer.   *a sour face*
2130 "Sir," he said, "wherefore and why
   Sholde we these proude wordes here?
Me think ye fare as cowardly
   As we ne durst no man nighe ner.   *As if we dared approach no man*

"Dight we us in rich array,   *dress*
2135   Both with spere and with sheld,
As swithe as ever that we may,
   And ride we out into the feld.
While my life laste may,
   This day I ne shall my wepen yeld; *weapon; surrender*
2140 Therefore my life I dare well lay   *wager*
   We two shall make them all to held."   *withdraw*

"Alas," quod Launcelot, "Wo is me,   *said*
   That ever sholde I see with sight
Again my lord for to be,

2145   The noble king that made me knight!
      Sir Gawain, I beseeche thee,
        As thou art man of muche might,
      In the feld let not my lord be, [1]
        Ne that thyself with me not fight."

2150   It may no lenger for to bide,
      But busked them and made all boun;   *hastened; ready*
      When they were redy for to ride,
        They raised spere and gonfanoun;   *banner*
      When these hostes gan samen glide,   *together*
2155   With vois and hidous hornes soun,   *voice; hideous; sound*
      Grete pitee was on either side,
        So fele good there were laid down.   *many; slain*

      Sir Lionel with muche main,   *strength*
        With a spere before gan found;
2160   Sir Gawain rides him again,
        Horse and man he bore to ground,
      That all men wend he had been slain;   *thought*
        Sir Lionel had such a wound
      Out of the feld was he drayn,   *drawn*
2165   For he was seke and sore unsound.

      In all the feld that ilke tide
        Might no man stand Launcelot again,
      And sithen as fast as he might ride [2]
        To save that no man sholde be slain.
2170   The king was ever ner beside
        And hew on him with all his main,   *hewed*
      And he so courtais was that tide
        O dint that he nolde smite again.   *would not strike in return*

      Bors de Gawnes saw at last,
2175   And to the king then gan he ride,
      And on his helm he hit so fast
        That ner he lost all his pride;   *he (Arthur)*
      The steede rigge under him brast,   *steed's backbone*
        That he to grounde fell that tide;
2180   And sithen wordes loud he cast,   *he (Bors)*

---

[1] *Let not my lord (Arthur) be in the field of battle / And see that you yourself do not fight with me*

[2] *And yet he rode about as fast as he could / To see that no man should be slain*

70

With Sir Launcelot to chide:

"Sir, shaltou all day suffer so   *shalt thou; allow*
   That the king thee assail,
And sithe his herte is so thro,   *fierce*
2185   Thy courtaisy may not avail?
Batailes shall there never be mo,
   And thou wilt do by my counsel: *If*
Giveth us leve them all to slo,   *slay*
   For thou hast vanquished this batail."

2190 "Alas," quod Launcelot, "Wo is me,   *said*
   That ever sholde I see with sight
Before me him unhorsed be,
   The noble king that made me knight!"
He was then so courtais and free
2195   That down of his steed he light;   *alighted*
The king there-on then horses he,   *puts Arthur back on a horse*
   And bade him flee, yif that he might.

When the king was horsed there,
   Launcelot lookes he upon,
2200 How courtaisy was in him more   *courtesy*
   Than ever was in any man.
He thought on thinges that had been ere;
   The teres from his eyen ran;
He said, "Alas," with sighing sore,
2205   "That ever yet this war began!"

The parties arn withdrawen away,   *are*
   Of knightes were they wexen thin;   *grown*
On morrow on that other day
   Sholde the batail eft begin;   *again*
2210 They dight them on a rich array
   And parted their hostes both in twinne;   *in two*
He that began this wretched play,
   What wonder though he had grete sin?

Bors was breme as any bore,   *fierce; boar*
2215   And out he rode to Sir Gawain;
For Lionel was wounded sore,
   Venge his brother he wolde full fain.   *Avenge; eagerly desired*
Sir Gawain gan again him fare,
   As man that muche was of main;

2220   Either through other body bore
        That well ner were they bothe slain.

    Both to ground they fell in fere;   *together*
        Therefore were fele folk full wo.
    The kinges party redy were
2225   Away to take them bothe two.
    Launcelot himself come ner,
        Bors rescues he them fro;
    Out of the feld men him bere;
        So were they wounded bothe two.

2230   Of this batail were to tell
        A man that it well understood,
    How knightes under saddles fell
        And sitten down with sorry mood;
    Steedes that were bold and snell   *fast*
2235   Among them waden in the blood;   *wade*
    But by the time of even-bell   *vespers (6 p.m.)*
        Launcelot party the better stood.

    Of this batail was no more,
        But thus departen they that day;
2240   Folk their frendes home led and bore,
        That slain in the feldes lay.
    Launcelot gan to his castle fare,
        The batail vanquished, for sooth to say;
    There was dole and weeping sore;
2245   Among them was no childes play.

    Into all landes north and south
        Of this war the word sprong,
    And yet at Rome it was full couthe   *well known*
        In Yngland was such sorrow strong;
2250   There-of the Pope had grete rewth;   *pity*
        A letter he seled with his hand: *sealed*
    But they accorded well in trewth   *Unless; truth*
        Enterdite he wolde the land. [1]

    Then was a bishop at Rome,
2255   Of Rochester, withouten lees;

---

[1] *He would place the land under interdict*

	Til Yngland he, the message, come,	*messenger*
	To Carlisle there the king was;	
	The Popes letter out he nome,	*took*
	In the palais, before the dese,	*palace; dais*
2260	And bade them do the Popes doom	*decree*
	And hold Yngland in rest and pees.	

	Redde it was before all bydene,	*Read; everyone*
	The letter that the Pope gan make,	
	How he must have again the queen	*he (Arthur)*
2265	And accord with Launcelot du Lake,	
	Make a pees them between	
	For ever more, and trewes make,	
	Or Yngland enterdited sholde ben	
	And turn to sorrow for their sake.	

2270	The king again it wolde not ben,	*against*
	To do the Popes commaundement,	*command*
	Blithely again to have the queen;	
	Wolde he not that Yngland were shent;	*destroyed*
	But Gawain was of herte so keen	
2275	That to him wolde he never assent	
	To make accord them between	
	While any life were in him lente.	*remained*

	Through the sent of all bydene,	*assent*
	Gan the king a letter make;	
2280	The bishop in message yede between	*as a messenger went*
	To Sir Launcelot du Lake,	
	And asked if he wolde the queen	
	Courtaisly to him betake,	*entrust*
	Or Yngland enterdite sholde ben	*interdicted*
2285	And turn to sorrow for their sake.	

	Launcelot answerd with grete favour,	
	As knight that hardy was and keen:	
	"Sir, I have stand in many a stour,	*stood; battle*
	Both for the king and for the queen;	
2290	Full cold had been his beste towr	*Destroyed; castle*
	Yif that I nadde myselfe been;	*If I had not been there*
	He quites me with little honour,	*repays*
	That I have served him all bydene."	*completely*

The bishop spake withoute fail,

73

2295	Though he were nothing afrought:	*afraid*
	"Sir, think that ye have vanquished many a batail,	
	Through grace that God hath for you wrought;	
	Ye shall do now by my counsel;	
	Think on Him that you dere bought;	
2300	Women are frele of their entail;	*frail; character*
	Sir, lettes not Yngland go to nought!"	
	"Sir Bishop, castelles for to hold,	*castles*
	Wite you well, I have no need;	
	I might be king, yif that I wolde,	
2305	Of all Benwick, that riche thede,	*nation*
	Ride into my landes bold,	
	With my knightes stiff on steed;	
	The queen, yif that I to them yolde,	*yield*
	Of her life I have grete drede."	
2310	"Sir, by Mary, that is maiden flowr,	*flower of maidens*
	And by God that all shall rede and right,	*teach; guide*
	She ne shall have no dishonour;	
	There-to my trowth I shall you plight,	*word; pledge*
	But boldly brought into her bowr,	
2315	To ladies and to maidens bright,	
	And holden in well more honour	
	Than ever she was by day or night."	
	"Now, yif I graunt such a thing	
	That I deliver shall the queen,	
2320	Sir Bishop, say my lord, the king,	
	Sir Gawain and them all bydene,	
	That they shall make me a sekering,	*give me assurance*
	A trews to holde us between."	*truce*
	Then was the bishop wonder blithe	
2325	That Launcelot gave him this answer;	
	Til his palfrey he went as swithe,	
	And til Carlisle gan he fare.	
	Tithandes soon were done to lithe,	*Tidings; proclaimed*
	Which that Launcelotes wordes were;	
2330	The king and court was all full blithe;	
	A trews they set and sekered there.	*truce; pledged themselves to it*
	Through the assent of all bydene	
	A seker trews there they wrought;	*sure truce*

74

Though Gawain were of herte keen,
2335   There-against was he nought,
To hold a trewes them between
    While Launcelot the queen home brought;
But cordement thar him never ween   *reconciliation; expected*
    Ere either other herte have sought. [1]

2340 A seker trews gonne they make   *sure truce*
    And with their seles they it band;   *seals; bound*
There-to they three bishoppes gonne take,
    The wisest that were in all the land,
And sent to Launcelot du Lake;
2345   At Joyous Gard then they him fand;   *found*
The lettres there they him betake,   *deliver*
    And there-to Launcelot held his hand.   *pledged himself*

The bishoppes then went on their way,
    To Carlisle there the king was;
2350 Launcelot shall come that other day,   *the next day*
    With the lady proud in press.   *amidst the company*
He dight him in a rich array,
    Wite ye well, withouten lees;   *Know*
An hundreth knightes, for sooth to say,
2355   The best of all his host he chese.   *chose*

Launcelot and the queen were cledde   *clad*
    In robes of a riche weed,   *material*
Of samite white, with silver shredde,   *silk; trimmed*
    Ivory saddle and white steed,
2360 Sambues of the same thred,   *Saddle-clothes; thread*
    That wrought was in the hethen thede;   *heathen lands*
Launcelot her bridle led,
    In the romaunce as we rede.   *romance (French book)*

The other knightes everychone,   *every one*
2365   In samite green of hethen land,   *silk; heathen*
And in their kirtels ride alone,   *gowns (i.e., without armor)*
    And iche knight a green garland;
Saddles set with riche stone;
    Ichon a braunch of olive in hand;
2370 All the feld about them shone;

---

[1] *Until one has sought (with a sword) the other's heart*

The knightes rode full loud singand.   *singing*

To the castle when they come
   In the palais gonne they light;   *alight*
Launcelot the queen off her palfrey nome;   *took*
2375   They said it was a seemly sight.
The king then salues he full soon,   *salutes*
   As man that was of muche might;
Fair wordes were there fone,   *few*
   But weeping stood there many a knight.

2380 Launcelot spake, as I you mene,   *tell*
   To the king of mikel might:
"Sir, I have thee brought thy queen,
   And saved her life with the right,
As lady that is fair and sheen
2385   And trew is both day and night;
If any man sayes she is not clene,   *pure*
   I proffer me therefore to fight."

The king Arthur answeres there
   Wordes that were keen and thro: *fierce*
2390 "Launcelot, I ne wend never more   *supposed*
   That thou wolde me have wrought this wo;
So dere as we samen were,   *were to each other*
   There-under that thou was my fo;   *I.e., despite this*
But nought-for-thy me rewes sore   *nevertheless it sorely pains me*
2395   That ever was war betwixt us two."

Launcelot then answerd he,
   When he had listened long:
"Sir, thy wo thou witest me,   *your troubles you blame on me*
   And well thou wost it is with wrong;   *you know well you do wrongly*
2400 I was never fer from thee   *far*
   When thou had any sorrow strong;
But liers listenes thou to lie,   *you listen to lying liars*
   Of whom all this word out sprong."

Then bespake him Sir Gawain,
2405   That was hardy knight and free:
"Launcelot, thou may it not withsayn   *deny*
   That thou hast slain my brethern three;
For-thy shall we prove our main

In feld whether shall have the gree. [1]

2410 Ere either of us shall other slayn,   *slay*
   Blithe shall I never be."

Launcelot answerd with herte sore,
   Though he were nothing afrought: *afraid*
"Gawain," he said, "Though I were there,
2415   Myself thy brethern slogh I nought;   *slew*
Other knightes fele there were   *many*
   That sithen this war dere han bought."   *have*
Launcelot sighed wonder sore;
   The teres of his eyen sought.   *ran from his eyes*

2420 Launcelot spake, as I you mene,
   To the king and Sir Gawain:
"Sir, shall I never of cordement ween,   *reconciliation*
   That we might frendes be again?"
Gawain spake with herte keen
2425   As man that muche was of main:
"Nay, cordement thar thee never ween [2]
   Til one of us have other slain!"

"Sithe it never may betide
   That pees may be us between,
2430 May I into my landes ride,
   Safely with my knightes keen?
Then will I here no lenger bide,
   But take leve of you all bydene;
Where I wend in worlde wide,
2435   Yngland will I never sen."   *see*

The king Arthur answerd there —
   The teres from his eyen ran —
"By Jesu Crist," he there swore,
   "That all this world wrought and won,
2440 Into thy landes when thou wilt fare,
   Thee shall let no livand man."   *No living man shall stop you*
He said, "Alas!" with sighing sore,
   "That ever yet this war began!"

---

[1] *[To see] on the field [of battle] who should have the prize*

[2] *Nay, you may never expect reconciliation*

"Sithe that I shall wend away,
2445   And in mine owne landes wonne,   *dwell*
May I safely wonne there ay,
   That ye with war not come me on?"
Sir Gawain then said: "Nay,
   By Him that made sun and moon,
2450   Dight thee well as ever thou may,   *Prepare yourself*
   For we shall after come full soon."

Launcelot his leve hath taken there;
   It was no lenger for to bide;
His palfrey fand he redy yare,   *quickly*
2455   Made him redy for to ride;
Out of the castel gonne they fare;   *castle*
   Grimly teres let they glide;
There was dole and weeping sore;
   At the parting was little pride.

2460   To the Joyous Gard, the riche town,   *fortified place*
   Rode Launcelot, the noble knight;
Busked them and made all boun,   *Hastened; ready*
   As men that were of muche might.
With spere in hand and gonfanoun   *banner*
2465   (Let they neither day ne night)   *Delayed*
To an haven hight Kerlioun;   *named Caerleon*
   Rich galleys there they fande dight.   *found prepared*

Now are they shipped on the flood,
   Launcelot and his knightes hende;
2470   Wederes had they fair and good   *Weathers (winds)*
   Where their will was for to wend,
To an haven there it stood,
   As men were levest for to lende; [1]
Of Benwick blithe was their mood,   *glad; mind*
2475   When Jesu Crist them thider send.   *sent*

Now are they arrived on the strand;
   Of them was fele folk full blithe;
Grete lordes of the land,
   Again him they come as swithe,   *quickly*

---

[1] *Where the men were most eager to stay*

2480	And fellen him to foot and hand; [1]	
	For their lord they gonne him kithe,	
	At his doomes for to stand,	
	And at his lawes for to lithe.	

	Bors made he king of Gawnes,	
2485	As it was both law and right;	
	Lionel made king of Fraunce,	
	By olde time Gawle hight;	*Gaul was called*
	All his folk he gan avaunce	*advance*
	And landes gave to ich a knight,	
2490	And stored his casteles for all chaunce,	*supplied; every emergency*
	For mikel he hoped more to fight.	

	Ector he crownes with his hand,	
	So says the book, withouten lees,	
	Made him king of his fader land,	*father's*
2495	And prince of all the riche press,	
	Bade nothing him sholde withstand,	
	But hold him king, as worthy was,	
	For there no more himself wolde fonde	*try [to do]*
	Til he wiste to live in pees.	*knew [he could]*

2500	Arthur will he no lenger abide;	*Arthur himself will*
	Night and day his herte was sore.	
	Messengeres did he go and ride,	*commanded; walk*
	Throughout Yngland to fare,	
	To erles and barons on ich a side,	
2505	Bade them busk and make all yare,	*hurry; ready*
	On Launcelot landes for to ride,	
	To bren and slee and make all bare.	*burn; slay*

	At his knightes all bydene	*From; together*
	The king gan his counsel take,	
2510	And bade them ordain them between	
	Who beste steward were for to make,	
	The reme for to save and yeme,	*realm; control*
	And beste were for Britaines sake;	
	Full mikel they drede them all bydene,	
2515	That aliens the land wolde take.	

---

[1] *And knelt and kissed Launcelot's foot and hand / And acknowledged him to be their lord, / And (promised) to obey his decrees / And to heed his laws*

The knightes answerd, withoute lees,
    And said, for sooth, that so them thought
That Sir Mordred the sekerest was   *most trustworthy*
    Though men the reme throughoute sought,
2520 To save the reme in trews and pees.
    Was a book before him brought;
Sir Mordred they to steward chese;   *as*
    That many a bold sithen abought.   *For that, many a bold one later paid*

It was no lenger for to bide,
2525   But buskes them and made all boun;   *they bustle about*
When they were redy for to ride,
    They raised spere and gonfanoun;   *banner*
Forth they went with mikel pride
    Til an haven hight Kerlioun,   *Caerleon*
2530 And graithes by the lande side   *prepare*
    Galleys grete of fele fasoun.   *many fashions*

Now are they shipped on the se
    And wenden over the water wide;
Of Benwick when they mighte see,
2535   With grete rout they gonne up ride;   *company*
Withstood them neither stone ne tree,
    But brent and slogh on ich a side;   *burned; slew; every*
Launcelot is in his best citee;
    There he batail will abide.

2540 Launcelot clepes his knightes keen,   *calls*
    His erles and his barons bold;
Bade them ordain them between,   *draw battle lines*
    To wite their will, what they wolde,
To ride again them all bydene   *together*
2545   Or their worthy walles hold,
For well they wiste, withouten ween,   *doubt*
    For no fantysé Arthur nolde fold. [1]

Bors de Gawnes, the noble knight,
    Sternly spekes in that stound: *time*
2550 "Doughty men, that ye be dight,   *(see) that*
    Foundes your worship for to fonde   *Prepare; test*
With spere and sheld and armes bright,

---

[1] *Arthur would not submit for lack of courage*

Again your fomen for to founde;   *go*
   King and duke, erl and knight,
2555 We shall them bete and bring to ground!"   *beat*

Lionel spekes in that tide,
   That was of warre wise and bold: *war*
"Lordinges, yet I rede we bide
   And our worthy walles hold;
2560 Let them prik with all their pride,   *spur*
   Til they have caught both hunger and cold;
Then shall we out upon them ride,
   And shred them down as sheep in fold."   *cut*

Sir Bangdemagew, that bolde king,
2565 To Launcelot spekes in that tide:
"Sir, courtaisy and your suffering
   Has wakend us wo full wide;   *brought us great woe*
Avise you well upon this thing;
   Yif that they over our landes ride,
2570 All to nought they might us bring,
   While we in holes here us hide."

Galyhod, that ay was good,
   To Launcelot he spekes there:
"Sir, here are knightes of kinges blood,
2575 That long will not droop and dare;   *crouch from fear*
Give me leve, for Cross on Rood,   *Body (?); Cross*
   With my men to them to fare;
Though they be worse than outlawes wode,
   I shall them slee and make full bare."   *slay and plunder*

2580 Of North-Gales were brethern seven,   *North Wales*
   Ferly mikel of strength and pride;   *Wondrously great*
Not full fele that men coude neven   *very many; name*
   Better durst in batail bide;   *dare*
And they said with one steven: *voice*
2585 "Lordinges, how long will ye chide?   *wrangle*
Launcelot, for Goddes love in Heven,
   With Galyhod forth let us ride!"

Then spake the lord that was so hende,
   Himself, Sir Launcelot du Lake:
2590 "Lordinges, a while I rede we lende   *advise; remain*
   And our worthy walles wake;   *watch*

81

A message will I to them send,
    A trews between us for to take;   *truce; offer*
My lord is so courtais and hende
2595   That yet I hope a pees to make.

"Though we might with worship win,   *honor*
    Of a thing mine herte is sore: *one*
This land is full of folk full thin,   i.e., *starving*
    Batailes have made it full bare;
2600   Wite ye well it were grete sin
    Cristen folk to slee thus more;   *slay*
With mildeness we shall begin
    And God shall wisse us well to fare."   *direct*

And at this assent all they were,
2605   And set a watch for to wake,   *guard; watch*
Knightes breme as any bore
    And derf of drede as is the drake; *fearsome as the dragon*
A damesel they did be yare,   *prepare*
    And hastely gonne her lettres make;
2610   A maid sholde on the message fare,   *travel*
    A trews between them for to take.   *offer*

The maid was full sheen to shew,   *be seen*
    Upon her steed when she was set;
Her parail all of one hew,   *apparel*
2615   Of a green velvet;
In her hand a braunch new,   *branch;* i.e., *green*
    For-why that no man sholde her let;   *stop*
There-by men messengeres knew,   *By that (*i.e., *green branch)*
    In hostes when that men them met.

2620   The king was loked in a feld,   *lodged*
    By a river brode and dregh;   *wide*
A while she hoved and beheld,   *paused*
    Pavaliouns that were pight on high; *pavilions; pitched*
She saw there many comely telde,   *tents*
2625   With pommels bright as goldes bee; [1]
On one hung the kinges sheld;
    That pavilioun she drew her nigh.

---

[1] *With knobs on the tent poles bright as golden rings*

The kinges banner out was set;
    That pavilioun she drew her ner;   *nearer*
2630 With a knight full soon she met,
    Hight Sir Lucan de Botteler;   *Called*
She hailsed him and he her grette,   *saluted; greeted*
    The maid with full mild cheer;
Her errand was not for to let;
2635   He wiste she was a messenger.

Sir Lucan down gan her take
    And in his armes forth gan lede;
Hendely to her he spake,
    As knight that wise was under weed: [1]
2640 "Thou comest from Launcelot du Lake,
    The best that ever strode on steed;
Jesu, for his Moderes sake,   *Mother's*
    Give thee grace well to speed!"

Fair was pight upon a plain   *pitched*
2645   The pavilioun in rich apparail;
The king himself and Sir Gawain
    Comely sitten in the hall;
The maiden kneeled the king again,
    So low to grounde gan she fall;
2650 Her lettres were not for to laine;
    They were yredde among them all.   *read*

Hendely and fair the maiden spake,
    Full fain of speche she wolde be speed: [2]
"Sir, God save you all from wo and wrake,
2655   And all your knightes in riche weed;
You greetes well Sir Launcelot du Lake,
    That with you hath been ever at need;
A twelve-month trews he wolde take,
    To live upon his owne lede,   *country*

2660 "And sithen, yif ye make an hest,   *promise*
    He will it hold with his hand   *i.e., swear*
Between you for to make pees,
    Stabely ever for to stand;

---

[1] *Like a knight who was wise in his armor*

[2] *She was very eager to succeed by (means of) her speech*

	He will rap him on a rese	*hasten in a rush*
2665	Mildly to the Holy Land,	
	There to live, withouten lees,	
	While he is man livand."	

	The king then cleped his counsel,	
	His doughty knightes all bydene;	
2670	First he said, withouten fail:	
	"Me think it were best to sen;	*see (about this)*
	He were a fool, withouten fail,	
	So fair forwardes for to fleme."	*To flee (reject) such fair offers*
	The king the messenger thus did assail:	*i.e., address*
2675	"It were pity to set war us between."	

	"Certes, nay!" said Sir Gawain,	
	"He hath wrought me wo ynow,	
	So traitourly he hath my brethern slain,	
	All for your love, sir; that is trouth!	*truth*
2680	To Yngland will I not turn again	
	Til he be hanged on a bough;	
	While me lasteth might or main,	
	There-to I shall find peple ynow."	*people*

	The king himself, withouten lees,	
2685	And ich a lord, is not to laine,	*doubt*
	All they spake to have pees,	
	But himselfe, Sir Gawain;	
	To batail hath he made his hest,	*promise*
	Or elles never to turn again.	*return*
2690	They made them redy to that rese;	*for that attack*
	Therefore was fele folk unfain.	*unhappy*

	The king is comen into the hall,	
	And in his royal see him set;	*seat (i.e., throne)*
	He made a knight the maiden call,	
2695	Sir Lucan de Botteler, withouten let:	*delay*
	"Say to Sir Launcelot and his knightes all,	
	Such an hest I have him hette,	*promise; promised*
	That we shall wend for no wall, [1]	
	Til we with mightes ones have met."	

---

[1] *That we shall turn aside for no obstacle*

84

2700	The maid had her answer;	
	With drery herte she gan her dight;	*prepare*
	Her fair palfrey fand she yare,	*found; ready*
	And Sir Lucan led her thider right.	
	So through a forest gan she fare	
2705	And hasted her with all her might,	
	There Launcelot and his knightes were,	
	In Benwick the brough with bemys bright.	*castle; trumpets brilliant*

	Now is she went within the wall,	
	The worthy damesel fair in weed;	
2710	Hendely she came into that hall;	
	A knight her took down off her steed.	
	Among the princes proud in palle	*costly cloth*
	She took her lettres for to rede;	*offered*
	There was no counsel for to call,	
2715	But redyly buskes them to that deed.	

	As folkes that preste were to fight,	*eager*
	From felde wolde they never flee;	
	But by the morrow that day was light,	
	About beseged was all their fee;	*All their holdings were besieged*
2720	Ichon them rayed in all rightes; [1]	
	Neither party thought to flee.	

	Erly as the day gan spring,	
	The trompets upon the walles went;	*trumpeters*
	There might they see a wonder thing,	
2725	Of teldes rich and many a tent.	*rich dwellings (tents)*
	Sir Arthur then, the comely king,	
	With his folkes there was lente,	*staying*
	To give assaut, without leesing,	
	With alblasters and bowes bent.	*cross-bows*

2730	Launcelot all forwondered was	*amazed*
	Of the folk before the wall;	
	But he had rather knowen that rese [2]	
	Out had run his knightes all.	
	He said: "Princes, beth in pees,	*be still*
2735	For follies fele that might befall;	*many*

---

[1] *Each one arranged himself correctly (for battle)*

[2] *But he had no sooner realized that attack, / Than out all his knights rushed*

Yif they will not their sege sese,   *cease*
 Full sore I hope forthink them shall." *I suppose they will regret it sorely*

Then Gawain, that was good at every need,
 Graithed him in his good armour,   *Prepared*
2740 And stiffly stert upon a steed,   *leaped*
 That seker was in ilk a stour;   *every battle*
Forth he sprang as spark on glede,   *live coal*
 Before the gates again the towr;   *next to*
He bade a knight come kithe main,   *prove his strength*
2745 A course of war for his honour.   *joust*

Bors de Gawnes buskes him boun, *makes himself ready*
 Upon a steed that sholde him bere,
With helme, sheld, and hauberk brown,   *shining*
 And in his hand a full good spere;
2750 Out he rode a grete randoun;   *at a rapid pace*
 Gawain kydde he coude of war;   *proved he knew of war*
Horse and man both bore he down,
 Such a dint he gave him there.

Sir Lionel was all redy then,
2755 And for his brother was wonder wo;
Redyly with his steed out ran,
 And wend Gawain for to slo.   *went*
Gawain him kept as he well can,[1]
 As he that ay was keen and thro;   *bold*
2760 Down he bore both horse and man,
 And every day some served he so.

And so more than half a yere,
 As long as they there layn,   *lay (remained)*
Every day men might see there
2765 Men wounded and some slain;
But how that ever in world it were,
 Such grace had Sir Gawain,
Ever he passed hole and clere; *whole; clear (of any wound)*
 There might no man stand him again.

2770 Then it befell upon a tide,
 Sir Gawain, that was hende and free,

---

[1] *Gawain protected himself as he well knows how*

He made him redy for to ride,
  Before the gates of the citee;
Launcelot of tresoun he becried,   *accused*
2775   That he had slain his brethern three;
That Launcelot might no lenger abide,
  But he ever a coward sholde be.   *Unless*

The lord that grete was of honour,
  Himself, Sir Launcelot du Lake,
2780 Above the gates upon the towr,
  Comely to the king he spake:
"My lord, God save your honour!
  Me is wo now for your sake,
Against thy kin to stand in stour,
2785   But needes I moste this batail take."   *must by necessity*

Launcelot armed him full well,
  For sooth, had full grete need,
Helme, hauberk, and all of steel,
  And stiffly stert upon a steed;   *quickly leapt*
2790 His harnes lacked he never a dele; [1]
  To warre wanted him no weed,
Ne wepen with all to dele;   *deal*
  Forth he sprang as spark on glede,   *live coal*

Then it was warned fast on high,   *proclaimed emphatically*
2795 How in world that it sholde fare,
That no man sholde come them nigh,
  Til the tone dede or yolden were. [2]
Folk withdrew them then by;
  Upon the feld, was brode and bare,
2800 The knightes met, as men it sigh   *saw*
  How they set their dintes sore.

Then had Sir Gawain such a grace —

---

[1] *He lacked not a bit of equipment; / He lacked no garment (armor) for war*

[2] *Until one of them was dead or had surrendered*

An holy man had bodden that boon —   *granted that gift*
When he were in any place
2805   There he sholde batail don,
His strength sholde wax in such a space,   *grow; space of time*
From the under-time til noon,   *about 9 a.m. until*
And Launcelot forbore for that case;
Again twenty strokes he gave not one.

2810   Launcelot saw there was no succour;
Needes moste he his venture abide;   *By necessity he had to wait his chance*
Many a dint he gan well endure
Til it drew near the noone tide;
Then he straught in that stour   *straightened up; battle*
2815   And gave Gawain a wounde wide;
The blood all covered his colour   *complexion (face)*
And he fell down upon his side.

Thorough the helm into the hede   *Through*
Was hardy Gawain wounded so
2820   That unnethe was him life leved;   *That life was hardly left to him*
On foot might he no ferther go;
But wightly his sword about he waved,   *stoutly*
For ever he was both keen and thro.
Launcelot then him lyand leved;   *left him lying (there)*
2825   For all the world he nolde him slo.   *would not slay him*

Launcelot then him drew on dryghe,   *back*
His sword in his hande drayn,   *drawn*
And Sir Gawain cried loud on high:
"Traitour and coward, come again,
2830   When I am hole and going on high;
Then will I prove with might and main;
And yet a thou woldest nighe me nigh, [1]
Thou shalt well wite I am not slain!"

"Gawain, while thou mightest stiffly stand,

---

[1] *And yet, if you would come near me*

88

2835	Many a stroke today of thee I stood,	
	And I forbore thee in every land,	
	For love and for the kinges blood; [1]	
	When thou art hole in herte and hand,	*whole*
	I rede thee turn and change thy mood;	*advise you; mind*
2840	While I am Launcelot and man livand,	
	God shelde me from workes wode!"	*mad deeds*
	"But have good day, my lord the king,	
	And your doughty knightes all;	
	Wendeth home and leve your warring;	
2845	Ye win no worship at this wall;	
	And I wolde my knightes oute bring,	
	I wot full sore rew it ye shall;	
	My lord, therefore think on such thing,	
	How fele folk therefore might fall."	
2850	Launcelot, that was much of main,	
	Boldly to his citee went;	
	His goode knightes there-of were fain	
	And hendely him in armes hent.	*took*
	The tother party tho took Sir Gawain;	*other*
2855	They wesh his woundes in his tent;	*washed*
	Ere ever he covered might or main,	*recovered*
	Unnethe was him the life lente. [2]	
	A fourtenight, the sooth to say,	*fortnight*
	Full passing seke and unsound	
2860	There Sir Gawain on leching lay	*in medical care*
	Ere he were hole all of his wound.	*healed*
	Then it befell upon a day,	
	He made him redy for to wonde;	*go*
	Before the gate he took the way,	
2865	And asked batail in that stound:	*time*

---

[1] *Because of love (for you) and because you are the king's kinsman*

[2] *Hardly any life remained in him*

"Come forth, Launcelot, and prove thy main,
   Thou traitour that hast tresoun wrought;
My three brethern thou hast slain
   And falsely them to grounde brought;
2870 While me lasteth might or main,
   This quarrel leve will I nought,
Ne pees shall there never be seen,
   Ere thy sides be thorough sought."   *pierced through*

Then Launcelot thought it nothing good,
2875   And for these wordes he was full wo;
Above the gates then he yode,
   And to the king he saide so:
"Sir, me rewes in my mood   *I grieve; mind*
   That Gawain is in herte so thro;   *severe*
2880 Who may me wite, for Cors on Rood,   *blame, by the Body on the Cross*
   Though I him in batail slo?"

Launcelot busked and made him boun;
   He will boldly the batail abide,
With helme, sheld, and hauberk brown,   *shining*
2885   None better in all this worlde wide,
With spere in hand and gonfanoun,   *banner*
   His noble sworde by his side;
Out he rode a grete randoun,   *at a rapid pace*
   When he was redy for to ride.

2890 Gawain grippes a full good spere,
   And in he glides glad and gay;
Launcelot kydde he coude of war, [1]
   And even to him he takes the way;
So stoutly they gan togeder bere
2895   That marvel it was, sooth to say;
With dintes sore gan they dere,   *blows severe; harm*
   And deepe woundes delten they.   *dealt*

---

[1] *Launcelot proved he knew about war*

When it was nighed ner-hand noon   *was nearly noon*
  Gawaines strength gan to increse;   *increase*
2900 So bitterly he hewed him upon,
  That Launcelot all for-wery was;   *tired out*
Then to his sword he grippes anon,
  And sithe that Gawain will not sese,   *since; cease*
Such a dint he gave him one,   *blow*
2905   That many a riche rewed that rese.   *nobleman rued that attack*

Launcelot stert forth in that stound,   *moment*
  And sithe that Gawain will not sese,   *cease*
The helm, that was rich and round,
  The noble sword rove that rese;   *pierced; rash onslaught*
2910 He hit him upon the olde wound
  That over the saddle down he went,
And grisly groned upon the ground,   *pitiably*
  And there was good Gawain shent.   *put to shame*

Yet Gawain, swooning there as he lay,
2915   Gripped to him both sword and sheld;
"Launcelot," he said, "soothly to say,
  And by Him that all this world shall weld,   *wield (control)*
While me lasteth life today,
  To thee me shall I never yeld;
2920 But do the worst that ever thou may,
  I shall defend me in the feld."

Launcelot then full stille stood,
  As man that was much of might:
"Gawain, me rewes in my mood   *mind*
2925   Men hold thee so noble a knight.
Weenestou I were so wode   *Do you think*
  Against a feeble man to fight?
I will not now, by Cross on Rood,
  Nor never yet did by day or night.

2930 "But have good day, my lord the king,
  And all your doughty knightes bydene;
Wendeth home and leve your warring,

91

For here ye shall no worship win.
  Yif I wolde my knightes oute bring,
2935   I hope full soon it sholde be seen;
But, good lord, think upon a thing,
  The love that hath us be between."   *been between us*

After was it monthes two,
  As freely folk it understand,   *noble*
2940 Ere ever Gawain might ride or go,
  Or had foot upon erthe to stand.
The thirde time he was full thro   *bold*
  To do batail with herte and hand;
But then was word comen them to
2945   That they moste home to Yngland.

Such message was them brought,
  There was no man that thought it good.
The king himself full soon it thought —
  Full muche morned he in his mood   *mind*
2950 That such tresoun in Yngland sholde be wrought —
  That he moste needes over the flood.   *cross over the sea*
They broke sege and homeward sought;   *went*
  And after they had much angry mood.

That false traitour, Sir Mordred,
2955   The kinges soster son he was   *king's sister's son*
And eek his own son, as I rede   *also*
  (Therefore men him for steward chese),
So falsely hath he Yngland led,
  Wite you well, withouten lees,
2960 His emes wife wolde he wed,   *uncle's*
  That many a man rewed that rese.   *course of action*

Festes made he many and fele,
  And grete giftes he gave also;
They said with him was joy and wele,
2965   And in Arthurs time but sorrow and wo;
And thus gan right to wronge go;
  All the counsel, is not to hele,   *hide*

92

Thus it was, withouten mo,
    To hold with Mordred in land with wele.

2970   False lettres he made be wrought,
    And caused messengeres them to bring,
    That Arthur was to grounde brought
    And chese they moste another king.
    All they said as them thought:
2975   "Arthur loved nought but warring
    And such thing as himselfe sought;
    Right so he took his ending."

Mordred let cry a parlement;   *called*
    The peple gan thider to come,   *people*
2980   And holly through their assent   *wholly*
    They made Mordred king with crown.
    At Canterbury, fer in Kent,   *afar*
    A fourtenight held the feste in town,   *fortnight; feast*
    And after that to Winchester he went;
2985   A riche bride-ale he let make boun.   *bridal feast; had prepared*

In sommer, when it was fair and bright,
    His faders wife then wolde he wed
    And her hold with main and might,
    And so her bring as bride to bed.
2990   She prayd him of leve a fourtenight —   *delay; fortnight*
    The lady was full hard bestedde —   *hard pressed*
    So to London she her dight,   *went*
    That she and her maidens might be cledde.[1]

The queen, white as lily flowr,
2995   With knightes fele of her kin,   *many*
    She went to London to the towr
    And sperred the gates and dwelled therein.   *barred the gates*
    Mordred changed all his colour;
    Thider he went and wolde not blinne;   *stop*
3000   There-to he made many a showr,   *shower (of arrows)*

---

[1] *So that she and her maidens could be clad [in new clothes for the wedding]*

But the walles might he never win.

The Archebishop of Canterbury thider yode   *went*
    And his cross before him brought;
He said: "Sir, for Crist on Rood,
3005   What have ye now in all your thought?
Thy faders wife, whether thou be wode,   *even if you are crazy*
    To wed her now mayst thou nought.
Come Arthur ever over the flood,   *If Arthur comes*
    Thou mayst be bold, it will be bought!" [1]

3010   "A, nice clerk," then Mordred said,   *foolish clergyman*
    "Trowest thou to warn me of my will? [2]
By Him that for us suffred pain,
    These wordes shalt thou like full ill!
With wilde horse thou shalt be drayn   *drawn apart*
3015   And hanged high upon a hill!"
The bishop to flee then was fain,   *eager*
    An suffred him his follies to fulfill.   *allowed*

Then he him cursed with book and bell   *excommunicated him*
    At Canterbury, fer in Kent.
3020   Soon, when Mordred herde thereof tell,
    To seech the bishop hath he sent;   *seek*
The bishop durst no lenger dwell,
    But gold and silver he hath hent;   *seized*
There was no lenger for to spell,   *talk*
3025   But to a wildernesse he is went.

The worldes wele there he will forsake;
    Of joy keepeth he never more,   *He cares no more for joy*
But a chapel he lette make   *commanded to be built*
    Between two highe holtes hore;   *grey woods*
3030   Therein wered he the clothes black,   *wore*
    In wood as he an ermite were;   *hermit*
Often gan he weep and wake

---

[1] *You can be sure it will be paid for*

[2] *Do you expect to forbid me my desire?*

For Yngland that had such sorrows sore.

Mordred had then lien full long, *lain (in siege)*
3035 But the towr might he never win,
With strengthe ne with stoure strong
 Ne with none other kinnes gin; *sort of trick*
His fader dredde he ever among; *dreaded*
 Therefore his bale he nill not blinne;[1]
3040 He wend to warn them all with wrong *expected to deny them*
 The kingdom that he was crowned in.

Forth to Dover gan he ride,
 All the costes well he kend; *coasts; knew*
To erles and to barons on ilk a side
3045 Grete giftes he gave and lettres sent
And forset the se on ilk a side *blockaded*
 With bolde men and bowes bent;
Fro Yngland, that is brode and wide,
 His owne fader he wolde defend. *deny (entry)*

3050 Arthur, that was mikel of might,
 With his folk come over the flood,
An hundreth galleys that were well dight
 With barons bold and high of blood;
He wend to have landed, as it was right,
3055 At Dover, there him thought full good,
And there he fand many an hardy knight *found*
 That stiff in stour again him stood. *strong in battle*

Arthur soon hath take the land
 That him was levest in to lende;[2]
3060 His fele fomen that he there fand *many enemies; found*
 He wend before had been his frend; *friends*
The king was wroth and well-nigh wode,
 And with his men he gan up wend;
So strong a stour was upon that strand

---

[1] *Therefore he will not stop his evil deeds*

[2] *Which he liked best to dwell in*

3065   That many a man there had his end.

     Sir Gawain armed him in that stound;
         Alas! Too long his hede was bare;
     He was seke and sore unsound;
         His woundes greved him full sore.
3070   One hit him upon the olde wound
         With a tronchon of an ore;   *handle; oar*
     There is good Gawain gone to ground,
         That speche spake he never more.

     Bolde men, with bowes bent,
3075   Boldly up in botes yode,   *went*
     And rich hauberkes they rive and rent   *cut; tear*
         That through-out brast the redde blood.   *red*
     Grounden glaives through them went;   *Sharpened spears*
         Tho games thought them nothing good;   *Those*
3080   But by that the stronge stour was stent,[1]
         The stronge stremes ran all on blood.   *rushing*

     Arthur was so much of might
         Was there none that him withstood;
     He hewed on their helmes bright
3085   That through their brestes ran the blood.   *breasts*
     By then ended was the fight;
         The false were felld and some were fled   *struck down*
     To Canterbury all that night
         To warn their master, Sir Mordred.

3090   Mordred then made him boun,   *ready*
         And boldly he will batail abide
     With helme, sheld, and hauberk brown;   *shining*
         So all his rout gan forthe ride;   *troop*
     They them met upon Barendown,   *Barlam Down (Kent)*
3095   Full erly in the morrow tide;   *early*
     With glaives grete and gonfanoun,   *spears*

---

[1] *But by the time that perilous battle was ended*

Grimly they gonne togeder ride.

Arthur was of rich array
   And hornes blewe loud on hight,   *on high*
3100 And Mordred cometh glad and gay,
   As traitour that was false in fight.
They fought all that longe day
   Til the night was nighed nigh;
Who had it seen well might say
3105 That such a stour never he sigh.   *saw*

Arthur then fought with herte good;
   A nobler knight was never none.
Through helmes into hede it yode   *i.e., a sword (Excalibur)*
   And sterred knightes both blood and bone. [1]
3110 Mordred for wrath was nighe wode,
   Called his folk and said to them one: *alone*
"Releve you, for Cross on Rood!   *Recover yourselves*
   Alas! This day so soon is gone!"

Fele men lieth on bankes bare,
3115 With brighte brandes through-oute borne; [2]
Many a doughty dede was there,
   And many a lord his life hath lorne.   *lost*
Mordred was full of sorrow and care;
   At Canterbury was he upon the morn;
3120 And Arthur all night he dwelled there;
   His freely folk lay him beforn.   *noble; before him*

Erly on the morrow tide   *Early*
   Arthur bade his hornes blow,
And called folk on every side,
3125 And many a dede buried on a row,
   In pittes that was deep and wide;

---

[1] *And stirred the blood and bones of knights*
[2] *Driven through with bright swords*

97

> On ich an hepe they laid them low, [1]
>> So all that ever gon and ride
>> Some by their markes men might know.

3130   Arthur went to his dinner then,
      His freely folk him followed fast,
   But when he fand Sir Gawain   *found*
      In a ship lay dede by a mast,
   Ere ever he covered might or main,   *recovered*
3135   An hundreth times his herte nigh brast.   *nearly broke*

   They laid Sir Gawain upon a bere,   *bier*
      And to a castle they him bore,
   And in a chapel amid the quere   *choir*
      That bold baron they buried there.
3140   Arthur then changed all his cheer;
      What wonder though his herte was sore!
   His soster son, that was him dere,   *sister's son*
      Of him sholde he here never more.

   Sir Arthur he wolde no lenger abide;
3145   Then had he all manner of ivil rest;
   He sought ay forth the southe side, [2]
      And toward Wales went he west.
   At Salisbury he thought to bide,
      At that time he thought was best,
3150   And call to him at Whitsuntide   *Pentecost*
      Barons bold to battail prest.   *eager*

   Unto him came many a doughty knight,
      For wide in world these wordes sprong,
   That Sir Arthur had all the right,
3155   And Mordred warred on him with wrong.
   Hidous it was to see with sight;

---

[1] *They made a mound over each body, / So that all that ever walk or ride by / Might know some of them by their markers (on the mounds)*

[2] *He went ever forth by the south side (of England)*

98

Arthures host was brode and long,
  And Mordred, that mikel was of might,
With grete giftes made him strong.

3160 Soon after the feste of the Trinitee,
  Was a batail between them set,
That a stern batail there sholde be;
  For no lede wolde they it let;   *man*
And Sir Arthur maketh game and glee,
3165 For mirth that they sholde be met;   *should meet [in battle]*
And Sir Mordred came to the countree
  With fele folk that fer was fette.   *were fetched from afar*

At night when Arthur was brought in bed
  (He sholde have batail upon the morrow),
3170 In stronge swevenes he was bestedde,   *By painful dreams; beset*
  That many a man that day sholde have sorrow,
Him thought he sat in gold all cledde,   *clad*
  As he was comely king with crown,
Upon a wheel that full wide spredde,   *spread*
3175 And all his knightes to him boun.   *stood [ready] by him*

The wheel was ferly rich and round;   *wondrously*
  In world was never none half so high;
Thereon he sat richly crowned,
  With may a besaunt, brooch, and bee;   *Byzantine coin; ring*
3180 He looked down upon the ground;
  A black water there under him he see,   *saw*
With dragons fele there lay unbound,
  That no man durst them nighe nigh.   *come near them*

He was wonder ferde to fall   *strangely afraid of falling*
3185 Among the fendes there that fought.   *fiends*
The wheel over-turned there with-all   *The wheel then turned*
  And everich by a limm him caught.[1]
The king gan loude cry and call,

---

[1] *And each (of the fiends) caught him by a limb*

99

As marred man of wit unsaught; [1]

3190 His chamberlains waked him there with-all,

And wodely out of his sleep he raught.   *madly; roused*

All nighte gan he wake and weep,

With drery herte and sorrowful steven,   *voice*

And against the day he fell on sleep.   *near day (-light)*

3195 About him was set tapers seven.   *candles*

Him thought Sir Gawain him did keep,   *await*

With mo folk than men can neven,   *name*

By a river that was brode and deep;

All seemed angeles come from heven.

3200 The king was never yet so fain,   *glad*

His soster son when that he sigh: *sister's son; saw*

"Welcome," he said, "Sir Gawain,

And thou might live, well were me.   *If*

Now, leve frend, withouten laine,   *dear; deceit*

3205 What are tho folk that follow thee?"

"Certes, sir," he said again,

"They bide in bliss there I mot be.   *where I must be*

"Lordes they were, and ladies hende

This worldes life that han forlorn;   *Who have lost this world's life*

3210 While I was man on life to lende,   *remain*

Against their fon I fought them forn;   *foes; for them*

Now find I them my moste frend;   *greatest friends*

They bless the time that I was born;

They asked leve with me to wend,

3215 To meet with you upon this morn.

"A monthe-day of trewes moste ye take   *month's truce*

And then to batail be ye bain;   *ready*

You cometh to help Launcelot du Lake,   *Launcelot is coming to help you*

With many a man mikel of main;

3220 To-morn the batail ye moste forsake,

Or elles, certes, ye shall be slain."

---

[1] *Like a troubled man with a disturbed mind*

100

The king gan woefully weep and wake,
    And said, "Alas, this rewful regne!"   *pitiful kingdom*

Hastely his clothes on him he did,
3225   And to his lordes gan he sayn:
"In stronge swevenes I have been stedde,[1]
    That glad I may not for no games gay.
We moste unto Sir Mordred send
    And fonde to take another day,[2]
3230   Or trewly this day I mon be shend;
    This know I in bed as I lay."

"Go thou, Sir Lucan de Botteler,
    That wise wordes hast in wold,   *in (your) power*
And look that thou take with thee here
3235   Bishoppes fele and barons bold;
Forth they went all in a fere,   *all together*
    In trewe bookes as it is told,
To Sir Mordred and his lordes, there they were,
    And an hundreth knightes all untold.   *beyond counting*

3240   The knightes that were of grete valour,
    Before Sir Mordred as they stood,
They greeten him with grete honour,
    As barons bold and high of blood:
"Right well thee greetes King Arthur,
3245   And prayeth thee with milde mood,
A monthe-day to stint this stour,   *To delay this battle for a month*
    For His love that died on Rood."

Mordred, that was both keen and bold,
    Made him breme as any bore at bay,
3250   And swore by Judas that Jesus sold:
    "Such sawes are not now to say;   *speeches*
That he hath hight he shall it hold;   *What; promised*

---

[1] *I have been beset by strong (painful) dreams*

[2] *And try to set another day (for the battle), / Or truly this day I must be put to shame*

The tone of us shall die this day;   *The one*
And tell him trewly that I told:
3255   I shall him mar, yif that I may."   *injure*

"Sir," they said, "withouten lees,
    Though thou and he to batail boun,   *for battle prepare*
Many a rich shall rew that rese,   *powerful knight; rue; attack*
    By all be delt upon this down, [1]
3260   Yet were it better for to sese,   *cease*
    And let him be king and bere the crown,   *him (Arthur)*
And after his dayes, full dredeless,   *without doubt*
    Ye to welde all Yngland, towr and town."   *You would rule*

Mordred tho stood still a while,
3265   And wrothly up his eyen there went,
And said: "Wiste I it were his will
    To give me Cornwall and Kent!
Let us meet upon yonder hill
    And talk togeder with good entent;   *intent*
3270   Such forwardes to fulfill   *agreements*
    There-to shall I me soon assent.

"And yif we may with speches speed,
    With trewe trouthes of entail,   *good character*
Hold the bode-word that we bede,   *Keep; agreements; made*
3275   To give me Kent and Cornwall,
Trewe love shall there leng and lende,   *stay and reside*
    And certes, forwardes yif we fail, [2]
Arthur to stert upon a steed
    Stiffly for to do batail."

3280   "Sir, will ye come in such manner,
    With twelve knightes or fourteen,
Or elles all your strength in fere,   *together*
    With helmes bright and hauberkes sheen?"

---

[1] *By the time all (blows) are dealt on this down*

[2] *And certainly, if we fail to keep our promises, / Let Arthur leap upon a steed*

"Certes, nay," then said he there,
3285   "Other work thou thar not ween,   *need not expect*
But both our hostes shall nighe ner,   *armies; approach near*
     And we shall talke them between."

They took their leve, withouten lees,
     And wightly upon their way they went;   *staunchly*
3290   To King Arthur the way they chese,
     There that he sat, within his tent:
"Sir, we have proffered pees,
     Yif ye will there-to assent;
Give him your crown after your dayes
3295   And in your life Cornwall and Kent.

"To his behest yif ye will hold
     And your trouth trewly there-to plight,
Maketh all redy your men bold,
     With helme, sword, and hauberk bright;
3300   Ye shall meet upon yon molde,   *ground*
     That either host may see with sight,
And yif your forward fail to hold,   *agreement*
     There is no boot but for to fight."   *remedy*

But when Arthur herde this neven,   *said*
3305   Trewly there-to he hath sworn,
And arrayed him with batailes seven,
     With brode banners before him borne;
They lemed bright as any leven   *gleamed; flash of lighting*
     When they sholde meet upon the morn.
3310   There lives no man under heven
     A fairer sight hath seen beforn.

But Mordred many men had mo;
     So Mordred, that was mikel of main,
He had ever twelve against him two,
3315   Of barons bold to batail bain.   *ready*
Arthur and Mordred — both were thro —   *bold*
     Sholde meete both upon a plain;
The wise sholde come to and fro,

To make accord, the sooth to sayn.

3320	Arthur in his herte hath cast,	*considered*
	And to his lordes gan he say:	
	"To yonder traitour have I no trust,	
	But that he will us falsely betray;	
	Yif we may not our forwardes faste,	i.e., *agree on our terms*
3325	And ye see any wepen drayn,	*And if; drawn*
	Presseth forth as princes preste,	*eager*
	That he and all his host be slain.	

	Mordred, that was keen and thro,	
	His freely folk he said toforn:	
3330	"I wot that Arthur is full wo	
	That he hath thus his landes lorn;	*lost*
	With fourteen knightes and no mo	
	Shall we meet at yonder thorn;	*hawthorn tree*
	Yif any tresoun between us go,	
3335	That brode banners forth be borne."[1]	

	Arthur with knightes fully fourteen	
	To that thorn on foot they founde,	*hawthorn tree*
	With helme, sheld, and hauberk sheen;	
	Right so they trotted upon the ground.	
3340	But as they accorded sholde have been,	
	An adder glode forth upon the ground;	*glided*
	He stang a knight, that men might sen	*stung; see*
	That he was seke and full unsound.	

	Out he brayed with sworde bright;	*drew*
3345	To kill the adder had he thought.	
	When Arthur party saw that sight,	
	Freely they togeder sought;	*Instantly; charged*
	There was no thing withstand them might;	
	They wend that tresoun had been wrought;	*thought*
3350	That day died many a doughty knight,	

---

[1] *Let broad banners be brought forth (as a signal to attack)*

104

And many a bold man was brought to nought.

	Arthur stert upon his steed;	*angrily; leaped*
	He saw no thing him withstand might;	
	Mordred out of wit ner yede,	*nearly went*
3355	And wrothly into his saddle he light;	*leaped*
	Of accord was nothing to bede,	*No peace was offered*
	But fewtered speres and togeder sprent;	*But they lowered their spears; rushed*
	Full many a doughty man of deed	
	Soon there was laid upon the bente.	*ground*

3360	Mordred ymarred many a man,	*injured*
	And boldly he gan his batail abide;	
	So sternly out his steede ran,	
	Many a rout he gan through ride.	*company*
	Arthur of batail never blanne	*ceased*
3365	To dele woundes wicke and wide,	*wicked*
	For the morrow that it began	
	Til it was ner the nightes tide.	

	There was many a spere sprent,	*splintered*
	And many a thro word they spake;	*fierce*
3370	Many a brand was bowed and bent,	*sword*
	And many a knightes helm they brake;	
	Riche helmes they rove and rente;	*cut; tore*
	The riche routes gan togeder raike,	*powerful companies; rush*
	An hundreth thousand upon the bente;	*ground*
3375	The boldes ere even was made right meek.	*before evening*

	Sithe Brutus out of Troy was sought	*Since; came*
	And made in Britain his owne wonne,	*dwelling*
	Such wonders never ere was wrought,	
	Never yet under the sun.	
3380	By even leved was there nought	*left*
	That ever sterred with blood or bone,	*stirred*
	But Arthur and two that he thider brought,	
	And Mordred was leved alone.	

	The tone was Lucan de Botteler,	*one*

105

3385   That bled at many a baleful wound,
         And his broder, Sir Bedivere,
            Was sely seke and sore unsound.   *wondrously*
         Than spake Arthur these wordes there:
            "Shall we not bring this thef to ground?"
3390   A spere he gripped with felle cheer,   *fierce expression*
         And felly they gan togeder founde. [1]

         He hit Mordred amid the breste
            And out at the backe bone him bore;
         There hath Mordred his life lost,
3395   That speche spake he never more;
         Then keenly up his arm he cast
            And gave Arthur a wounde sore,
         Into the hede through the helm and crest,
            That three times he swooned there.

3400   Sir Lucan and Sir Bedivere
            Between them two the king upheld;
         So forthe went tho three in fere,   *together*
            And all were slain that lay in feld.
         The doughty king that was them dere
3405   For sore might not himselfe weld;   *pain; wield (move)*
         To a chapel they went in fere;
            Of boot they saw no better beld.   *For a remedy; comfort*

         All night they in the chapel lay,
            By the se side, as I you neven,   *tell*
3410   To Mary mercy cryand aye,
            With drery herte and sorrowful steven,   *sound*
         And to her leve Son gonne they pray: *dear*
            "Jesu, for thy names seven,
         Wisse his soul the righte way,   *Teach (direct)*
3415   That he lese not the bliss of Heven."   *lose*

         As Sir Lucan de Botteler stood,

---

[1] *And fiercely they began to test each other*

106

	He sigh folk upon plaines hie;	*hasten*
	Bolde barons of bone and blood	
	They reft them of besaunt, brooch, and bee; [1]	
3420	And to the king again they yode	
	Him to warn with wordes slee.	*sly (wise)*

	To the king spake he full still,	
	Rewfully as he might then roun:	*speak*
	"Sir, I have been at yon hill,	
3425	There fele folk drawen to the down;	
	I not whether they will us good or ill;	*know not*
	I rede we busk and make us boun,	
	Yif it were your worthy will	
	That we wende to some town."	

3430	"Now, Sir Lucan, as thou redde,	*advised*
	Lift me up, while I may last."	
	Both his armes on him he spredde,	*spread*
	With all his strength to hold him fast.	
	The king was wounded and forbledde,	*bled freely*
3435	And swooning on him his eyen he cast;	
	Sir Lucan was hard bestedde;	*hard beset*
	He held the king to his own herte brast.	*until; burst*

	When the king had swooned there,	
	By an auter up he stood;	*altar*
3440	Sir Lucan, that was him dere,	
	Lay dede and fomed in the blood.	*foamed*
	His bolde broder, Sir Bedivere,	
	Full mikel morned in his mood;	*mourned*
	For sorrow he might not nighe him ner,	
3445	But ever weeped as he were wode.	

	The king turned him there he stood,	
	To Sir Bedivere with wordes keen:	
	"Have Excaliber, my sworde good,	

---

[1] *They robbed them of Byzantine coins, brooches, and rings*

107

A better brand was never seen;
3450 Go cast it in the salte flood,
And thou shalt see wonder, as I ween;
Hie thee fast, for Cross on Rood,   *hasten*
And tell me what thou hast there seen."

The knight was bothe hende and free;
3455 To save that sword he was full glad,
And thought: "Whether I better be,   *Would I be any better*
Yif never man it after had?
And I it cast into the se,   *If*
Of molde was never man so mad."   *earth*
3460 The sword he hid under a tree,
And said: "Sir, I did as ye me bade."

"What saw thou there?" then said the king,
"Tell me now, yif thou can."
"Certes, sir," he said, "nothing
3465 But watres deep and wawes wan."   *pale waves*
"A, now thou hast broke my bidding!
Why hast thou do so, thou false man?
Another bode thou must me bring."   *message*
Then carefully the knight forth ran,

3470 And thought the sword yet he wolde hide
And cast the scauberk in the flood: *scabbard*
"Yif any aventures shall betide,   *adventures*
Thereby shall I see tokenes good."
Into the se he let the scauberk glide;
3475 A while on the land he there stood;
Then to the king he went that tide
And said: "Sir, it is done, by the Rood."   *Cross*

"Saw thou any wondres more?"
"Certes, sir, I saw nought."
3480 "A, false traitour!" he said there,
"Twice thou hast me tresoun wrought;
That shall thou rewe sely sore,   *wondrously*

108

And, be thou bold, it shall be bought." [1]
The knight then cried, "Lord, thine ore!"   *mercy*
3485   And to the sworde soon he sought.

Sir Bedivere saw that boot was best,   *i.e., keeping his word*
    And to the goode sword he went;
Into the se he it cast;
    Then might he see what that it ment.
3490 There came an hand withouten rest,
    Out of the water, and fair it hent,   *seized*
And braundished as it sholde brast,   *shook; break*
    And sithe, as glem, away it glent.   *then, like a gleam; glided*

To the king again went he there
3495 And said: "Leve sir, I saw an hand;   *Dear*
Out of the water it came all bare
    And thrice braundished that riche brand."   *shook*
"Help me, soon that I were there."
    He led his lord unto that strand;
3500 A riche ship, with mast and ore,   *oar*
    Full of ladies there they fand.   *found*

The ladies, that were fair and free,
    Courtaisly the king gan they fonge;   *take*
And one that brightest was of blee   *complexion*
3505 Weeped sore and handes wrang.   *wrung*
"Broder," she said, "wo is me!
    Fro leching hastou be too long; [2]
I wot, that gretly greveth me,   *I know*
    For thy paines are full strong."

3510 The knight cast a rewful roun,   *speech*
    There he stood, sore and unsound,
And said: "Lord, whider are ye boun?   *whither are you bound?*
    Allas! Whider will ye fro me found?"

---

[1] *And, you can be sure, it must be paid for*

[2] *You have been too long away from medical attention*

The king spake with sorry soun:

3515 "I will wend a little stound

Into the vale of Aveloun,

A while to hele me of my wound."

When the ship from the land was brought,

Sir Bedivere saw of them no more.

3520 Through the forest forth he sought

On hilles and holtes hore.   *hoary (gray) forests*

Of his life rought he right nought;   *reckoned*

All night he went weeping sore;

Against the day he fand there wrought   *Before daybreak*

3525 A chapel between two holtes hore.

To the chapel he took the way,

There he might see a wonder sight;

Then saw he where an ermite lay,

Before a tomb that was new dight,

3530 And covered it was with marble gray,

And with riche lettres rayled aright;   *rightly adorned*

There-on an herse, soothly to say,   *bier (hearse)*

With a hundreth tapers light.   *candles*

Unto the ermite went he there

3535 And asked who was buried there.

The ermite answerd swithe yare: *quite readily*

"Thereof can I tell no more;

About midnight were ladies here,

In world ne wiste I what they were;

3540 This body they brought upon a bere   *bier*

And buried it with woundes sore.

"Besauntes offred they here bright,   *Coins*

I hope an hundreth pound and more,   *suppose*

And bade me pray both day and night

3545 For him that is buried in these moldes hore   *this hoary ground*

Unto our Lady both day and night

That she his soul help sholde."

The knight redde the lettres aright;   *read*

110

For sorrow he fell unto the folde. *ground*

3550 "Ermite," he said, "without leesing,
 Here lieth my lord that I have lorn, *lost*
Bold Arthur, the beste king
 That ever was in Britain born.
Give me some of thy clothing,
3555 For Him that bore the crown of thorn,
And leve that I may with thee lenge, *grant; stay*
 While I may live, and pray him forn." *pray for him*

The holy ermite wolde not wonde; *delay*
 Some time Archebishop he was,
3560 That Mordred flemed out of land, *put to flight*
 And in the wood his wonning chese; *dwelling chose*
He thanked Jesu all of his sound *good fortune*
 That Sir Bedivere was comen in pees;
He received him with herte and hand,
3565 Togeder to dwell, withouten lees.

When Queen Gaynor, the kinges wife,
 Wiste that all was gone to wrake, *ruin*
Away she went, with ladies five,
 At Aumsbury, a nun her for to make. *Almesbury*
3570 There-in she lived an holy life,
 In prayers for to weep and wake;
Never after she coude be blithe; *could*
 There wered she clothes white and black. *wore; a nun's habit*

When this tidinges was to Launcelot brought,
3575 What wonder though his herte were sore?
His men, his frendes, to him sought,
 And all the wise that with him were.
Their galleys were all redy wrought;
 They busked them and made yare; *hurried; ready*
3580 To help Arthur was their thought
 And make Mordred of bliss full bare.

Launcelot had crowned kinges seven,

111

Erles fele and barons bold;
The number of knightes I can not neven,   *tell*
3585   The squires too fele to be told;
They lemed light as any leven;   *gleamed as bright as any lightning*
The wind was as themselve wolde;   *they desired*
Through the grace of God of Heven,
    At Dover they took haven and hold.   *protection*

3590   There herde tell Launcelot in that town,
    In land it is not for to laine,   *The news is not to be concealed*
How they had fought at Barendown
    And how buried was Sir Gawain,
And how Mordred wolde be king with crown,
3595   And how either of them had other slain,
And all that were to batail boun,   *ready*
    At Salisbury lay dede upon the plain.

Also in lande herde it kithe   *he heard it said*
    That made his herte wonder sore:
3600   Queen Gaynor, the kinges wife,
    Much had lived in sorrow and care;
Away she went with ladies five,
    In land they wiste not whider where,   *knew not where*
Dolven dede or to be on life;   *Whether dead and buried or still living*
3605   That made his morning much the more.   *mourning*

Launcelot cleped his kinges with crown;
    Sir Bors stood him ner beside;
He said: "Lordinges, I will wend toforn,   *before (onward)*
    And by these bankes ye shall abide
3610   Unto fifteen dayes at the morn.
    In land whatsoever us betide [1]
To herken what lord his life hath lorn,   *hear; lost*
    Look ye rappe you not up to ride."

---

[1] *Whatever may happen to us in this land (as we go) / To hear what lord has lost his life, / See that you do not rush to ride out (to help us)*

	There had he neither roo ne rest,	*peace*
3615	But forth he went with drery mood,	
	And three dayes he went even west	*straight*
	As man that coude neither ivel nor good. [1]	*knew*
	Then sigh he where a towr by west	*on the west*
	Was bigged by a burnes flood;	*built; stream's flood basin*
3620	There he hoped it were best	
	For to get him some lives stood.	*support for life (food)*

	As he came through a cloister clere —	
	Almost for weeping he was mad —	
	He sigh a lady bright of lere,	*complexion*
3625	In nunnes clothing was she cledde;	*clad*
	Thrice she swooned swiftly there,	
	So stronge paines she was in stedde	*places*
	That many a nun then nighed her ner,	
	And to her chamber was she led.	

	"Mercy, madame," they said all,	
	"For Jesu, that is King of bliss,	
	Is there any bride in bowr or hall	*maiden*
	Hath wrathed you?" She said: "Nay, iwis."	*angered*
	Launcelot to her gan they call,	
3635	The abbess and the other nunnes, iwis,	
	They that wonned within the wall.	*dwelt*
	In counsel there then said she thus:	

	"Abbess, to you I knowlech here	*acknowledge*
	That through this ilke man and me,	
3640	For we togeder han loved us dere,	
	All this sorrowful war hath be;	
	My lord is slain, that hath no peer,	
	And many a doughty knight and free;	
	Therefore for sorrow I died ner,	
3645	As soon as I ever gan him see.	

---

[1] *Like one who did not know good from evil (in a daze)*

113

"When I him see, the sooth to say,   *saw*
   All my herte began to colde;   *grow cold*
That ever I sholde abide this day,
   To see so many barons bold
3650 Sholde for us be slain away!
   Our will hath be too sore bought sold; [1]
But God, that all mightes may,
   Now hath me set where I will hold.   *abide*

"Yset I am in such a place   *Set*
3655 My soule hele I will abide,   *soul's healing; await*
Til God send me some grace,
   Through mercy of his woundes wide,
That I may do so in this place,
   My sinnes to amend this ilke tide,
3660 After to have a sight of His face,
   At Doomes-day on His righte side.   *Judgment Day*

"Therefore, Sir Launcelot du Lake,
   For my love now I thee pray,
My company thou ay forsake,
3665 And to thy kingdom thou take thy way,
And keep thy reme from war and wrake,   *realm*
   And take a wife with her to play,
And love well then thy worldes make;   *worldly mate*
   God give you joy togeder, I pray!

3670 "Unto God I pray, Allmighty King,
   He give you togeder joy and bliss;
But I beseech thee in alle thing
   That never in thy life after this
Ne come to me for no sokering,   *comfort*
3675 Nor send me sonde, but dwell in bliss;   *message*
I pray to God Everlasting
   To graunt me grace to mend my misse."   *sins*

---

[1] *Our desire (passion) has been too painfully bought and paid for*

114

"Now, sweet madame, that wolde I not do
    To have all the world unto my meed;   *as my reward*
3680 So untrew find ye me never mo;
    It for to do Crist me forbede!

"Forbede it God that ever I sholde
    Against you work so grete unright,   *great a wrong*
Sinne we togeder upon this molde   *Since; earth*
3685   Have led our life by day and night!
Unto God I give a hest to hold: *promise*
    That same destainy that you is dight   *destiny*
I will receive in some house bold   *i.e., receive monkhood*
    To plese hereafter God Allmight.   *please*

3690 "To plese God all that I may   *please*
    I shall hereafter do mine entent,   *make my intent*
And ever for you specially pray,
    While God will me life lente."   *grant*
"A, wilt thou so," the queen gan say,
3695   "Fulfill this forward that thou has ment?"   *promise; said*
Launcelot said: "Yif I said nay,
    I were well worthy to be brent."   *burned (in Hell)*

"Brent to ben worthy I were,
    Yif I wolde take none such a life,
3700 To bide in penaunce, as ye do here,   *penance*
    And suffer for God sorrow and strife;
As we in liking lived in fere,   *in pleasure; together*
    By Mary, Moder, maid, and wife,
Til God us depart with dethes dere,
3705   To penaunce I yeld me here as blithe.   *pain*

"All blyve to penaunce I will me take,   *quickly*
    As I may find any ermite
That will me receive for Goddes sake,
    Me to clothe with black and white."
3710 The sorrow that the tone to the tother gan make   *one; other*
    Might none erthely man see it.
"Madame," then said Launcelot du Lake,

115

"Kiss me, and I shall wend as-tite."   *go quickly away*

"Nay," said the queen, "that will I not;
3715   Launcelot, think on that no more;
To abstain us we moste have thought [1]
     Fro such we have delited in ere.
Let us think on Him that us hath bought,   *redeemed*
     And we shall plese God therefore.   *please*
3720 Think on this world, how there is nought
     But war and strife and batail sore."

What helpeth lenger for to spell?   *speak*
     With that they gan depart in twain;
But none erthely man coude tell
3725   The sorrow that there began to ben;
Wringing their handes and loud they yell,
     As they never more sholde blinne,   *cease*
And sithe in swoon both down they fell;
     Who saw that sorrow ever might it mene. [2]

3730 But ladies then, with morning cheer,   *mournful face*
     Into the chamber the queen they bore,
And all full busy made them there
     To cover the queen of her care.   *recover*
But many also that with Launcelot were,
3735   They comfort him with rewful care;
When he was covered he took his gere   *gear (equipment)*
     And went from thence withouten more.

His herte was hevy as any lede,   *lead*
     And lever he was his life have lorn.   *rather he would; lost*
3740 He said: "Rightuous God, what is my rede?   *what shall I do*
     Alas, forbore, why was I born?"   *misbegotten (creature)*
Away he went, as he had fled,
     To a forest that was him beforn;

---

[1] *We must be determined to abstain / From what we once delighted in*

[2] *He who saw that sorrow could tell of it forever*

116

His life fain he wolde have leved;   *gladly; departed*
3745   His rich attire he wolde off-torn.   *have torn off*

All night gan he weep and wring   *wring his hands*
    And went about as he were wode;
Erly, as the day gan spring,
    Tho sigh he where a chapel stood;   *Then saw*
3750   A bell herde he rewfully ring;
    He hied him then and thider yode;   *hastened; went*
A prest was redy for to sing,
    And mass he herde with drery mood.

The Archebishop was ermite there,
3755   That flemed was for his workes trew;   *banished; loyal deeds*
The mass he sang with sighing sore,
    And oft he changed hide and hew;   *complexion; hue*
Sir Bedivere had sorrow and care
    And oft morned for tho workes new;   *those recent events*
3760   After mass was morning more,   *more mourning*
    When ech of them other knew.

When the sorrow was to the end,
    The bishop took his habit there
And welcomed Launcelot as the hende,   *as a courteous person should*
3765   And on his knees down gan he fare:
"Sir, ye be welcome as our frend,
    Unto this bigging in bankes bare;   *building*
Were it your will with us to lende
    This one night, yif ye may no more!"

3770   When they knew him at the last,
    Fair in armes they gan him fold,
And sithe he asked freely fast
    Of Arthur and of other bold;
An hundreth times his herte ner brast,
3775   While Sir Bedivere the tale told.
To Arthures tomb he cast;   *went*
    His careful corage wexed all cold.   *sorrowful heart*

He threw his armes to the walle,   *walls*
    That riche were and bright of blee;   *color*
3780 Before the ermite he gan down fall
    And comely kneeled upon his knee;
Then he shrove him of his sinnes all,   *confessed himself*
    And prayd he might his broder be,
To serve God in bowr and hall,
3785   That might-full King of mercy free.

The holy bishop nolde not blinne,   *would not refuse*
    But blithe was to do his boon;   *fulfill his request*
He received him with wele and winne,   *rejoicing*
    And thanked Jesu trew in trone,   *throne*
3790 And shrove him there of his sin,   *absolved*
    As clene as he had never done none;
And sithe he kiste him cheek and chin
    And an habit there did him upon.   *monastic habit put on him*

His grete host at Dover lay,   *army*
3795   And wend he sholde have come again,
Til after befell upon a day,
    Sir Lionel, that was mikel of main,
With fifty lordes, the sooth to say,
    To seek his lord he was full fain;
3800 To London he took the righte way;
    Alas, for wo! There was he slain.

Bors de Gawnes wolde no lenger abide
    But busked him and made all boun,   *prepared himself; ready*
And bade all the host homeward ride —
3805   God send them wind and weder round!   *ample wind*
To seek Launcelot will he ride;
    Ector and he diverse wayes yode,
And Bors sought forth the weste side,
    As he that coude neither ivel nor good.   *knew not evil from (i.e., in a daze)*

3810 Full erly in a morrow tide
    In a forest he fand a well;
He rode ever forth by the river side,

Til he had sight of a chapel;
There at mass thought he abide;
3815   Rewfully he herde ring a bell;
There Launcelot he fand with mikel pride,
And prayd he might with him there dwell.

Ere the half yere were comen to the end,
There was comen of their fellowes seven,
3820 Where ichon had sought their frend,
With sorrowful herte and drery steven;   *voice*
Had none never will away to wend,
When they herde of Launcelot neven,   *heard tell of Lancelot*
But all togeder there gan they lende,
3825   As it was Goddes will of heven.

Holich all tho seven yeres   *Wholly*
Launcelot was prest and mass song,   *priest and sang mass*
In penaunce and in diverse prayers;
That life him thought nothing long;
3830 Sir Bors and his other feres   *companions*
On bookes redde and belles rong.   *read; rang*
So little they wex of lin and leres   *thin; grew; loin; face*
Them to know it was strong.   *difficult*

It fell again an even-tide   *happened one evening*
3835   That Launcelot sekened sely sore.   *sickened wondrously*
The bishop he cleped to his side,
And all his fellows less and more;
He said: "Brethern, I may no lenger abide;
My baleful blood of life is bare;
3840 What boot is it to hele and hide?   *What good is it to conceal and hide it?*
My foul flesh will to erthe fare.

"But, brethern, I pray you tonight,
Tomorrow, when ye find me dede,
Upon a bere that ye will me dight,   *bier; prepare (embalm)*
3845   And to Joyous Gard then me lede;
For the love of God Almight,
Bury my body in that stede;   *place*

119

Some time my trouth there-to I plight;[1]
  Alas! Me forthinketh that I so did!"

3850 "Mercy, sir," they said all three,
  "For His love that died on Rood;
Yif any ivel have greved thee,
  It is but hevyness of your blood; *heaviness*
Tomorrow ye shall better be;
3855 When were ye but of comfort good?"
Merrily spake all men but he,
  But straight unto his bed he yode.

And cleped the bishop him until, *to him*
  And shrove him of his sinnes clene,[2]
3860 Of all his sinnes loud and still,
  And of his sinnes much did he mene; *speak*
There he received with goode will
  God, Maryes Son, maiden clene. *pure*
Then Bors of weeping had never his fill;
3865 To bed they yede then all bydene.

A little while before the day,
  As the bishop lay in his bed,
A laughter took him there he lay, *where*
  That all they were right sore adredde; *frightened*
3870 They wakened him, for sooth to say,
  And asked yif he were hard bestedde. *pressed*
He said: "Alas, and wele-away!
  Why ne had I lenger thus be led? *been led (in dreams)*

"Alas! Why nighed ye me nigh
3875 To awake me in word or steven? *sound*
Here was Launcelot bright of blee *countenance*
  With angeles thirty thousand and seven;
Him they bore up on high;

_____

[1] *Once I pledged my word to that; / Alas, I repent that I did so!*
[2] *And cleansed himself of his sins by confession*

120

Against him opened the gates of heven;
3880 Such a sight right now I see,
Is none on erthe that might it neven."   *describe*

"Sir," they said, "for Cross on Rood,
Doth such wordes clene away.
Sir Launcelot aileth nothing but good;
3885 He shall be hole by prime of day."   *the first hour*
Candle they light and to him yode,
And fand him dede, for sooth to say,
Red and fair of flesh and blood,
Right as he in sleeping lay.

3890 "Alas!" said Bors, "That I was born!
That ever I sholde see this in-deed!
The beste knight his life hath lorn
That ever in stour bestrode steed!
Jesu, that crowned was with thorn,
3895 In heven his soul foster and feed!"
Unto the fifth day at the morn
They left not for to sing and rede,   *chant*

And after they made them a bere,   *bier*
The bishop and these other bold,
3900 And forth they went, all in fere,
To Joyous Gard, that riche hold;   *stronghold*
In a chapel, amiddes the quere,   *amid the choir*
A grave they made as they wolde,
And three dayes they waked him there,   *gave him a wake*
3905 In the castel with cares cold.   *chilled with grief*

Right as they stood about the bere   *bier*
And to burying him sholde have brought,
In came Sir Ector, his broder dere,
That seven yere afore had him sought.
3910 He looked up into the quere;   *choir*
To here a mass then had he thought;

121

For that they all ravished were [1]
    They knew him and he them nought.

Sir Bors both wept and sang,
3915   When they that faire fast unfold; [2]
There was none but his handes wrang,   *wrung*
    The bishop nor none of the other bold.
Sir Ector then thought long;
    What this corpse was fain wite he wolde; [3]
3920   An hundreth times his herte nigh sprang,   *nearly broke*
    By that Bors had him the tale told.

Full hendely Sir Bors to him spake,
    And said: "Welcome, Sir Ector, iwis;
Here lieth my lord Launcelot du Lake,
3925   For whom that we have morned thus."
Then in armes he gan him take,
    The dede body to clipp and kiss,   *embrace*
And prayed all night he might him wake,   *watch by him*
    For Jesu love, King of bliss.

3930   Sir Ector of his wit ner went,   *nearly went out of his mind*
    Wallowed and wrang as he were wode;   *wrung his hands*
So wofully his mone he ment   *said*
    His sorrow minged all his mood;   *confused; mind*
When the corpse in armes he hent,   *seized*
3935   The teres out of his eyen yode;   *went*
At the last they might no lenger stent,   *delay*
    But buried him with drery mood.

Sithen on their knees they kneeled down —
    Grete sorrow it was to see with sight:
3940   "Unto Jesu Crist I ask a boon,
    And to his Moder, Mary bright:

---

[1] *Because they were all in a religious ecstasy, / They neither knew him nor did he know them*

[2] *When they closely embrace that fair one (Ector, Bors' brother)*

[3] *He wanted very much to know who this corpse was*

Lord, as thou madest both sun and moon,
  And God and Man art most of might,
Bring this soul unto Thy trone,   *throne*
3945 And ever Thou rewdest on gentle knight."   *If; You had pity*

Sir Ector tent not to his steed,   *paid no attention*
  Wheder he wolde stint or run away,   *stand still*
But with them all to dwell and lede, [1]
  For Launcelot all his life to pray.
3950 On him did he ermites weed,   *himself he put hermit's*
  And to their chapel went their way;
A fourtenight on foot they yede,
  Ere they home come, for sooth to say.

When they came to Aumsbury,   *Almesbury*
3955 Dede they found Gaynor the queen,
With rodes fair and red as cherry,   *cheeks*
  And forth they bore her them between,
And buried her with mass full merry
  By Sir Arthur, as I you mene;
3960 Now hight their chapel Glastonbury,   *is named*
  An abbey full rich, of order clene.   *pure (monastic) order*

Of Launcelot du Lake tell I no more,
  But thus beleve these ermites seven.   *remain; hermits*
And yet is Arthur buried there,
3965 And Queen Gaynor, as I you neven,
With monkes that are right of lore;
  They rede and sing with milde steven:
"Jesu, that suffred woundes sore,
  Graunt us all the bliss of heven!"
            Amen

        Explicit le Morte Arthur
      (Here ends the Death of Arthur)

---

[1] *But decided to dwell with them all and lead his life there*

123

Notes

In the textual notes, corrections and emendations made by J. D. Bruce (see Bibliography) are accepted without comment. Additional changes made by Larry D. Benson in the edition on which this volume is based (see Preface to the Revised Edition) are indicated: Be.

Explanatory notes are Benson's, either verbatim or with minor changes to fit the format of this revision. Additional explanatory material is cited as follows:

F: Edward E. Foster, editor of this revision

M: Charles and Ruth Moorman, *An Arthurian Dictionary*. Oxford, Mississippi: University of Mississippi Press, 1978.

OED: *Oxford English Dictionary*

1   *Lordinges*: a familiar form of address for the audience at the beginning of romances. See, e.g., *Havelok* and the Pardoner's address to the other pilgrims in *The Canterbury Tales*. It implies nothing about the social status of the audience. (F)

43   *Galehod*. Malory's Galyhodyn, king of Surluse and kinsman of Galehaut. See lines 225, 261, 2572, and 2587.

152   The convention noted in lines 147-152 was not the case in actual life.

245   *aunt*. Ascolot's sister, to whom they return when Launcelot is wounded, line 321.

284   *brown*: the word is used in the sense of "shining, gleaming, or burnished" only with regard to swords or steel. (F)

309   MS *hitte: hit him*. (Be)

          hood: "The part of a suit of armor that covers the head; applied to the helmet itself, or to a flexible head-covering inside the helmet" (*OED*).

361   The stanza beginning at 361 has only seven lines as does the stanza beginning at 1483; the stanza beginning at 3678 has only four lines; the stanzas beginning at 1176, 1318, 1490, 1920, 2318, 2716, 3130, and 3416 have only six lines. Nothing seems lost to the sense by these omissions or variations, although the six line stanzas beginning at 1176 and 1318 are at the beginning and end of the long gap in the MS.

457   The boards are set on trestles to form tables. Permanently assembled tables were still rare at this time.

603   *Launcelotes sheld du Lake:* Launcelot du Lake's shield. The inflectional ending is placed on the primary noun rather than on the last word of the noun phrase. The construction was disappearing in the fourteenth century but can be observed in Chaucer's "Wyves Tale of Bath" ("Wife of Bath's Tale"). (F)

764   *Cross and Rood.* The redundancy perhaps implies urgency. Benson notes, however, that the expression *Cross on* (or *and*) *Rood* is frequently used in this poem; the word *cross* is probably a metathesis of *cors* — body, as in line 2880, where *Cors on Rood* does appear.

840   No reason is provided as to why the squire wishes to poison Gawain and, within the narrative conventions of romance, none is needed: our interest is in what the effects will be for Guinevere. (F)

916   Guinevere has two choices: to be "defended" in combat or be tried by a group of the knights. She knows that if the latter occurs she is doomed.

1105   *ender* (Be). MS: *?ender.*

1350   *Cross on Rood.* See note to line 764.

1377   *aguilte* (Be). MS: *gilte.*

1396   Identical to line 1380.

1414   A missing line is provided here by Furnivall's conjecture, accepted by Br and Be. (F)

1472   Sometimes *blake* has the meaning white and Be glosses it thus. I think, how-
         ever, that it is more likely that Lancelot is dressed in black and the more ordi-
         nary meaning can stand. (F)

1617-18 Compare Priamus's words to Gawain in the *Alliterative Morte Arthure*, lines
         2646-49.

1831   *hauberk*: "Originally intended for the defense of the neck and shoulders; but
         already in the twelfth and thirteenth centuries developed into a long coat of
         mail, or military tunic, usually of ring or chain mail, which adapted itself read-
         ily to the motions of the body" (*OED*).

1951   The smock is a loose, usually white, simple sleeveless dress over which the
         other garments were put; the counterpart of a modern slip, though it would
         usually show beneath the vest, sleeves, cloaks, and such that were put over it.

2025   Launcelot apparently thinks Gaheriet fought against him.

2052   Launcelot offers to take part in a judicial duel of the sort he previously fought
         to prove Guenevere's innocence of the charge of poisoning.

2253   A papal interdict would deny the sacraments of the Church to everyone in the
         country.

2305   *Benwick* is Bayonne (or Beune), a city in southwestern France. See *Alliterative
         Morte Arthure*, line 587. (F)

2345   *Joyous Gard then they* (Be). MS: *Ioyus gard the they.* Joyous Gard is Lancelot's
         castle (fortress) in Northern England. (F)

2361   The heathen nations are in the Orient, from which silk came.

2466   Caerleon, in South Wales on the River Usk near the Bristol Channel, was one
         of the chief Arthurian cities. See *Alliterative Morte Arthure*, note to line 61. (F)

2639   The phrase *wise . . . under weed* has little real meaning and conveys only the
         idea of a "good knight."

2837   Gawain is Arthur's nephew.

2934   *oute*. Br reads *cute*.

2954   *That false traitour,* applied here to Mordred, is a commonplace epithet for Satan, who led the rebellion against God. (F)

2955   Mordred was the product of an incestuous union between Arthur and his own sister. Though little is made of it in this poem, Arthur's fall is partly a consequence of his own sin.

2957   The motif of the false steward, who evilly abuses his stewardship, is a familiar literary and folk motif. (F)

2960   Thus Mordred intends to commit incest, made worse since Guenevere is also his father's wife. (Compare line 2987.)

3121   *his* (Be). MS: *hye*.

3160   The Feast of the Trinity is the first Sunday after Pentecost.

3179   *Besaunt*: a coin of Byzantine origin, sometimes used as ornamental jewelry. (F)

3357   *fewtered*: placed spears against the "fewter," the spear rest on the saddle, into which the spear would be placed when the knight prepared to attack.

3376   *Brutus*. MS: *Britain*. Be notes the error but does not emend (F). Brutus is the legendary hero who, according to Geoffrey of Monmouth's *History of the Kings of Britain* (Book I), conquered what is now England from a race of giants and founded the nation to which he gave his name.

3413   *names seven*. The number seven commonly signifies a totality. Thus the seven names implies *all the names of Jesus*. But traditions reaching far back into the rabbinical commentaries often, in fact, identify seven specific names for God. According to *The Jewish Encyclopedia*, "The number of divine names that require the scribe's special care is seven: El, Elohim, Adonai, YHWH, Ehyeh-Asher-Ehyeh, Shaddai, and Zeba'ot" (9, 163). The seven names of the Lord are also referred to in *The Second Shepherd's Play* (lines 190–91), where Mak says: "Now lord, for thy naymes sevyn, that made both moyn and starnes /Well mo then I can neuen thi will, lorde, of me tharnys [is unclear]." See also Brian P. Copenhaver, "Names of God," in *A Dictionary of Biblical Traditions in Eng-*

lish Literature, ed. David Lyle Jeffrey (Grand Rapids: William B. Eerdmans, 1992), pp. 535–37, who notes more than one hundred and fifty substitute names for God and, in the New Testament, more than forty names and titles for Jesus.

3504   Possibly Morgan le Fay, Arthur's half-sister. Although often antagonistic to Arthur and Guenevere, she often helps heal Arthurian knights and assists in transporting Arthur to Avalon. (M)

3507   *leching*. In the fourteenth century, leeching had no necessary connection with the therapeutic application of leeches. It means simply "medical care" from OE *laece*, to heal.

3569   *Aumsbury*: Almesbury (or Amesbury): a town in Wiltshire where Guenevere retreats to a convent after Arthur's death. (M, F)

3628   *nun* (Be). MS: *man.*

3709   *black and white* (Be). MS: *whyte and blak.*

3759   The "recent events" are Mordred's treachery and Arthur's death.

3815   *ring a bell* (Be). MS: *a bell ring.*

3862   *received* in this line refers to receiving the sacrament of the Eucharist, the body and blood of Christ, after having been forgiven (shriven) one's sins.

3896   *fifth* (Be). MS: *fyfty.*

Alliterative Morte Arthure

Select Bibliography

Manuscript

Lincoln Cathedral 91 (Thornton Manuscript), fols. 53a–98b; c. 1440. (Lincoln Cathedral Library)

Editions

Morte Arthure, or The Death of Arthur. Ed. Edmund Brock. EETS o.s. 8. New York, London, Toronto: Oxford University Press, 1871; rpt. 1961. [Very close to the manuscript, but with few notes.]

Morte Arthure. Ed. Erik Björkman. Alt- und mittelenglische Texte, 9. Heidelberg: Carl Winters and New York: G. E Stechert and Company, 1915. [Heavily emended, often to improve rhythm or alliteration; excellent notes and glossary.]

The Alliterative Morte Arthure: A Critical Edition. Ed. Valerie Krishna. New York: Burt Franklin, 1976. [An excellent conservative edition with full documentation and notes.]

Morte Arthure: A Critical Edition. Ed. Mary Hamel. Garland Medieval Texts, 9. New York and London: Garland, 1984. [Full apparatus; uses Winchester manuscript of Malory to elucidate the text of the alliterative poem.]

Criticism

Benson, Larry D. "The Alliterative *Morte Arthure* and Medieval Tragedy." *Tennessee Studies in Literature* 11 (1966), 75–87. [Argues that the conflict is between two goods and that Arthur's fall is the consequence of the heroic system that comes into conflict with Christian ideals.]

Alliterative Morte Arthure

Göller, Karl Heinz, ed. *The Alliterative Morte Arthure: A Reassessment of the Poem*. Arthurian Studies, 2. Cambridge: D. S. Brewer, 1981.

Hamel, Mary. "Adventure as Structure in the Alliterative *Morte Arthure*." *Arthurian Interpretations* 3 (1988), 37–48.

Jember, Gregory K. "Tone as Meaning in the *Morte Arthure*." *Studies in Medieval English Language and Literature* 2 (1987), 95–100.

Keiser, George R. "The Theme of Justice in the Alliterative *Morte Arthure*." *Annuale Medievale* 16 (1975), 94–109.

Kennedy, Edward Donald. "Generic Intertextuality in the English Alliterative *Morte Arthure*: The Italian Connection." In *Text and Intertext in Medieval Arthurian Literature*. Ed. Norris J. Lacy. New York: Garland, 1996. Pp. 41–56.

Lumiansky, Robert M. "The Alliterative *Morte Arthure*, the Concept of Medieval Tragedy, and the Cardinal Virtue Fortitude." In *Medieval and Renaissance Studies*. Ed. John M. Headley. Chapel Hill: University of North Carolina Press, 1968. Pp. 95–118. [Sees the poem as an "exemplum" of fortitude.]

Matthews, William. *The Tragedy of Arthur*. Berkeley and Los Angeles: University of California Press, 1960. [Still the only comprehensive, full-length study of the poem.]

Peck, Russell A. "Willfulness and Wonders: Boethian Tragedy in the Alliterative *Morte Arthure*." In *The Alliterative Tradition in the Fourteenth Century*. Ed. Bernard S. Levy and Paul E. Szarmach. Kent: Kent State University Press, 1981. Pp. 153–82. [Examines geometric structure of the plot whereby the second half of the poem on Arthur's willful decline mirrors in reverse the first half on good kingship.]

Westover, Jeff. "Arthur's End: The King's Emasculation in the Alliterative *Morte Arthure*." *Chaucer Review* 32 (1998), 310–24.

For a complete bibliography of *The Alliterative Morte Arthure*, see the electronic Introduction to the poem at http://www.lib.rochester.edu/camelot/teams/alstint.htm

For more materials on Arthurian literature see The Camelot Project: http://www.lib.rochester.edu/camelot/cphome.stm

Alliterative Morte Arthure

Here beginnes Morte Arthure. In Nomine Patris et Filii et Spiritus Sancti. Amen
pur Charite. Amen.

Now grete glorious God through grace of Himselven	*great*
And the precious prayer of his pris Moder	*excellent*
Sheld us fro shamesdeede and sinful workes	*shameful deeds*
And give us grace to guie and govern us here	*guide*
5 In this wretched world, through virtuous living	
That we may kaire til his court, the kingdom of heven	*go to*
When our soules shall part and sunder fro the body	*from*
Ever to beld and to bide in bliss with Himselven;	*dwell; abide*
And wisse me to warp out some word at this time	*teach; utter*
10 That nother void be ne vain but worship til Himselven	*neither; honor*
Plesand and profitable to the pople that them heres.	*Pleasing; people; hear*
Ye that lust has to lithe or loves for to here	*desire; listen*
Of elders of olde time and of their awke deedes,	*strange*
How they were lele in their law and loved God Almighty	*loyal; religion*
15 Herkenes me hendely and holdes you stille,	*Hearken; courteously*
And I shall tell you a tale that trew is and noble	*true*
Of the real renkes of the Round Table	*royal men*
That chef were of chivalry and cheftains noble	*chief; chieftains*
Both wary in their workes and wise men of armes,	*skilled*
20 Doughty in their doings and dredde ay shame,	*dreaded always*
Kind men and courtais and couth of court thewes,	*courteous; skilled; manners*
How they won with war worshippes many,	*honors*
Slogh Lucius the lithere that lord was of Rome,	*Slew; wicked*
And conquered that kingrik through craftes of armes;	*kingdom*
25 Herkenes now hiderward and heres this story!	*Listen; here; hear*
When that the king Arthur by conquest had wonnen	*won*
Casteles and kingdomes and countrees many,	*countries*
And he had covered the crown of that kith riche	*recovered; country*
Of all that Uter in erthe ought in his time:	*Uther; earth; owned*

131

30	Argayle and Orkney and all these oute-iles,	*outer-isles*
	Ireland utterly, as Ocean runnes,	*entirely; where the*
	Scathel Scotland by skill he skiftes as him likes,[1]	
	And Wales of war he won at his will,	*by; to*
	Bothe Flaunders and Fraunce free til himselven	*to*
35	Holland and Hainault they held of him bothen,	*both*
	Burgoigne and Brabaunt and Bretain the less	*Brittany*
	Guienne and Gothland and Grace the rich,	*Grasse*
	Bayonne and Bourdeaux he belded full fair,	*dwelt in*
	Touraine and Toulouse with towres full high,	*towers*
40	Of Poitiers and Provence he was prince holden;	*considered*
	Of Valence and Vienne, of value so noble,	
	Of Overgne and Anjou, those erldoms rich,	*Auvergne; earldoms*
	By conquest full cruel they knew him for lord	*acknowledged*
	Of Navarre and Norway and Normandy eek	*also*
45	Of Almaine, of Estriche, and other ynow;	*Germany; Austria; many others*
	Denmark he dressed all by drede of himselven	*directed; dread*
	Fro Swynne unto Swetherwike, with his sword keen![2]	

	When he these deedes had done, he dubbed his knightes,	
	Devised ducheries and delt in diverse rewmes,[3]	
50	Made of his cosins kinges annointed	*relatives*
	In kithes there they covet crownes to bere.	*countries where; bear*
	When he these rewmes had ridden and rewled the pople,	*realms; ruled; people*
	Then rested that real and held the Round Table;	*royal (one)*
	Sujourns that seson to solace himselven	*Sojourns; season*
55	In Bretain the brodder, as him best likes;	*Great Britain; pleases*
	Sithen went into Wales with his wyes all,	*Then; men*
	Sways into Swaldie with his snell houndes	*Moves; South Wales; swift*
	For to hunt at the hartes in those high landes,	*stags*
	In Glamorgan with glee there gladship was ever,	*where gladness*
60	And there a citee he set, by assent of his lordes	*city; established*
	That Caerlion was called, with curious walles,	*Caerleon; skillfully made*
	On the rich river that runnes so fair,	*great*

---

[1] *Harmful Scotland with skill he rules as it pleases him*

[2] *From Swynn (an arm of the North Sea near Zeeland) to Sweden, with his sharp sword*

[3] *Created and gave out dukedoms in diverse realms*

There he might semble his sorte to see when him liked.[1]

Then after at Carlisle a Christenmass he holdes,   *Christmas*

65   This ilk kidd conquerour and held him for lord   *same famous*

With dukes and douspeeres of diverse rewmes,   *high nobles; realms*

Erles and erchevesques and other ynow,   *Earls; archbishops*

Bishoppes and bachelers and bannerettes noble[2]

That bowes to his banner, busk when him likes.   *go when it pleases him*

70   But on the Christenmass-day when they were all sembled,

That comlich conquerour commaundes himselven   *comely*

That ilk a lord sholde lenge and no leve take   *each; should remain; leave*

To the tende day fully were taken to the end.   *tenth*

Thus on real array he held his Round Table   *royal*

75   With semblaunt and solace and selcouthe metes;   *splendor; rare foods*

Was never such noblay in no mannes time   *nobleness*

Made in mid-winter in tho West Marches!   *those*

But on the New-Yere day, at the noon even,   *New Year's; exactly*

As the bold at the borde was of bred served,[3]

80   So come in sodenly a senatour of Rome,   *suddenly*

With sixteen knightes in a suite, sewand him one;   *company following; alone*

He salued the soveraign and the sale after   *saluted; hall*

Ilk a king after king, and made his inclines;   *Each; bows*

Gaynor in her degree he grette as him liked   *greeted; pleased*

85   And sinn again to the gome he gave up his needes:[4]

"Sir Lucius Iberius, the Emperour of Rome,

Salues thee as subjet, under his sele rich;   *Salutes; subject; seal*

It is credens, Sir King, with cruel wordes;   *credentials*

Trow it for no troufles, his targe is to shew![5]

90   Now in this New-Yeres Day, with notaries sign,

I make thee summons in sale to sew for thy landes,   *hall; plead*

That on Lamass Day there be no let founden   *August 1; hindrance found*

That thou be redy at Rome with all thy Round Table   *ready*

---

[1]*Where he might assemble his followers to go to sea when it pleased him*

[2] *Bishops and young knights (bachelers) and noble senior knights (bannerettes)*

[3] *As the bold men at the table were served with bread (the first course)*

[4] *And then (he bowed) again to the man (Arthur) and delivered his message*

[5] *Think it not a trifle, his shield (armorial device) is to be seen hereon*

	Appere in his presence with thy pris knightes	*Appear; excellent*
95	At prime of the day, in pain of your lives,	*first hour; on*
	In the kidd Capitoil before the king selven	*famous; himself*
	When he and his senatours bes set as them likes,	*are; it pleases them*
	To answer only why thou occupies the landes	*alone*
	That owe homage of old til him and his elders,	*to*
100	Why thou has ridden and raimed and ransound the pople	*robbed; ransomed*
	And killed down his cosins, kinges annointed;	*kinsmen*
	There shall thou give reckoning for all thy Round Table,	
	Why thou art rebel to Rome and rentes them with-holdes!	*revenue*
	Yif thou these summons withsit, he sendes thee these wordes:	*if; resist*
105	He shall thee seek over the se, with sixteen kinges,	*sea*
	Brin Bretain the brode and britten thy knightes[1]	
	And bring thee buxomly as a beste with brethe where him likes,	
	That thou ne shall route ne rest under the heven rich	
	Though thou for reddour of Rome run to the erthe!	
110	For if thou flee into Fraunce or Frisland other,	*Frisia either*
	Thou shall be fetched with force and overset forever!	*overthrown*
	Thy fader made fewtee we find in our rolles,	*father; fealty; records*
	In the regestré of Rome, who-so right lookes;	*registry*
	Withouten more troufling the tribute we ask	*trifling*
115	That Julius Cesar won with his gentle knightes!"	*noble*
	The king blushed on the berne with his brode eyen,[2]	
	That full bremly for brethe brent as the gledes,	
	Cast colours as the king with cruel lates	*Turned pale; features*
	Looked as a lion and on his lip bites.	
120	The Romanes for radness rusht to the erthe,	*fear; ground*
	For ferdness of his face as they fey were;	*fear; fated to die*
	Couched as kennetes before the king selven;	*Crouched like hounds*
	Because of his countenaunce confused them seemed!	*they seemed*
	Then covered up a knight and cried full loud:	*got up (on his knees)*
125	"King, crowned of kind, courtais and noble,	*by nature courteous*

---

[1] *Burn Britain the broad (Great Britain) and beat down your knights / And with anger bring you compliantly as a beast where he pleases / And you shall not sleep nor rest under the great heaven, / Though for fear of Rome you run to the earth (like a hunted animal)*

[2] *The king looked on the man with his large eyes, / Which burned very fiercely like coals because of (his) anger*

	Misdo no messanger for mensk of thyselven,	*Harm; honor*
	Senn we are in thy manrede and mercy thee beseekes;	*Since; power; beseech*
	We lenge with Sir Lucius, that lord is of Rome,	*belong*
	That is the marveloustest man than on molde lenges;	*most marvelous; earth*
130	It is lelful til us his liking til work;[1]	
	We come at his commaundment; have us excused."	

	Then carpes the conquerour cruel wordes:	*says*
	"Ha! cravand knight, a coward thee seemes!	*craven; you seem*
	There is some segge in this sale, and he were sore greved[2]	
135	Thou durst not for all Lumbardy look on him ones!"	

	"Sir," says the senatour, "so Crist mot me help,	*As; may*
	The vout of thy visage has wounded us all!	*expression*
	Thou art the lordliest lede that ever I on looked.	*man*
	By looking, withouten lees, a lion thee seemes!"	*In appearance; lies; you seem*

140	"Thou has me summoned," quod the king, "and said what thee likes.	
	For sake of thy soveraign I suffer thee the more;	
	Senn I crowned was in kith with crisom annointed,	*Since; country; holy oil*
	Was never creature to me that carped so large!	*spoke so freely*
	But I shall take counsel at kinges annointed	*from*
145	Of dukes and douspeeres and doctours noble,	*high noblemen; theologians*
	Of peeres of the parlement, prelates and other	*parliament*
	Of the richest renkes of the Round Table;	*most powerful men*
	Thus shall I take avisement of valiant bernes,	*advice; men*
	Work after the wit of my wise knightes.	*Do according to*
150	To warp wordes in waste no worship it were,	*utter; honor*
	Ne wilfully in this wrath to wreken myselven.	*Nor; avenge*
	Forthy shall thou lenge here and lodge with these lordes	*Therefore; remain*
	This seven-night in solace to sujourn your horses,	*pleasure; rest*
	To see what life that we lede in these low landes."	*lead; humble*
155	For by the realtee of Rome, that richest was ever,	*royalty; most powerful*
	He commaundes Sir Kayous, "Take keep to those lordes	*care of*

---

[1] *It is loyal (our duty) for us to do his pleasure*

[2] *There is a certain man in this hall, and he was sorely grieved / That you dared not look on him once for all Lombardy (as a reward)*

To stightel tho stern men as their state askes,   *arrange those; requires*
That they be herbered in haste in those high chambres,   *lodged; noble*
Sithen sittandly in sale served thereafter,   *Then suitably in hall*
160   That they find no faute of food to their horses,   *lack*
Nother wine ne wax ne welth in this erthe;   *candles*
Spare for no spicery, but spend what thee likes[1]
That there be largess on loft and no lack founden;   *generosity prevailing*
If thou my worship wait, wye, by my trewth,[2]
165   Thou shall have gersoms full grete that gain shall thee ever!"

Now are they herbered in high and in host holden,[3]
Hastily with hende men within these high walles.   *courteous; noble*
In chambers with chimpnees they changen their weedes,[4]
And sithen the chaunceller them fetched with chevalry noble;   *then*
170   Soon the senatour was set as him well seemed,   *befit*
At the kinges own borde; two knightes him served,   *table*
Singulere, soothly, as Arthur himselven,   *Singly (alone)*
Richly on the right hand at the Round Table.
By resoun that the Romans were so rich holden,   *reason; powerful*
175   As of the realest blood that regned in erthe.   *most royal; reigned*
There come in at the first course, before the king selven,   *himself*
Borehevedes that were bright, burnisht with silver   *Boar-heads; adorned*
All with taught men and towen in togges full rich,[5]
Of sank real in suite, sixty at ones;
180   Flesh flourisht of fermison, with frumentee noble,[6]
There-to wild to wale, and winlich briddes,
Pacockes and plovers in platters of gold   *Peacocks*
Pigges of pork despine that pastured never;   *Piglets; porcupine*

---

[1] *Don't save money on spices, but spend what you please*

[2] *If you guard my honor, man, by my pledged word, / You shall have very great rewards that will profit you forever*

[3] *Now are they nobly lodged and regarded as guests*

[4] *In chambers with chimneys (heat), they change their clothes*

[5] *All with men trained and taught, in very rich clothes, / All of royal blood in a troop, sixty together*

[6] *Flesh fattened in season with noble frumentee (a wheat dish), / Along with wild (game) to choose, and pleasant birds*

	Sithen herons in hedoyne heled full fair,	*Then; plumage concealed*
185	Grete swannes full swithe in silveren chargeours,[1]	*platters*
	Tartes of Turky, taste whom them likes;	*pies; Turkey; pleases*
	Gumbaldes graithly, full gracious to taste;	*Beef pies readily*
	Senn bowes of wild bores with the brawn leched,[2]	
	Bernakes and botoures in batterd dishes,	
190	Thereby braunchers in bred, better was never,	*young hawks; bread*
	With brestes of barrowes that bright were to shew;	*breasts; pigs; be seen*
	Senn come there sewes sere with solace thereafter,	*Then; stews various*
	Ownde of azure all over and ardaunt them seemed;[3]	
	Of ilk a leche the lowe launched full high,	
195	That all ledes might like that looked them upon;	*men; who*
	Then cranes and curlewes craftily rosted,	*roasted*
	Connies in cretoyne coloured full fair,	*Rabbits; milk and spices*
	Fesauntes enflourished in flamand silver,	*Pheasants adorned; flaming*
	With darielles endored and dainties ynow;[4]	
200	Then Claret and Crete clergially rennen[5]	
	With condethes full curious all of clene silver,	
	Osay and Algarde and other ynow	*Alsatian and Spanish wines; many others*
	Rhenish wine and Rochelle, richer was never,	
	Vernage of Venice, virtuous, and Crete,	*White wine; full-bodied*
205	In faucetes of fine gold, fonde who-so likes;	*vessels; to try*
	The kinges cup-bord was closed in silver,	*enclosed*
	In grete gobletes overgilt, glorious of hew;[6]	
	There was a chef butler, a chevaler noble	*chief; chevalier*
	Sir Kayous the courtais, that of the cup served;	*courteous*
210	Sixty cuppes of suite for the king selven,	*cups in a set*
	Crafty and curious, corven full fair,	*Skillfully made; carved*

---

[1] *Very many large swans on silver platters, / Pies of Turkey, to be tasted by whomever it pleases*

[2] *Then shoulders of wild boars, with the lean meat sliced, / Barnacle geese and bitterns in pastry-covered dishes*

[3] *Wavy with azure-colored sauce all over, and they appeared to be flaming; / From each slice the flame leaped very high*

[4] *With pastries glazed with egg yolks and many (other) dainties*

[5] *Then Claret and Cretan wine were cunningly made to flow / By conduits that were skillfully made, all of pure silver*

[6] *With great jewels gilded over, glorious of hue*

	In ever-ilk a party pight with precious stones,	*each part adorned*
	That none enpoison sholde go privily there-under[1]	
	But the bright gold for brethe sholde brist all to peces,	
215	Or else the venom sholde void through virtue of the stones;	
	And the conquerour himselven, so clenly arrayed,	*handsomely*
	In colours of clene gold cledde, with his knightes,	*pure; clad*
	Dressed with his diadem on his dese rich,	*dais*
	For he was deemed the doughtiest that dwelled in erthe.	

220	Then the conquerour kindly carped to those lordes,	*spoke*
	Reheted the Romans with real speche:	*Cheered; royal speech*
	"Sirs, bes knightly of countenaunce and comfortes yourselven;	*be*
	We know nought in this countree of curious metes;	*exotic meats*
	In these barrain landes breedes none other;	*barren*
225	Forthy, withouten feining, enforce you the more[2]	
	To feed you with such feeble as ye before find."	*poor food*

	"Sir," says the senatour, "so Crist mot me help,	*As; may*
	There regned never such realtee within Rome walles!	*reigned; royalty*
	There ne is prelate ne pope ne prince in this erthe	*is no; nor*
230	That he ne might be well payed of these pris metes!"	*pleased; excellent foods*

	After their welth they wesh and went unto chamber,	*bounteous feast; washed*
	This ilk kidd conquerour with knightes ynow;	*same famous; many knights*
	Sir Gawain the worthy Dame Waynor he ledes,	*Guinevere; leads*
	Sir Owghtreth on tother side, of Turry was lord.	*the other*
235	Then spices unsparely they spended thereafter,	*unsparingly; expended*
	Malvesy and Muskadell, those marvelous drinkes,	*Malmsey and Muscatel*
	Raiked full rathely in rosset cuppes[3]	
	Til all the rich on row, Romans and other.	*To; in turn*
	But the soveraign soothly, for solace of himselven,	*pleasure*
240	Assigned to the senatour certain lordes	

---

[1] *So that if any poison should go secretly under them (in the cup), / The bright gold would burst all to pieces with anger, / Or else the poison should lose its power because of the virtue of the precious stones*

[2] *Therefore, without pretending (that you are enjoying it), force yourself all the more*

[3] *Went round very quickly in russet-colored (gold) cups*

To lede to his levere, when he his leve askes,   *lead; desired place; leave*
With mirth and with melody of minstralsy noble.   *musicians*

Then the conquerour to counsel kaires thereafter   *goes*
With lordes of his legeaunce that to himself longes   *allegiance; belong*
245   To the Giauntes Towr jollily he wendes   *Tower; goes*
With justices and judges and gentle knightes.   *noble*

Sir Cador of Cornwall to the king carpes,   *speaks*
Laugh on him lovely with likand lates;[1]
"I thank God of that thro that thus us thretes!   *trouble; threatens*
250   You must be trailed, I trow, but yif ye tret better!   *dragged; believe; unless*
The lettres of Sir Lucius lightes mine herte.   *lighten; heart*
We have as losels lived many long day   *wastrels*
With delites in this land with lordshippes many   *delights*
And forlitened the los that we are laited.   *lessened; praise; esteemed*
255   I was abashed, by our Lord, of our best bernes,   *by; men*
For grete dole of deffuse of deedes of armes.   *sadness because of the ban*
Now wakenes the war! Worshipped be Crist!   *reawakens*
And we shall win it again by wightness and strength!"   *vigor*

"Sir Cador," quod the king, "thy counsel is noble;   *said*
260   But thou art a marvelous man with thy merry wordes!
For thou countes no case ne castes no further,[2]
But hurles forth upon heved, as thy herte thinkes;   *spout off; heart*
I moste trete of a trews touchand these needes,   *consider; truce; matters*
Talk of these tithandes that teenes mine herte.   *tidings; grieve*
265   Thou sees that the emperour is angerd a little;
It seemes by his sandesman that he is sore greved;   *messenger; grieved*
His senatour has summond me and said what him liked,
Hethely in my hall, with heinous wordes,   *Scornfully; hateful*
In speche despised me and spared me little;   *speech*
270   I might not speke for spite, so my herte trembled!   *could not speak*
He asked me tyrauntly tribute of Rome,
That teenfully tint was in time of mine elders,   *painfully lost*

---

[1] *Smiles at him pleasantly with pleasing features*

[2] *You take account of no circumstances, nor consider (the matter) any further*

	There alienes, in absence of all men of armes,	*foreigners*
	Coverd it of commouns, as cronicles telles.	*Obtained; commoners*
275	I have title to take tribute of Rome;	
	Mine auncestres were emperours and ought it themselven,	*owned*
	Belin and Bremin and Bawdewyne the third;	
	They occupied the empire eight score winters,	
	Ilkon eier after other, as old men telles;	*Each one heir*
280	They covered the Capitol and cast down the walles,	*seized*
	Hanged of their hedesmen by hundrethes at ones;	*head men; hundreds; once*
	Senn Constantine, our kinsman, conquered it after,	*Then*
	That eier was of Yngland and emperour of Rome,	*heir; England*
	He that conquered the cross by craftes of armes,	
285	That Crist was on crucified, that King is of heven.	*heaven*
	Thus have we evidence to ask the emperour the same,	
	That thus regnes at Rome, what right that he claimes."	*reigns*

	Then answerd King Aungers to Arthur himself:	
	"Thou ought to be overling over to all other kinges,	*overlord*
290	For wisest and worthyest and wightest of handes,	*strongest*
	The knightlyest of counsel that ever crown bore.	
	I dare say for Scotland that we them scathe limped;	*suffered harm from them*
	When the Romans regned they ransound our elders	*reigned; ransomed*
	And rode in their riot and ravished our wives,	
295	Withouten resoun or right reft us our goodes;	*reason; bereft us of*
	And I shall make my avow devotly to Crist	*devoutly*
	And to the holy vernacle, virtuous and noble,	*St. Veronica's kerchief*
	Of this grete vilany I shall be venged ones,	*villainy; avenged at once*
	On yon venomous men with valiant knightes!	
300	I shall thee further of defence fostred ynow	*well trained*
	Twenty thousand men within two eldes	*ages*
	Of my wage to wend where-so thee likes,	*At my expense; travel*
	To fight with thy fomen that us unfair ledes!"	*foes; treat*

	Then the burlich berne of Bretain the Little	*stately man; Brittany*
305	Counsels Sir Arthur and of him beseekes	*beseeches*
	To answer the alienes with austeren wordes,	*bold*
	To entice the emperour to take over the mountes.	
	He said: "I make mine avow verily to Crist,	*vow*
	And to the holy vernacle, that void shall I never	*image of Veronica; retreat*

310	For radness of no Roman that regnes in erthe,	*fear; reigns*
	But ay be redy in array and at erest founden;	*ready; the first*
	No more dout the dintes of their derf wepens	*fear the blows; grim*
	Than the dew that is dank when that it down falles;	
	Ne no more shoun for the swap of their sharp swordes	*shrink; sweep*
315	Than for the fairest flowr that on the folde growes!	*flower; ground*
	I shall to batail thee bring of brenyed knightes	*battle; armored*
	Thirty thousand by tale, thrifty in armes,	*count, prosperous*
	Within a month-day, into what march	*whatever country*
	That thou will soothly assign, when thyself likes.”	

320	“A! A!” says the Welsh king; “worshipped be Crist!	
	Now shall we wreke full well the wrath of our elders!	*avenge; injury to*
	In West Wales, iwis, such wonders they wrought	
	That all for wandreth may weep that on that war thinkes.	*sorrow*
	I shall have the avauntward witterly myselven,	*vanguard certainly*
325	Til that I have vanquisht the Viscount of Rome,	
	That wrought me at Viterbo a vilany ones,	*villainy once*
	As I past in pilgrimage by the Pount Tremble.	*Pontremoli*
	He was in Tuskane that time and took of our knightes,	*Tuscany; some of*
	Arrest them unrightwisly and ransound them after.[1]	
330	I shall him surely ensure that saghtel shall we never	*be reconciled*
	Ere we sadly assemble by ourselven ones	*ourselves alone*
	And dele dintes of deth with our derf wepens!	*deal; strong*
	And I shall wage to that war of worshipful knightes,	*bring at my expense*
	Of Wyghte and of Welshland and of the West Marches,	*Isle of Wight*
335	Two thousand in tale, horsed on steedes,	*number*
	Of the wightest wyes in all yon West Landes!”	*strongest men*

	Sir Ewain fitz Urien then egerly fraines,	*eagerly; asks*
	Was cosin to the conquerour, corageous himselven:	*kinsman; courageous*
	“Sir, and we wiste your will we wolde work thereafter;	*if we knew; would*
340	Yif this journee sholde hold or be ajourned further,	*journey; adjourned*
	To ride on yon Romans and riot their landes,	*ravage*
	We wolde shape us therefore, to ship when you likes.”	*would prepare us*

---

[1] *Arrested them unjustly and afterwards held them for ransom*

141

"Cosin," quod the conquerour, "kindly thou askes   *kinsman; said*
Yif my counsel accord to conquer yon landes.

345   By the kalendes of Juny we shall encounter ones   *first day of June*
With full cruel knightes, so Crist mot me help!   *as; may*
Thereto I make mine avow devotly to Crist   *devoutly*
And to the holy vernacle, virtuous and noble;   *image of Veronica*
I shall at Lamass take leve to lenge at my large[1]

350   In Lorraine or Lumbardy, whether me leve thinkes;
Merk unto Meloine and mine down the walles   *Go; Milan; undermine*
Both of Petersand and of Pis and of the Pount Tremble;   *(see note)*
In the Vale of Viterbo vitail my knights,   *supply (victual)*
Sujourn there six weekes and solace myselven,   *Sojourn; refresh*

355   Send prikers to the pris town and plant there my sege   *riders; excellent; siege*
But if they proffer me the pees by process of time."   *Unless; peace*

"Certes," says Sir Ewain, "and I avow after,   *Certainly; vow*
And I that hathel may see ever with mine eyen   *If; man; eyes*
That occupies thine heritage, the empire of Rome,

360   I shall aunter me ones his egle to touch   *venture; eagle-standard*
That borne is in his banner of bright gold rich,
And rase it from his rich men and rive it in sonder,   *snatch; cut it asunder*
But he be redily rescued with riotous knightes.[2]
I shall enforce you in the feld with fresh men of armes,   *reinforce; field*

365   Fifty thousand folk upon fair steedes,
On thy fomen to founde there thee fair thinkes,   *foemen to go where*
In Fraunce or in Frisland, fight when thee likes!"   *Frisia*

"By our Lord," quod Sir Launcelot, "now lightes mine herte!   *lightens*
I lowe God of this love these lordes has avowed!   *praise*

370   Now may less men have leve to say what them likes,   *lesser; leave*
And have no letting by law; but listenes these wordes: *hindrance*
I shall be at journee with gentle knightes   *the day's fight; noble*
On a jamby steed full jollily graithed,   *active; equipped*

---

[1] *At Lamas (August 1) I shall take my leave, to remain freely / In Lorraine or Lombardy, whichever seems preferable to me*

[2] *Unless he (the eagle) is quickly rescued by vigorous knights*

Ere any journee begin to joust with himselven[1]

375 Among all his giauntes, Genivers and other,   *giants, Genoese*

Strike him stiffly fro his steed with strenghe of mine handes, *stoutly from*

For all the steren in stour that in his stale hoves![2]

Be my retinue arrayed, I reck it but a little   *reckon*

To make route into Rome with riotous knightes.

380 Within a seven-night day, with six score helmes,[3]

I shall be seen on the se, sail when thee likes."   *sea*

Then laughes Sir Lot and all on loud meles: *speaks*

"Me likes that Sir Lucius longes after sorrow;   *for*

Now he wilnes the war his wandreth beginnes;   *desires; sorrow*

385 It is our werdes to wreke the wrath of our elders!   *fates to avenge*

I make mine avow to God and to the holy vernacle: *image of Veronica*

And I may see the Romans that are so rich holden,[4]

Arrayed in their riotes on a round feld,

I shall at the reverence of the Round Table   *for*

390 Ride through all the rout, rereward and other,[5]

Redy wayes to make and renkes full rowm,

Runnand on red blood, as my steed rushes!   *Running with*

He that followes my fare and first comes after   *route*

Shall find in my fare-way many fey leved!"   *path; dead left*

395 Then the conquerour kindly comfortes these knightes,

Alowes them gretly their lordly avowes;   *Praises; vows*

"Allweldand God worship you all!   *All-ruling; honor*

And let me never want you, whiles I in world regn;   *be without you*

My mensk and my manhed ye maintain in erthe,   *honor; manhood*

400 Mine honour all utterly in other kinges landes;

---

[1] *Before any day's fight (the major battle) begins, to joust with himself (Lucius)*

[2] *Despite the strong (ones) in battle that remain in his troop*

[3] *Within a week from today with one hundred and twenty knights*

[4] *If I can see the Romans, who are considered so powerful, / Arrayed in their riotous groups on a broad field.*

[5] *Ride through all the company, rear guard and the rest, / To make a ready way and paths full spacious*

My wele and my worship of all this world rich,   *prosperity*

Ye have knightly conquered that to my crown longes.   *belongs*

Him thar be ferd for no foes that swilk a folk ledes,   *He needs be afraid; such*

But ever fresh for to fight in feld when him likes.   *field*

405   I account no king that under Crist lives;   *take account of*

Whiles I see you all sound, I set by no more."   *depend on*

When they trustily had treted they trumped up after,[1]

Descended down with a daunce of dukes and erles.   *group (dance); earls*

Then they sembled to sale and souped als swithe,   *met; hall; dined quickly*

410   All this seemly sorte, with semblaunt full noble.   *company; splendor*

Then the roy real rehetes these knightes   *royal king regales*

With reverence and riot of all his Round Table   *respect; revelry*

Til seven dayes was gone. The senatour askes

Answer to the Emperour with austeren wordes.   *bold*

415   After the Epiphany, when the purpose was taken   *January 6*

Of peeres of the parlement, prelates and other,   *parliament*

The king in his counsel, courtais and noble,   *courteous*

Uters the alienes and answers himselven: *Brings out*

"Greet well Lucius, thy lord, and laine not these wordes;   *conceal*

420   If thou be legemen lele, let him wite soon   *liege-man loyal; know*

I shall at Lamass take leve and lodge at my large   *August 1; freely*

In delite in his landes with lordes ynow,   *delight; many lords*

Regne in my realtee and rest when me likes;   *Reign; royalty*

By the river of Rhone hold my Round Table,

425   Fang the fermes in faith of all tho fair rewmes[2]

For all the menace of his might and maugree his eyen!

And merk sithen over the mountes into his main landes,   *go; mountains*

To Miloine the marvelous and mine down the walles;   *Milan; undermine*

In Lorraine ne in Lumbardy leve shall I nother   *Lombardy; leave; neither*

430   Nokine lede upon life that there his lawes yemes;   *No kind of man; keeps*

And turn into Tuskane when me time thinkes,   *Tuscany*

Ride all those rowm landes with riotous knightes.   *spacious; vigorous*

---

[1] *When they had confidently discussed (this business), they blew on trumpets afterwards (conclusion of the council)*

[2] *Seize the revenues, in faith, of all those fair realms, / Despite the threat of his power and regardless of his resistance*

	Bid him make rescues for mensk of himselven,	*honor*
	And meet me for his manhed in those main landes!	*manhood; strong*
435	I shall be founden in Fraunce, fraist when him likes!	*try*
	The first day of Feveryer in those fair marches!	*February*
	Ere I be fetched with force or forfeit my landes,	
	The flowr of his fair folk full fey shall be leved!	*dead; left*
	I shall him sekerly ensure under my sele rich	*certainly; seal*
440	To sege the citee of Rome within seven winter	*besiege; city*
	And that so sekerly ensege upon sere halves	*securely besiege; all sides*
	That many a senatour shall sigh for sake of me one!	*alone*
	My summons are certified and thou art full served	*provided*
	Of cundit and credens; kaire where thee likes.[1]	
445	I shall thy journee engist, enjoin them myselven,[2]	
	Fro this place to the port there thou shall pass over:	*from*
	Seven days to Sandwich I set at the large;	*as a maximum time*
	Sixty mile on a day, the sum is but little!	
	Thou moste speed at the spurs and spare not thy fole;	*must; foal*
450	Thou wendes by Watling Street and by no way elles;	*travel; else*
	There thou nyghes on night needes moste thou lenge;[3]	
	Be it forest or feld, found thou no further;	*field; go*
	Bind thy blonk by a busk with thy bridle even,	*horse; bush*
	Lodge thyselven under linde as thee lefe thinkes;[4]	
455	There owes none alienes to ayer upon nightes,	*ought; wander*
	With such a ribawdous rout to riot thyselven.	*ribald; company*
	Thy license is limit in presence of lordes,	*limited*
	Be now loth or lette, right as thee thinkes,[5]	
	For both thy life and thy limm ligges thereupon,	*limb lie*
460	Though Sir Lucius had laid thee the lordship of Rome,	*laid on you*
	For be thou founden a foot withoute the flood marches	*edge of the sea*
	After the aughtende day when undern is rungen,	*eighteenth; nine a.m.*

---

[1] *With safe-conduct and credentials; go where you please*

[2] *I shall assign the resting-places for your journey, order them myself*

[3] *Wherever you set down by night you must by necessity remain*

[4] *Lodge yourself under trees, wherever it seems good to you*

[5] *Whether (my order) is now hateful or a hindrance in your mind*

Thou shall be heveded in hie and with horse drawen,[1]
And senn hiely be hanged, houndes to gnawen!

465 The rent ne red gold that unto Rome longes   *tax; belongs*
Shall not redily, renk, ransoun thine one!"   *man, ransom you alone*

"Sir," says the senatour, "so Crist mot me help,   *as; may*
Might I with worship win away ones   *Could; go*
I sholde never for Emperour that on erthe lenges   *should; remains*
470 Eft unto Arthur ayer on such needes;   *Again; go; a message*
But I am singely here with sixteen knightes;   *singly*
I beseek you, sir, that we may sound pass.   *beseech; safely*
If any unlawful lede let us by the way,   *man hinder*
Within thy license, lord, thy los is inpaired."   *fame is impaired*

475 "Care not," quod the king; "thy cundit is knowen   *said; safe conduct*
Fro Carlisle to the coste there thy cogge lenges;   *From; coast; ship*
Though thy coffers were full, crammed with silver,
Thou might be seker of my sele sixty mile further."   *secure; seal*

They enclined to the king and congee they asked,   *bowed; leave*
480 Kaires out of Carlisle, catches on their horses;   *Go*
Sir Cador the courtais kend them the wayes,   *courteous; taught*
To Catrik them conveyed and to Crist them bekenned.   *entrusted*
So they sped at the spurres they sprangen their horses,   *exhausted*
Hires them hackenayes hastily thereafter.   *horses*
485 So for reddour they ridden and rested them never,   *fear; rode*
But yif they lodged under linde whiles them the light failed;   *Unless; tree*
But ever the senatour forsooth sought at the gainest.   *nearest (way)*
By the sevende day was gone the citee they reched.   *By (the time)*
Of all the glee under God so glad were they never
490 As of the sound of the se and Sandwich belles.   *sea; curfew*
Withouten more stunting they shipped their horses;   *delay*
Wery to the wan se they went all at ones.   *Weary; pale sea*
With the men of the wale they weighted up their ankers   *gunwale; anchors*
And fled at the fore flood; in Flaunders they rowed   *first high tide; to*

---

[1] *You shall be speedily beheaded and torn apart by horses, / And then quickly hanged for dogs to gnaw.*

146

495	And through Flaunders they found, as them fair thought,	*went*
	Til Aachen in Almaine, in Arthur landes;	*To; Germany*
	Gos by Mount Goddard full grevous wayes,	*They go; grievous*
	And so into Lumbardy, likand to shew.	*pleasant to be seen*
	They turn through Tuskane with towres full high;	*Tuscany*
500	In pris appairelles them in precious weedes.[1]	
	The Sononday in Sutere they sujourn their horses	*Sunday; Sutri; rest*
	And seekes the saintes of Rome by assent of knightes;	
	Sithen prikes to the palais with portes so rich,	*spur; palace; gates*
	There Sir Lucius lenges with lordes ynow;	*Where; many lords*
505	Loutes to him lovely and lettres him bedes	*Bows; properly; offers*
	Of credens enclosed with knightlich wordes.	*credentials; knightly*
	Then the Emperour was eger and enkerly fraines;	*eager; ardently asks*
	The answer of Arthur he askes him soon,	*immediately*
	How he arrayes the rewm and rewles the pople,	*orders the realm*
510	Yif he be rebel to Rome, what right that he claimes;	*If*
	"Thou sholde his sceptre have sesed and sitten aboven	*seized; above*
	For reverence and realtee of Rome the noble;	*royalty*
	By certes thou was my sandes and senatour of Rome,	*Because; messenger*
	He sholde for solempnitee have served thee himselven."	*decorum*
515	"That will he never for no wye of all this world rich	*man*
	But who may win him of war, by wightness of handes;	*Except; strength*
	Many fey shall be first upon the feld leved,	*dead; left*
	Ere he appere in this place, proffer when thee likes.	*appears*
	I say thee, sir, Arthur is thine enmy forever,	*tell you; enemy*
520	And ettles to be overling of the empire of Rome,	*intends; overlord*
	That all his auncestres ought but Uter himselven.	*owned; except*
	Thy needes in this New Yere I notified myselven	*message; made knowen*
	Before that noble of name and nine sum of kinges;	*nine in all*
	In the most real place of the Round Table	*royal*
525	I summond him solemnly on-seeand his knightes;[2]	
	Senn I was formed, in faith, so ferd was I never,	*Since; born; fearful (afraid)*
	In all the places there I passed of princes on erthe.	*where*

---

[1] *They dress themselves worthily in precious clothes*

[2] *I summoned him solemnly (to appear in Rome) with his knights looking on*

I wolde forsake all my suite of seignoury of Rome   *following; lordship*

Ere I eft to that soveraign were sent on such needes!   *again; errand*

530   He may be chosen cheftain, chef of all other   *chieftain; chief*

Both by chaunces of armes and chevalry noble,

For wisest and worthyest and wightest of handes.   *strongest*

Of all the wyes that I wot in this world rich —   *men; know*

The knighliest creature in Cristdendom holden   *considered*

535   Of king or of conquerour crowned in erthe,

Of countenaunce, of corage, of cruel lates,   *courage; expressions*

The comlyest of knighthood that under Crist lives!

He may be spoken in dispens despiser of silver,   *called in his expenditures*

That no more of gold gives than of grete stones,

540   No more of wine than of water that of the well runnes,

Ne of welth of this world but worship alone.   *wealth; except for*

Such countenance was never knowen in no kith riche   *country*

As was with this conquerour in his court holden;

I counted at this Cristenmass of kinges annointed,

545   Hole ten at his table that time with himselven.   *Ten in all*

He will warray, iwis, be ware yif thee likes;   *make war*

Wage many wight men and watch thy marches,   *Pay; borders*

That they be redy in array and at erest founden,   *at the earliest time*

For yif he reche unto Rome, he ransouns it forever.   *if; reach*

550   I rede thou dress thee therefore and draw no let longer;[1]

Be seker of thy soudeours and send to the mountes;   *sure; mercenaries*

By the quarter of this yere, and him quert stand,   *year, if; health remains*

He will wightly in a while on his wayes hie."   *stoutly; hasten*

    "By Ester," says the Emperour, "I ettle myselven   *Easter; intend*

555   To hostay in Almaine with armed knightes;   *lead a host; Germany*

Send frekly into Fraunce, that flowr is of rewmes;   *boldly*

Fonde to fette that freke and forfeit his landes,   *Try; fetch; man*

For I shall set keepers, full cunnand and noble,   *guards; cunning*

Many giaunt of Gene, jousters full good.   *Genoa*

560   To meet him in the mountes and martyr his knightes,   *mountains*

Strike them down in straites and stroy them forever.   *narrow places; destroy*

---

[1] *I advise you to prepare yourself therefore and delay no longer*

	There shall upon Goddard a garret be rered[1]	
	That shall be garnisht and keeped with good men of armes,	*furnished*
	And a becon aboven to brin when them likes,	*beacon; burn*
565	That none enmy with host shall enter the mountes.	*enemy*
	There shall on Mount Bernard be belded another,	*built*
	Busked with bannerettes and bachelers noble.[2]	
	In at the portes of Pavia shall no prince pass	*gates*
	Through the perilous places for my pris knightes.”	*excellent*

570	Then Sir Lucius lordlich lettres he sendes	
	Anon into the Orient with austeren knightes	*bold*
	Til Ambyganye and Orcage and Alisaundere eek[3]	
	To Inde and to Ermonye, as Eufrates runnes,	
	To Asia and to Afrike, and Europe the large,	
575	To Irritaine and Elamet, and all those oute iles,	*Hyrcania; Elam; outer isles*
	To Arraby and Egypt, til erles and other	*to*
	That any erthe occupies in those este marches	*eastern countries*
	Of Damaske and Damiet, and dukes and erles.	*Damascus; Damietta*
	For drede of his daunger they dressed them soon;	
580	Of Crete and of Capados the honourable kinges	*Cappadocia (in Turkey)*
	Come at his commaundement clenly at ones;	*completely*
	To Tartary and Turkey when tithinges is comen	*China; tidings*
	They turn in by Thebay, tyrauntes full huge,	*Thebes*
	The flowr of the fair folk of Amazonnes landes;	*land of the Amazons*
585	All that failes on the feld be forfeit forever.	*are lacking*
	Of Babylon and Baldake the burlich knightes	*Cairo; Bagdad; stately*
	Bayous with their baronage bides no longer;	*Men of Bayonne*
	Of Perse and of Pamphile and Preter John landes[4]	
	Ech prince with his power appertlich graithed;	*Each; openly prepared*
590	The Sowdan of Surry assembles his knightes	*Sultan; Syria*
	Fro Nilus to Nazareth, numbers full huge;	*From Nile*
	To Garyere and to Galilee they gader all at ones,	*Gadara; gather; once*

---

[1] *A watch-tower shall be raised on Mount Goddard (in the Alps)*

[2] *Equipped with noble bachelors and bannerets (see note to line 68)*

[3] *To Ambyganye and Orcage (Albania?) and Alexandria as well, / To India and to Armenia, where the Euphrates runs*

[4] *From Persia and Pamphilia and Prester John's lands*

	The sowdanes that were seker soudeours to Rome;	*sultans; trusty mercenaries*
	They gadered over the Greekes Se with grevous wepens,	
595	In their grete galleys, with glitterande sheldes;	*glittering shields*
	The King of Cyprus on the se the Sowdan abides,	*awaits*
	With all the reales of Rhodes arrayed with him one;	*royal (ones); alone*
	They sailed with a side wind over the salt strandes,	*ample*
	Sodenly the Sarazenes, as themselve liked;	*Quickly; Saracens*
600	Craftyly at Cornett the kinges are arrived,	*Corneto*
	Fro the citee of Rome sixty mile large.	*away*
	By that the Greekes were graithed, a full grete number,	*By this time; prepared*
	The mightiest of Macedone, with men of tho marches,	*those*
	Pulle and Prussland, presses with other,	*Apulia; Prussia; hasten*
605	The lege-men of Lettow with legions ynow.	*liege-men; Lithuania*
	Thus they semble in sortes, summes full huge;	*assemble; companies*
	The sowdanes and Sarazenes out of sere landes	*sultans; Saracens; various*
	The Sowdan of Surry and sixteen kinges	*Sultan; Syria*
	At the citee of Rome assembled at ones.	

	Then ishews the Emperour, armed at rightes	*issues; completely*
610	Arrayed with his Romans upon rich steedes;	
	Sixty giauntes before, engendered with fendes,	*by fiends*
	With witches and warlaws, to watchen his tentes	*warlocks*
	Aywere where he wendes wintres and yeres.	*Anywhere; years*
615	Might no blonkes them bere, those bustous churles,	*horses; bear; wild*
	But coverd cameles of towrs, enclosed in mailes;	*camels covered with towers*
	He ayeres out with alienes, hostes full huge	*goes*
	Even into Almaine, that Arthur had wonnen,	*Directly; Germany*
	Rides in by the river and riotes himselve,	
620	And ayeres with a huge will all those high landes;	*goes*
	All Westfale by war he winnes as him likes,	*Westphalia*
	Drawes in by Danuby and dubbes his knightes,	*Danube*
	In the countree of Coloine castelles enseges	*Cologne; besieges*
	And sujourns that sesoun with Sarazenes ynow.	

	At the utas of Hillary Sir Arthur himselven[1]	
625	In his kidd counsel commaunde the lordes:	*famous; commanded*

---

[1] *At the Octave of St. Hillary's day (i.e., a week after January 24) Sir Arthur himself*

"Kaire to your countrees and semble your knightes,   *Go; assemble*
And keepes me at Constantine, clenlich arrayed,   *await; completely*
Bides me at Barflete upon the blithe stremes   *peaceful streams*
630 Boldly within borde, with your best bernes;   *aboard (ships); men*
I shall menskfully you meet in those fair marches."   *honorably*

He sendes forth sodenly sergeauntes of armes   *quickly*
To all his mariners in row to arrest him shippes;   *commandeer*
Within sixteen dayes his fleet was assembled,
635 At Sandwich on the se, sail when him likes.
In the palais of York a parlement he holdes   *palace*
With all the peeres of the rewm, prelates and other;   *realm*
And after the preching, in presence of lordes,   *preaching*
The king in his counsel carpes these wordes: *speaks*
640 "I am in purpose to pass perilous wayes,
To kaire with my keen men to conquer yon landes,   *go*
To outraye mine enmy, yif aventure it shew,[1]
That occupies mine heritage, the empire of Rome.
I set you here a soveraign, assent yif you likes,   *if*
645 That is my sib, my sister son; Sir Mordred himselven   *kin; sister's son*
Shall be my leutenant, with lordshippes ynow   *lieutenant; enough authority*
Of all my lele lege-men that my landes yemes."   *loyal liege-men; possess*

He carpes to his cosin then, in counsel himselven: *says; kinsman*
"I make thee keeper, Sir Knight, of kingrikes many,   *guardian; kingdoms*
650 Warden worshipful to weld all my landes,   *wield (rule)*
That I have wonnen of war in this world rich.
I will that Waynor, my wife, in worship be holden.   *desire; Guinevere*
That her want no wele ne welth that her likes;   *prosperity*
Look my kidd casteles be clenlich arrayed,   *famous; completely equipped*
655 There sho may sujourn herselve with seemlich bernes;   *she; fair knights*
Fonde my forestes be frithed, of frendship for ever,[2]
That none warray my wild but Waynor herselven,

---

[1] *To outrage my enemy, if a chance should appear*

[2] *See that my forests are enclosed (from poachers), on pain of losing my favor, / That no one be allowed to hunt the game except for Guinevere herself, / And even she is to hunt only at the season when the game are fat enough to be hunted, / So that she will take her pleasure at appropriate times*

151

And that in the sesoun when grees is assigned,
That sho take her solace in certain times.
660 Chaunceller and chamberlain change as thee likes,
Auditours and officers, ordain them thyselven,
Both jurees and judges, and justices of landes;   juries
Look thou justify them well that injury workes.   do justice to; do
If me be destained to die at Drightens will,   fated; God's
665 I charge thee my sektour, chef of all other,   executor, chief
To minister my mobles for meed of my soul   goods; reward
To mendinauntes and misese in mischef fallen.   mendicants; those in misery
Take here my testament of tresure full huge;
As I traist upon thee, betray thou me never!   trust
670 As thou will answer before the austeren Judge   austere
That all this world winly wisse as Him likes,   pleasantly directs
Look that my last will be lely perfourned!   loyally performed
Thou has clenly the cure that to my crown longes   completely; care
Of all my wordles wele and my wife eek;   earthly prosperity; as well
675 Look thou keep thee so clere there be no cause founden   clear; complaint
When I to countree come, if Crist will it thole;   come home; allow
And thou have grace goodly to govern thyselven,   If
I shall crown thee, knight, king with my handes."

Then Sir Mordred full mildly meles himselven,   speaks
680 Kneeled to the conquerour and carpes these wordes:
"I beseek you, sir, as my sib lord,   beseech; related by blood
That ye will for charitee chese you another,   chose
For if ye put me in this plitt, your pople is deceived;   plight; people
To present a prince estate my power is simple;   princely
685 When other of war-wisse are worshipped hereafter,   cunning in warfare
Then may I, forsooth, be set but at little.   be little regarded
To pass in your presence my purpose is taken   travel
And all my perveance appert for my pris knightes."   provisions ready

"Thou art my nevew full ner, my nurree of old,   nephew; near; nursling
690 That I have chastied and chosen, a child of my chamber;   disciplined; praised
For the sibreden of me, forsake not this office;   blood relationship to
That thou ne work my will, thou wot what it menes."   If; know; means

Now he takes his leve and lenges no longer

	At lordes, at lege-men that leves him behinden;	*With; leaves*
695	And senn that worthiliche wye went unto chamber	*then; worthy man*
	For to comfort the queen that in care lenges.	
	Waynor waikly weepand him kisses,	*weakly weeping*
	Talkes to him tenderly with teres ynow;	*tears*
	"I may werye the wye that this war moved,	*curse; person*
700	That warnes me worship of my wedde lord;	*denies; wedded*
	All my liking of life out of land wendes,	*pleasure*
	And I in langour am left, leve ye, forever!	*believe*
	Why ne might I, dere love, die in your armes,	
	Ere I this destainy of dole sholde drie by mine one!"	*destiny; suffer; alone*

	"Greve thee not, Gaynor, for Goddes love of heven,	
705	Ne grouch not my ganging; it shall to good turn!	*begrudge; going*
	Thy wandrethes and thy weeping woundes mine herte;	*sorrows*
	I may not wite of this wo for all this world rich;	*depart (turn aside from)*
	I have made a keeper, a knight of thine owen,	*guardian; own*
710	Overling of Yngland, under thyselven,	*Overlord*
	And that is Sir Mordred, that thou has mikel praised,	*much*
	Shall be thy dictour, my dere, to do what thee likes."	*spokesman*

	Then he takes his leve at ladies in chamber,	*from*
	Kissed them kindlich and to Crist beteches;	*kindly; entrusts (them)*
715	And then sho swoones full swithe when he his sword asked,	*she; requested*
	Sways in swooning, swelte as sho wolde!	*as if she would die*
	He pressed to his palfrey, in presence of lordes,	*hastened*
	Prikes of the palais with his pris knightes	*Spurs from; palace*
	With a real rout of the Round Table,	*company*
720	Sought toward Sandwich; sho sees him no more.	*Went; she*

	There the grete were gadered with galiard knightes,	*gathered; jolly*
	Garnished on the green feld and graitheliche arrayed;	*drawn up suitably*
	Dukes and douspeeres daintely rides,	*high noblemen*
	Erles of Yngland with archers ynow.	
725	Shirreves sharply shiftes the commouns,[1]	

---

[1] *Sheriffs sharply move the common soldiers about, / Give orders (to their men) before the powerful (men) of the Round Table*

Rewles before the rich of the Round Table,

Assignes ilk a countree to certain lordes,   *the soldiers from each country*

In the south on the se bank sail when them likes.

Then barges them buskes and to the bank rowes,   *prepare*

730 Bringes blonkes on borde and burlich helmes   *horses aboard; stately*

Trusses in tristly trapped steedes,   *securely; equipped*

Tentes and other tooles, and targes full rich,   *siege-engines; shields*

Cabanes and cloth-sackes and cofferes full noble,   *Cabins; sacks of clothes*

Hackes and hackeneys and horses of armes;

735 Thus they stow in the stuff of full steren knightes.   *stern*

When all was shipped that sholde, they shunt no lenger,   *hold back; longer*

But unteld them tite, as the tide runnes;   *untied; quickly*

Cogges and crayers then crosses their mastes,[1]

At the commaundement of the king uncovered at ones;   *unfurled (sails)*

740 Wightly on the wale they wie up their ankers,[2]

By wit of the watermen of the wale ythes.   *surging waves*

Frekes on the forestaine faken their cables   *Men; bow coil*

In floynes and fercostes and Flemish shippes,   *small ships; merchantmen*

Titt sailes to the top and turnes the luff,   *Pull; bow*

745 Standes upon steerbord, sternly they songen.   *starboard sternly; sang*

The pris shippes of the port proven their deepness,   *test*

And foundes with full sail over the fawe ythes;   *go; bounding waves*

Holly withouten harm they hale in botes,   *Wholly; haul; boats*

Shipmen sharply shutten their portes,   *shut; portholes*

750 Launches lede upon luff latchen their deepes,[3]

Lookes to the lode-stern when the light failes,   *North Star*

Castes courses by craft when the cloud rises

With the needle and the stone on the night tides.   *i.e., with a compass*

For drede of the dark night they dreched a little   *slowed down*

755 And all the steren of the streme steken at ones.[4]

The king was in a grete cogge with knightes full many,   *ship*

---

[1] *Large ships and small boats then hoist their sails*

[2] *Stoutly on the gunwale they weigh up their anchors*

[3] *Launch the lead on the luff (the bow) to measure the depth of the water*

[4] *And all the stern men of the stream (sailors) struck sail at once*

	In a cabane enclosed, clenlich arrayed;	*cabin; completely*
	Within on a rich bed restes a little,	
	And with the swogh of the se in swefning he fell.	*swaying; dreaming*
760	Him dremed of a dragon, dredful to behold,	*He dreamed*
	Come drivand over the deep to drenchen his pople,	*driving; drown*
	Even walkand out the West landes,	*Directly walking*
	Wanderand unworthyly over the wale ythes;	*Wandering unbecomingly; surging waves*
	Both his hed and his hals were holly all over	*neck; wholly*
765	Ounded of azure, enamelled full fair;[1]	
	His shoulders were shaled all in clene silver	
	Shredde over all the shrimp with shrinkand pointes;	
	His womb and his winges of wonderful hewes,	*belly; hues*
	In marvelous mailes he mounted full high.	
770	Whom that he touched he was tint forever!	*lost*
	His feet were flourished all in fine sable	*decorated*
	And such a venomous flaire flow from his lippes	*flame flowed*
	The flood of the flawes all on fire seemed!	*outpouring; flames*
	Then come out of the Orient, even him againes,[2]	
775	A black bustous bere aboven in the cloudes,	
	With ech a paw as a post and paumes full huge	
	With pikes full perilous, all pliand them seemed;	
	Lothen and lothly, lockes and other,	
	All with lutterd legges, lokkerd unfair,	
780	Filtered unfreely, with fomand lippes —	
	The foulest of figure that formed was ever!	
	He baltered, he blered, he braundished thereafter;	*danced about; grimaced*
	To batail he bounes him with bustous clawes;	*prepares himself; wild*
	He romed, he rored, that rogged all the erthe,	*bellowed; roared; rocked*
785	So rudely he rapped at to riot himselven![3]	

---

[1] *Covered with waves of azure, enamelled (colored) very fair; / His shoulders were all covered with scales of pure silver / That clothed the monster with shrinking points (like mail)*

[2] *Then came out of the East, directly against him, / A wild, black bear above in the clouds, / With each paw as big as a post, and palms very huge, / With very perilous claws that seemed all curling; / Hateful and loathly, his hair and the rest, / With legs all bowed, covered with ugly hair / That was churlishly matted, with foaming lips*

[3] *So violently he stamped on it (the earth) to enjoy himself*

155

	Then the dragon on dregh dressed him againes	*finally came against him*
	And with his duttes him drove on dregh by the welken;	*blows; afar; sky*
	He fares as a faucon, frekly he strikes;	*falcon; boldly*
	Both with feet and with fire he fightes at ones.	
790	The bere in the batail the bigger him seemed,	*bear*
	And bites him boldly with baleful tuskes;	
	Such buffetes he him reches with his brode klokes,	*reaches to (gives); claws*
	His breste and his brayell was bloody all over.	*breast; waist*
	He ramped so rudely that all the erthe rives,[1]	
795	Runnand on red blood as rain of the heven!	*Running*
	He had weried the worm by wightness of strenghe	*wearied; serpent; stoutness*
	Ne were it not for the wild fire that he him with defendes.	*himself*

	Then wanders the worm away to his heightes,	*serpent*
	Comes glidand fro the cloudes and coupes full even,	*strikes directly*
800	Touches him with his talones and teres his rigge,	*tears; back*
	Betwix the taile and the top ten foot large!	*long*
	Thus he brittened the bere and brought him o live,[2]	
	Let him fall in the flood, fleet where him likes.	*float*
	So they thring the bold king binne the ship-borde,[3]	
805	That ner he bristes for bale on bed where he ligges.	

	Then waknes the wise king, wery fortravailed,	*wakens; wearily exhausted*
	Takes him two philosophers that followed him ever,	
	In the seven science the sutelest founden,	*most subtle*
	The cunningest of clergy under Crist knowen;	*most learned of scholars*
810	He told them of his torment that time that he sleeped:	
	"Dreched with a dragon and such a derf beste,	*Harassed; dire beast*
	Has made me full wery, as wisse me Our Lord;	*guide me*
	Ere I mon swelt as swithe, ye tell me my swefen!"[4]	

	"Sir," said they soon then, these sage philosophers,	*immediately; wise*

---

[1] *He reared up on his hind legs so rudely that all the earth was shaken*

[2] *Thus he beat down the bear and killed him*

[3] *These dreams so oppress the king aboard the ship / That he nearly bursts for pain on the bed where he lies*

[4] *Before I must die quickly, interpret my dream for me*

815   "The dragon that thou dremed of, so dredful to shew,   *dreamed; behold*
       That come drivand over the deep to drenchen thy pople,   *driving; drown*
       Soothly and certain thyselven it is,
       That thus sailes over the se with thy seker knightes.   *trusty*
       The coloures that were casten upon his clere winges   *clear (shining)*
820   May be thy kingrikes all, that thou has right wonnen,   *kingdoms*
       And the tattered tail, with tonges so huge,   *tongues*
       Betokens this fair folk that in thy fleet wendes.   *Signifies*
       The bere that brittened was aboven in the cloudes   *beaten down*
       Betokenes the tyrauntes that tormentes thy pople   *people*
825   Or elles with some giaunt some journee shall happen,   *else; day's fight*
       In singular batail by yourselve one;   *battle; alone*
       And thou shall have the victory, through help of Our Lord,
       As thou in thy vision was openly shewed.
       Of this dredful dreme ne drede thee no more,   *dream*
830   Ne care not, sir conquerour, but comfort thyselven
       And these that sailes over the se with thy seker knightes."

       With trumpes then tristly they trussen up their sailes   *trumpet calls; boldly*
       And rowes over the rich se, this rout all at ones;   *company*
       The comly coste of Normandy they catchen full even   *coast; reach*
835   And blithely at Barflete these bold are arrived,   *Barfleur*
       And findes a fleet there of frendes ynow,
       The flowr and the fair folk of fifteen rewmes,   *kingdoms*
       For kinges and capitaines keeped him fair,   *awaited*
       As he at Carlisle commaunded at Cristenmass himselven.

840   By they had taken the land and tentes up rered,   *By the time; reared*
       Comes a Templar tite and touched to the king;   *quickly; told*
       "Here is a tyraunt beside that tormentes thy pople,
       A grete giaunt of Gene, engendered of fendes;   *Genoa; by fiends*
       He has freten of folk mo than five hundreth,   *devoured; more; hundred*
845   And als fele fauntekins of free-born childer.[1]
       This has been his sustenaunce all this seven winteres,
       And yet is that sot not sad, so well him it likes!   *rogue*
       In the countree of Constantine no kind has he leved   *family; left*

---

[1] *And as many infants (baptized babies) of noble children*

Withouten kidd casteles, enclosed with walles,

850 That he ne has clenly distroyed all the knave childer,　　*male children*

And them carried to the crag and clenly devoured.

The duchess of Bretain today has he taken,　　*Brittany*

Beside Reines as sho rode with her rich knightes,　　*Rennes; she*

Led her to the mountain there that lede lenges　　*man*

855 To lie by that lady ay whiles her life lastes.

We followed o ferrome mo than five hundreth　　*from afar*

Of bernes and of burges and bachelers noble,　　*townsmen*

But he covered the crag; sho cried so loud　　*got to*

The care of that creature cover shall I never　　*recover*

860 Sho was the flowr of all Fraunce or of five rewmes,

And one of the fairest that formed was ever,

The gentilest jowell ajudged with lordes　　*most noble jewel; by*

Fro Gene unto Gerone by Jesu of heven!　　*Genoa; Gironne*

Sho was thy wifes cosin, know it if thee likes,　　*relative; acknowledge*

865 Comen of the richest that regnes in erthe;　　*reigns*

As thou art rightwise king, rew on thy pople　　*righteous; have pity*

And fonde for to venge them that thus are rebuked!"　　*endeavor; avenge*

"Alas," says Sir Arthur, "so long have I lived!

Had I witten of this, well had me cheved.　　*known; achieved*

870 Me is not fallen fair but me is foul happened

That thus this fair lady this fend has destroyed!　　*fiend*

I had lever than all Fraunce this fifteen winter[1]

I had been before that freke a furlong of way

When he that lady had laght and led to the mountes;　　*siezed*

875 I had left my life ere sho had harm limped.　　*suffered*

But wolde thou ken me to that crag there that keen lenges,　　*show; keen one*

I wolde kaire to that coste and carp with himselven,

To trete with that tyraunt for tresoun of landes　　*treat; treason*

And take trews for a time til it may tide better."　　*truce; betide*

880 "Sir, see ye yon forland with yon two fires?　　*promontory*

There filsnes that fend, fraist when thee likes,　　*lurks; try*

---

[1] *I would give the revenues of all of France for the past fifteen years / To have been even a furlong from that man*

158

Upon the crest of the crag by a cold well
That encloses the cliff with the clere strandes;   *clear (shining)*
There may thou find folk fey withouten number,   *dead*
885 Mo florines, in faith, than Fraunce is in after,   *More coins*
And more tresure untrewly that traitour has getten   *dishonestly; gotten*
Than in Troy was, as I trow, that time that it was wonnen."   *believe*

Then romes the rich king for rewth of the pople,   *bellows; pity*
Raikes right to a tent and restes no lenger;   *Goes; longer*
890 He welteres, he wresteles, he wringes his handes;   *writhes; wrestles*
There was no wye of this world that wiste what he mened.   *knew; meant*
He calles Sir Kayous that of the cup served
And Sir Bedvere the bold that bore his brand rich: *sword*
"Look ye after even-song be armed at rightes   *completely*
895 On blonkes by yon buscaile, by yon blithe stremes,   *horses; brush; calm*
For I will pass in pilgrimage privily hereafter,
In the time of souper, when lordes are served,   *dinner*
For to seeken a saint by yon salt stremes,
In Saint Michel mount, there miracles are shewed."

900 After even-song Sir Arthur himselven
Went to his wardrope and warp off his weedes   *wardrobe; threw; clothes*
Armed him in a aketoun with orfrayes full rich;   *padded jacket; gold trim*
Aboven, on that, a jerin of Acres out over;   *Upon that, a leather jacket*
Aboven that a gesseraunt of gentle mailes,   *coat of mail*
905 A jupon of Jerodine jagged in shredes;   *gipon; shreds*
He braides on a bacenett burnisht of silver   *draws; helmet*
The best that was in Basel, with bordours rich;   *borders*
The crest and the coronal enclosed so fair   *diadem*
With claspes of clere gold, couched with stones;   *clear (shining); set*
910 The vesar, the aventail, enarmed so fair,   *visor; face guard; plated*
Void withouten vice, with windowes of silver;   *Devoid of defects*
His gloves gaylich gilt and graven at the hemmes   *gayly; decorated*
With graines and gobelets, glorious of hew.   *seed pearls; jewels*
He braces a brode sheld and his brand askes,[1]
915 Bouned him a brown steed and on the bente hoves;   *went to; ground waits*

---

[1] *He puts on the arm straps (braces) of a broad shield and asks for his sword*

159

He stert til his stirrup and strides on loft,		*leaped; aloft*
Straines him stoutly and stirres him fair,		
Broches the bay steed and to the busk rides,		*Spurs; bush*
And there his knightes him keeped full clenlich arrayed.		*awaited*

920	Then they rode by that river that runned so swithe,	*swiftly*
	There the rindes over-reches with real boughes;	*trees reach over; stately*
	The roe and the reindeer reckless there runnen,	*roe deer*
	In ranes and in rosers to riot themselven;	*bushes; rose bushes; amuse*
	The frithes were flourisht with flowres full many,	*woods; flowered*
925	With faucons and fesauntes of ferlich hewes;	*falcons; pheasants; wondrous*
	All the fowles there flashes that flies with winges,	
	For there galed the gouk on greves full loud;	*sang; cuckoo; groves*
	With alkine gladship they gladden themselven;	*all sorts of gladness*
	Of the nightingale notes the noises was sweet;	
930	They threped with the throstels three hundreth at ones!	*debated; thrushes*
	That whate swowing of water and singing of birds,	*swift sound*
	It might salve him of sore that sound was never!	

	Then ferkes this folk and on foot lightes,	*goes*
	Fastenes their fair steedes o ferrom between;[1]	
935	And then the king keenly commaunded his knightes	
	For to bide with their blonkes and boun no further;	*horses; go*
	"For I will seek this saint by myselve one	
	And mele with this master man that this mount yemes,	*speak; possesses*
	And senn shall ye offer, either after other[2]	
940	Menskfully at Saint Michel, full mighty with Crist."	*Honorably to*

	The king covers the crag with cloughes full high,	*gets to; ravines*
	To the crest of the cliff he climbes on loft,	
	Cast up his umbrere and keenly he lookes,	*visor*
	Caught of the cold wind to comfort himselven.	
945	Two fires he findes flamand full high;	
	The fourtedele a furlong between them he walkes;	*quarter to*
	The way by the well-strandes he wanderd him one	*welling water*

---

[1] *They tie their horses with a good distance between them*

[2] *And afterwards you shall make your offerings, each after the other*

	To wite of the warlaw, where that he lenges.	*learn; warlock; dwells*
	He ferkes to the first fire and even there he findes	*goes*
950	A wery woful widow wringand her handes,	
	And gretand on a grave grisly teres,	*weeping*
	New merked on molde, senn mid-day it seemed.	*Newly dug in the earth*
	He salued that sorrowful with sittand wordes	*saluted; fitting*
	And fraines after the fend fairly thereafter.	*asks; fiend*
955	Then this woful wife unwinly him greetes,	*woman unhappily*
	Coverd up on her knees and clapped her handes,	
	Said: "Careful, careman, thou carpes too loud!	*man*
	May yon warlaw wite, he warrays us all!	*warlock know; attacks*
	Weryd worth the wight ay that thee thy wit reved,	*Cursed be; man; stole*
960	That mas thee to waife here in these wild lakes!	*makes; wander*
	I warn thee, for worship, thou wilnes after sorrow!	*desire*
	Whider buskes thou, berne? unblessed thou seemes!	*Whither go*
	Weenes thou to britten him with thy brand rich?	*Expect; destroy; sword*
	Were thou wighter than Wade or Wawain either,	*fiercer*
965	Thou winnes no worship, I warn thee before.	
	Thou sained thee unsekerly to seek to these mountes;[1]	
	Such six were too simple to semble with him one,	
	For, and thou see him with sight, thee serves no herte	
	To saine thee sekerly, so seemes him huge.	
970	Thou art freely and fair and in thy first flowres,	*noble*
	But thou art fey, by my faith, and that me forthinkes!	*fated to die; grieves*
	Were such fifty on a feld or on a fair erthe,	*fifty such (as you)*
	The freke wolde with his fist fell you at ones.	*man*
	Lo! Here the duchess dere — today was sho taken —	*dear*
975	Deep dolven and dede, diked in moldes.	*buried; buried; ground*
	He had murthered this mild by mid-day were rungen,[2]	
	Withouten mercy on molde, I not what it ment;	*ground; knew not; meant*
	He has forced her and filed and sho is fey leved;	*raped; defiled; left dead*
	He slew her unslely and slit her to the navel.	*crudely*

---

[1] *You crossed yourself unsafely (started out wrong) to go to these mountains; / Six such as you would be too weak to attack him alone, / For, if you see him with sight (of your eyes), you will not have the heart / To cross yourself securely, so huge does he seem*

[2] *He had murdered this mild one by the time that midday (bell) was rung*

980	And here have I baumed her and buried thereafter.	*embalmed*
	For bale of the bootless, blithe be I never!	*sorrow; the helpless*
	Of all the frendes sho had there followed none after	
	But I, her foster moder, of fifteen winter.	*mother*
	To ferk off this forland fonde shall I never,	*go; promontory; endeavor*
985	But here be founden on feld til I be fey leved."	
	Then answers Sir Arthur to that old wife:	*woman*
	"I am comen fro the conquerour, courtais and gentle,	
	As one of the hathelest of Arthure knightes,	*most manly*
	Messenger to this mix, for mendement of the pople	*dung; amendment*
990	To mele with this master man that here this mount yemes,	*speak; possesses*
	To trete with this tyraunt for tresure of landes	
	And take trew for a time, to better may worthe."	*truce; until; be*
	"Ya, thir wordes are but waste," quod this wife then,	*these; woman*
	"For both landes and lythes full little by he settes;	*nations he thinks little of*
995	Of rentes ne of red gold reckes he never,	*reckons*
	For he will lenge out of law, as himself thinkes,	*live outside the law*
	Withouten license of lede, as lord in his owen.	*prince; own (right)*
	But he has a kirtle on, keeped for himselven,	*gown*
	That was spunnen in Spain with special birdes	*by maidens*
1000	And sithen garnisht in Greece full graithely togeders;	*sewn; readily*
	It is hided all with here, holly all over	*covered; hair; wholly*
	And borderd with the berdes of burlich kinges,	*beards; stately*
	Crisped and combed that kempes may know	*Curled; warriors*
	Ich king by his colour, in kith there he lenges.	*Each; country*
1005	Here the fermes he fanges of fifteen rewmes,	*revenues; siezes*
	For ilke Estern even, however that it fall,	*Easter Eve*
	They send it him soothly for saught of the pople,	*peace*
	Sekerly at that sesoun with certain knightes.	
	And he has asked Arthure all this seven winter;	*asked for Arthur's (beard)*
1010	Forthy hurdes he here to outraye his pople	*Therefore dwells; outrage*
	Til the Britones king have burnisht his lippes	*i.e., shaved*
	And sent his berde to that bold with his best bernes;	
	But thou have brought that berde boun thee no further,	

162

For it is a bootless bale thou biddes ought elles, [1]

1015 For he has more tresure to take when him likes

Than ever ought Arthur or any of his elders. — *owned*

If thou have brought the berde he bes more blithe — *will be*

Than thou gave him Borgoine or Britain the More; — *Burgundy; Great Britain*

But look now, for charitee, thou chasty thy lippes — *discipline (close)*

1020 That thee no wordes escape, whatso betides.

Look thy present be preste and press him but little, — *swift*

For he is at his souper; he will be soon greved. — *dinner; easily annoyed*

And thou my counsel do, thou dos off thy clothes — *If; take; i.e., armor*

And kneel in thy kirtle and call him thy lord. — *gown*

1025 He soupes all this sesoun with seven knave childer, — *dines; on; male children*

Chopped in a chargeur of chalk-white silver, — *serving dish*

With pickle and powder of precious spices,

And piment full plenteous of Portingale wines; — *spiced wine; Portuguese*

Three balefull birdes his broches they turn, — *sad maidens; spits*

1030 That bides his bedgatt, his bidding to work; — *bedtime; do*

Such four sholde be fey within four houres — *dead*

Ere his filth were filled that his flesh yernes." — *satisfied; yearns*

"Ya, I have brought the berde," quod he, "the better me likes;

Forthy will I boun me and bere it myselven — *go; bear*

1035 But, lefe, wolde thou lere me where that lede lenges? — *dear; teach; man*

I shall alowe thee, and I live, Our Lord so me help!" — *praise thee if*

"Ferk fast to the fire," quod sho, "that flames so high; — *Go*

There filles that fend him, fraist when thee likes. [2]

But thou moste seek more south, sidlings a little, — *go; sidewise*

1040 For he will have scent himselve six mile large." — *away*

To the source of the reek he sought at the gainest, — *smoke; went; quickest*

Sained him sekerly with certain wordes, — *Crossed himself*

And sidlings of the segge the sight had he reched; — *sidewise; man; reached*

How unseemly that sot sat soupand him one! — *dining alone*

1045 He lay lenand on long, lodgand unfair, — *stretched out; lodging*

[margin annotation: Arthur finds the warlock]

---

[1] *For it will be a sorrow without remedy if you offer him anything else*

[2] *There that fiend fills himself, to try when you please*

The thee of a mans limm lift up by the haunch;   *thigh; limb*
His back and his beuschers and his brode lendes   *buttocks; loins*
He bakes at the bale-fire and breekless him seemed;   *warms; without trousers*
There were rostes full rude and rewful bredes,   *roasts; roast meats*
1050   Bernes and bestail broched togeders,   *Men; beasts spitted*
Cowle full crammed of crismed childer,   *Tub; baptized children*
Some as bred broched and birdes them turned.   *roasts spitted; maidens*

And then this comlich king, because of his pople,   *comely*
His herte bleedes for bale on bente where he standes;   *pain; ground*
1055   Then he dressed on his sheld, shuntes no lenger,   *holds back no longer*
Braundisht his brode sword by the bright hiltes,
Raikes toward that renk right with a rude will   *Rushes; man*
And hiely hailses that hulk with hautain wordes: *hastily greets; proud*
"Now, All-weldand God that worshippes us all   *All-ruling; honors*
1060   Give thee sorrow and site, sot, there thou ligges,   *grief; lie*
For the foulsomest freke that formed was ever!   *foulest man*
Foully thou feedes thee! The Fend have thy soul!
Here is cury unclene, carl, by my trewth,   *cooking; churl; word*
Caff of creatures all, thou cursed wretch!   *Chaff*
1065   Because that thou killed has these crismed childer,   *baptized children*
Thou has martyrs made and brought out of life
That here are broched on bente and brittened with thy handes,[1]
I shall merk thee thy meed as thou has much served,   *assign; reward; deserved*
Through might of Saint Michel that this mount yemes!   *possesses*
1070   And for this fair lady that thou has fey leved   *As*
And thus forced on folde for filth of thyselven,   *raped; earth*
Dress thee now, dog-son, the devil have thy soul!   *Prepare yourself*
For thou shall die this day through dint of my handes!"

Then glopined the glutton and glored unfair;   *was terrified; glared*
1075   He grenned as a grayhound with grisly tuskes;   *snarled (grinned)*
He gaped, he groned fast with grouchand lates   *groaned; grudging expressions*
For gref of the good king that him with grame greetes.   *anger*
His fax and his foretop was filtered togeders   *hair; forelock; matted*
And out of his face fom an half foot large;   *foam; long*

---

[1] *Those who are roasted on spits in the field and broken with your hands*

1080	His front and his forheved, all was it over	*face; forehead*
	As the fell of a frosk and frakned it seemed;	*skin; frog; freckled*
	Hook-nebbed as a hawk, and a hore berde,	*Hook-nosed; gray (hoar)*
	And hered to the eyen-holes with hangand browes;	*haired; eye-holes*
	Harsk as a hound-fish, hardly who-so lookes,	*Harsh; intently*
1085	So was the hide of that hulk holly all over;	*wholly*
	Erne had he full huge and ugly to shew	*Ears; be seen*
	With eyen full horrible and ardaunt for sooth;	*eyes; flaming*
	Flat-mouthed as a fluke with fleriand lippes,	*flounder; sneering*
	And the flesh in his fore-teeth fouly as a bere;	*foul; bear*
1090	His berde was brothy and blak that til his breste reched;	*fierce*
	Grassed as a mere-swine with carkes full huge	*Fat; dolphin; carcass*
	And all faltered the flesh in his foul lippes,	*quivered*
	Ilke wrethe as a wolf-heved it wrath out at ones! [1]	
	Bull-necked was that berne and brode in the shoulders,	
1095	Brok-brested as a brawn with bristeles full large,	*Spotted-breasted; boar*
	Rude armes as an oke with ruskled sides,	*oak; wrinkled*
	Limm and leskes full lothen, leve ye for sooth; [2]	
	Shovel-footed was that shalk and shaland him seemed,	*man; bowlegged*
	With shankes unshapely shovand togeders;	*shoving (i.e., knock-kneed)*
1100	Thick thees as a thurse and thicker in the haunch,	*thighs; giant*
	Grees-growen as a galt, full grillich he lookes!	*Fat; pig; horrible*
	Who the lenghe of the lede lely accountes,	*length; man carefully*
	Fro the face to the foot was five fadom long!	*fathoms*
	Then stertes he up sturdily on two stiff shankes,	*leaps*
1105	And soon he caught him a club all of clene iron;	
	He wolde have killed the king with his keen wepen,	*fierce weapon*
	But through the craft of Crist yet the carl failed;	*churl*
	The crest and the coronal, the claspes of silver,	*diadem*
	Clenly with his club he crashed down at ones!	
1110	The king castes up his sheld and covers him fair,	
	And with his burlich brand a box he him reches;	*stately; reaches to him*
	Full butt in the front the fromand he hittes	*face; enemy*

---

[1] *Each fold (in the quivering skin of his lips) at once twisted out like the head of a wolf*

[2] *Limbs and loins very loathesome, believe you, truly*

That the burnisht blade to the brain runnes;

He feyed his fysnamie with his foul handes — *wiped; face*

1115 And frappes fast at his face fersly there-after! — *strikes; Arthur's; fiercely*

The king changes his foot, eschewes a little; — *retreats*

Ne had he eschaped that chop, cheved had evil; — *escaped; achieved (won)*

He follows in fersly and fastenes a dint — *strikes a blow*

High up on the haunch with his hard wepen — *weapon*

1120 That he heled the sword half a foot large; — *buried; deep*

The hot blood of the hulk unto the hilt runnes;

Even into the in-mete the giaunt he hittes — *in-meat (intestines)*

Just to the genitals and jagged them in sonder! — *Right up to; cut; asunder*

Then he romed and rored and rudely he strikes — *bellowed; roared*

1125 Full egerly at Arthur and on the erthe hittes; — *eagerly*

A sword-lenghe within the swarth he swappes at ones — *ground; strikes*

That ner swoones the king for swough of his dintes! — *sound*

But yet the king sweperly full swithe he beswenkes, — *swiftly; quickly; works*

Swappes in with the sword that it the swang bristed; — *Strikes; loins burst*

1130 Both the guttes and the gore gushes out at ones.

ew! {That all englaimes the grass on ground there he standes! — *makes slimy*

, He's not dead yet?!

Then he castes the club and the king hentes; — *throws away; seizes*

On the crest of the crag he caught him in armes,

And encloses him clenly to crushen his ribbes;

1135 So hard holdes he that hende that ner his herte bristes! — *noble; bursts*

Then the baleful birdes bounes to the erthe, — *sad maidens fall*

Kneeland and cryand and clapped their handes; — *clasped*

"Crist comfort yon knight and keep him fro sorrow,

And let never yon fend fell him o life!" — *fiend; kill him*

1140 Yet is that warlaw so wight he welters him under; — *warlock; rolls*

Wrothly they writhen and wrestle togeders,

Welters and wallows over within those buskes, — *bushes*

Tumbelles and turnes fast and teres their weedes, — *Tumble; tear; clothes*

Untenderly fro the top they tilten togeders, — *topple*

1145 Whilom Arthur over and other while under, — *At times*

Fro the heghe of the hill unto the hard rock, — *height*

They feyne never ere they fall at the flood marches;

But Arthur with an anlace egerly smites — *dagger*

166

And hittes ever in the hulk up to the hiltes.

1150 The thef at the ded-throwes so throly him thringes[1]

That three ribbes in his side he thrustes in sonder! *breaks asunder*

Then Sir Kayous the keen unto the king stertes, *leaps*

Said: "Alas! We are lorn! My lord is confounded, *lost*

Over-fallen with a fend! Us is foul happned! *Over-thrown; by*

1155 We mon be forfeited, in faith, and flemed forever!" *must; exiled*

They heve up his hawberk then and handelles there-under *lift; handle*

His hide and his haunch eek on height to the shoulders, *also; up*

His flank and his felettes and his fair sides, *loins*

Both his back and his breste and his bright armes.

1160 They were fain that they fande no flesh entamed *glad; found injured*

And for that journee made joy, thir gentle knightes. *day's fighting; these*

"Now certes," says Sir Bedvere, "it seemes, by my Lord,

He seekes saintes but selden, the sorer he grippes, *seldom; more severely*

That thus clekes this corsaint out of thir high cliffes, *drags; holy body; these*

1165 To carry forth such a carl at close him in silver; *churl to enclose*

By Michel, of such a mak I have much wonder *fellow*

That ever our soveraign Lord suffers him in heven!

And all saintes be such that serves our Lord *If*

I shall never no saint be, by my fader soul!" *father's*

1170 Then bourdes the bold king at Bedvere wordes: *jokes; Bedevere's*

"This saint have I sought, so help me our Lord!

Forthy braid out thy brand and broche him to the herte; *draw; spit*

Be seker of this sergeaunt; he has me sore greved! *fellow*

I fought not with such a freke this fifteen winter;

1175 But in the mountes of Araby I met such another;

He was forcier by fer that had I nere founden;[2]

Ne had my fortune been fair, fey had I leved!

Anon strike off his heved and stake it thereafter;[3]

[1] *In his death throes the thief squeezes him so fiercely*

[2] *He was stronger by far than any I had ever found*

[3] *Quickly strike off his head and put it on a stake thereafter*

Give it to thy squier, for he is well horsed,　　　　　*squire*

1180　Bere it to Sir Howell that is in hard bondes　　　　*bonds of sorrow*

And bid him herte him well; his enmy is destroyed!　　*hearten; enemy*

Senn bere it to Barflete and brace it in iron　　　　*Barfleur*

And set it on the barbican bernes to shew.　　　　*main-gate tower*

sword ⌐　My brand and my brode sheld upon the bente ligges,　　*ground lie*

1185　On the crest of the crag there first we encountered,

And the club there-by, all of clene iron,

That many Cristen has killed in Constantine landes;　　*Peninsula of Cotentin*

Ferk to the fore-land and fetch me that wepen　　*Go; promontory; weapon*

And let found to our fleet in flood there it lenges.　　*let us go*

1190　If thou will any tresure, take what thee likes;　　*want; treasure*

Have I the kirtle and the club, I covet nought elles."　　*gown; else*

Now they kaire to the crag, these comlich knightes,　　*comely*

And brought him the brode sheld and his bright wepen,

The club and the cote als, Sir Kayous himselven,[1]

1195　And kaires with the conquerour the kinges to shew.

That in covert the king held close to himselven　　*Yet*

While clene day fro the cloud climbed on loft.

By that to court was comen clamour full huge,　　*By that time*

And before the comlich king they kneeled all at ones:

1200　"Welcome, our lege lord, to long has thou dwelled!　　*liege*

Governour under God, graithest and noble,　　*most active*

To whom grace is graunted and given at His will

Now thy comly come has comforted us all!　　*coming*

Thou has in thy realtee revenged thy pople!　　*royalty*

1205　Through help of thy hand thine enmies are stroyed,　　*destroyed*

That has thy renkes over-run and reft them their childer;　　*bereft*

Was never rewm out of array so redyly releved!"　　*disordered realm; relieved*

Then the conquerour Cristenly carpes to his pople:　　*Christianly*

"Thankes God," quod he, "of this grace and no gome elles,　　*man*

1210　For it was never mans deed, but might of Himselven

Or miracle of his Moder, that mild is til all!"

attributes all victories to religion

---

[1] *Sir Kay himself brings the club and the coat as well*

168

He summond then the shipmen sharply thereafter,
To shake forth with the shire-men to shift the goodes: *go; men of the shire*
"All the much tresure that traitour had wonnen
1215 To commouns of the countree, clergy and other,
Look it be done and delt to my dere pople   *dealt out*
That none plain of their part o pain of your lives."   *complain; on*

He commaunde his cosin, with knightlich wordes,   *commanded*
To make a kirk on that crag, there the corse ligges   *church; body*
1220 And a covent there-in, Crist for to serve,   *monastery*
In mind of that martyr that in the mount restes.   *memory; i.e., the duchess*

When Sir Arthur the king had killed the giaunt,
Then blithely fro Barflete he buskes on the morn,   *goes*
With his batail on brede by tho blithe stremes;[1]
1225 Toward Castel Blank he cheses him the way,   *chooses (i.e., goes)*
Through a fair champain under chalk hilles;   *open plain*
The king fraistes a furth over the fresh strandes,   *seeks; ford*
Foundes with his fair folk over as him likes;   *goes*
Forth steppes that steren and strekes his tents   *stern (one); stretches out*
1230 On a strenghe by a streme, in those strait landes.   *strong-hold; narrow*

Anon after mid-day, in the mene-while,   *meanwhile*
There comes two messengers of tho fer marches,   *from those far*
Fro the Marshal of Fraunce, and menskfully him greetes,   *honorably*
Besought him of succour and said him these wordes:
1235 "Sir, thy Marshal, thy minister, thy mercy beseekes,   *Commander-in-chief*
Of thy mikel magistee, for mendment of thy pople,   *great majesty; amendment*
Of these marches-men that thus are miscarried   *men of the marches*
And thus marred among maugree their eyen;   *harmed in spite of*
I witter thee the Emperour is enterd into Fraunce   *assure*
1240 With hostes of enmies, horrible and huge;
Brinnes in Burgoine thy burges so rich,   *Burns; Burgundy; cities*
And brittenes thy baronage that beldes there-in;   *beats down; dwells*
He encroches keenly by craftes of armes   *invades*
Countrees and casteles that to thy crown longes,   *belong*

---

[1] *With his battalion spread out by those calm streams*

1245	Confoundes thy commouns, clergy and other;	*Destroys; citizens*
	But thou comfort them, Sir King, cover shall they never!	*Unless; recover*
	He felles forestes fele, forrays thy landes,	*many; plunders*
	Frithes no fraunches, but frayes the pople;	*Spares; liberty; affrights*
	Thus he felles thy folk and fanges their goodes;	*slays; seizes*
1250	Fremedly the French tonge fey is beleved. [1]	
	He drawes into douce Fraunce, as Dutch-men telles,	*sweet; Germans*
	Dressed with his dragons, dredful to shew;	
	All to dede they dight with dintes of swordes,	*death; put*
	Dukes and douspeeres that dreches there-in;	*stay*
1255	Forthy the lordes of the land, ladies and other,	
	Prayes thee for Petere love, the apostle of Rome,	
	Senn thou art present in place, that thou will proffer make	*i.e., make war*
	To that perilous prince by process of time.	*Against*
	He ayers by yon hilles, yon high holtes under,	*goes*
1260	Hoves there with hole strenghe of hethen knightes;	*Waits; force*
	Help now for His love that high in heven sittes	
	And talk tristly to them that thus us destroyes!"	*boldly*

There knights fight who Romans occupying France?

	The king biddes Sir Bois: "Busk thee belive!	*Go; quickly*
	Take with thee Sir Berille and Bedvere the rich,	
1265	Sir Gawain and Sir Grime, these galiard knightes,	*jolly*
	And graith you to yon green woodes and gos on thir needes;	*do this errand*
	Says to Sir Lucius too unlordly he workes	
	Thus litherly againes law to lede my pople;	*wickedly; treat*
	I let him ere ought long, yif me the life happen, [2]	says this a lot
1270	Or many light shall low that him over land followes;	
	Commaund him keenly with cruel wordes	
	Kaire out of my kingrik with his kidd knightes;	*Go; kingdom*
	In case that he will not, that cursed wretch,	
	Come for his courtaisy and counter me ones;	*courtesy; encounter*
1275	Then shall we reckon full rathe what right that he claimes,	*quickly*
	Thus to riot this rewm and ransoun the pople!	*ravage*
	There shall it derely be delt with dintes of handes;	*dearly; dealt*
	The Drighten at Doomesday dele as Him likes!"	*Lord; deal*

---

[1] *By foreigners the French tongue is destroyed*

[2] *I shall stop him before much longer if life is granted to me (if I live)*

	Now they graith them to go, these galiard knightes,	*prepare; jolly*
1280	All glitterand in gold, upon grete steedes	
	Toward the green wood, with grounden wepen,	*sharpened*
	To greet well the grete lord that wolde be greved soon.	

	These hende hoves on a hill by the holt eves [1]	
	Beheld the housing full high of hethen kinges;	*noble; heathen*
1285	They herde in their herberage hundrethes full many	*dwellings*
	Hornes of olyfantes full highlich blowen;	*elephants; loudly*
	Palaises proudly pight, that paled were rich [2]	
	Of pall and of purpure, with precious stones;	
	Pensels and pomells of rich princes armes	*pennons; tent-pommels*
1290	Pight in the plain mede the pople to shew.	*Placed; meadow*
	And then the Romans so rich had arrayed their tentes	
	On row by the river under the round hilles,	
	The Emperour for honour even in the middes,	*exactly*
	With egles all over ennelled so fair;	*eagles; decorated*
1295	And saw him and the Sowdan and senatours many	*Sultan*
	Seek toward a sale with sixteen kinges	*Go; hall*
	Syland softly in, sweetly by themselven,	*Gliding*
	To soupe with that soverain full selcouthe metes.	*dine; rare foods*

describes rich Roman setting

	Now they wend over the water, these worshipful knightes,	
1300	Through the wood to the wonne there the wyes restes;	*dwelling*
	Right as they had weshen and went to the table,	*washed*
	Sir Wawain the worthy unwinly he spekes:	*unfriendly; speaks*
	"The might and the majestee that menskes us all,	*honors*
	That was merked and made through the might of Himselven,	*formed*
1305	Give you site in your sete, Sowdan and other,	*grief; seat*
	That here are sembled in sale; unsaught mot ye worthe!	*hall; troubled; be*
	And the false heretik that Emperour him calles,	
	That occupies in errour the Empire of Rome,	
	Sir Arthure heritage, that honourable king	
1310	That all his auncestres ought but Uter him one,	*ancestors owned*

Arthur should rule Rome

---

[1] *These courteous ones wait on a hill by the edge of the wood*

[2] *Palaces (rich tents) proudly pitched, / That had rich walls of silk and purple cloth adorned with precious stones*

171

That ilke cursing that Caim caught for his brother — *Cain*
Cleve on thee, cuckewald, with crown there thou lenges, — *Cleave; cuckold*
For the unlordliest lede that I on looked ever!
My lord marveles him mikel, man, by my trewth, — *much; word*
1315 Why thou murtheres his men that no misse serves, — *murder; trouble deserve*
Commouns of the countree, clergy and other,
That are nought coupable there-in, ne knowes nought in armes, — *guilty*
Forthy the comlich king, courtais and noble,
Commaundes thee keenly to kaire of his landes — *out of*
1320 Or elles for thy knighthede encounter him ones. — *knighthood*
Senn thou covetes the crown, let it be declared!
I have discharged me here, challenge who likes, — *done my duty*
Before all thy chevalry, cheftaines and other.
Shape us an answer, and shunt thou no lenger, — *hold back*
1325 That we may shift at the short and shew to my lord." — *go quickly*

The Emperour answerd with austeren wordes: — *austere*
"Ye are with mine enmy, Sir Arthur himselven;
It is none honour to me to outraye his knightes, — *do violence to*
Though ye be irous men that ayers on his needes; — *angry; go; errands*
1330 Ne were it not for reverence of my rich table,
Thou sholde repent full rathe of thy rude wordes! — *quickly*
Such a rebawd as thou rebuke any lordes — *low fellow*
With their retinues arrayed, full real and noble!
But say to thy soveraign I send him these wordes:
1335 Here will I sujourn, whiles me lefe thinkes, — *it seems good*
And sithen seek in by Seine with solace thereafter, — *then go*
Ensege all the citees by the salt strandes, — *Besiege*
And senn ride in by Rhone that runnes so fair,
And of his rich casteles rush down the walles;
1340 I shall nought leve in Paris, by process of time,[1]
His part of a pecheline, prove when him likes!"

"Now certes," says Sir Wawain, "much wonder have I
That such a alfin as thou dare speke such wordes! — *foolish person*

---

[1] *Within a short time I shall not leave him in Paris / So much as a tiny spot; let him test this when he pleases*

I had lever than all Fraunce, that heved is of rewmes,   *rather; head*
1345   Fight with thee faithfully on feld by our one!"

Then answers Sir Gayous full gabbed wordes —   *foolish*
Was eme to the Emperour and erl himselven: *uncle*
"Ever were these Bretons braggers of old!   *Britons*
Lo, how he brawles him for his bright weedes,   *garments (i.e., armor)*
1350   As he might britten us all with his brand rich!   *beat down; sword*
Yet he barkes much boste, yon boy there he standes!"   *boast; knave*

Then greved Sir Gawain at his grete wordes,
Graithes toward the gome with grouchand herte;   *Goes; man; angry*
With his steelen brand he strikes off his heved,   *steel*
1355   And stertes out to his steed, and with his stale wendes.   *leaps; company*
Through the watches they went, these worshipful knightes,
And findes in their fare-way wonderlich many;   *path wondrously*
Over the water they went by wightness of horses,
And took wind as they wolde by the wood hemmes.   *edges of the wood*
1360   Then follows frekly on foot frekes ynow,   *fiercely; warriors*
And of the Romans arrayed upon rich steedes
Chased through a champain our chevalrous knightes   *open field*
Til a chef forest on chalk-white horses.   *large (chief)*
But a freke all in fine gold and fretted in sable   *adorned*
1365   Come furthermost on a Freson in flamand weedes;   *Frisian horse; bright armor*
A fair flourisht spere in fewter he castes,   *spear-rest*
And followes fast on our folk and freshly ascries.   *eagerly; cries*

Then Sir Gawain the good upon a gray steed
He grippes him a grete spere and graithly him hittes;   *readily*
1370   Through the guttes into the gore he girdes him even,   *smites*
That the grounden steel glides to his herte!   *sharpened*
The gome and the grete horse at the ground ligges,   *man; lies*
Full grislich gronand for gref of his woundes.   *grisly; groaning; grief*
Then presses a priker in, full proudly arrayed,   *rider*
1375   That beres all of purpure, paled with silver [1]

---

[1] *That bears on his shield a heraldic device all of purple, striped with silver*

Bigly on a brown steed he proffers full large. [1]

He was a paynim of Perse that thus him persewed;   *pagan; Persia*

Sir Boys, unabaist all, he buskes him againes;   *unabashed*

With a bustous launce he beres him through,   *wild*

1380   That the breme and the brode sheld upon the bente ligges!   *fierce (one)*

And he bringes forth the blade and bounes to his fellowes.   *goes*

Then Sir Feltemour, of might a man mikel praised,   *much*

Was moved on his manner and menaced full fast;

He graithes to Sir Gawain graithly to work,   *charges at; readily*

1385   For gref of Sir Gayous that is on ground leved.

Then Sir Gawain was glad; again him he rides;

With Galuth, his good sword, graithly him hittes;   *readily*

The knight on the courser he cleved in sonder,   *cleaved in two*

Clenlich fro the crown his corse he devised,   *Cleanly; body he divided*

1390   And thus he killes the knight with his kidd wepen.   *famous*

Then a rich man of Rome relied to his bernes: *rallied*

"It shall repent us full sore and we ride further!   *if*

Yon are bold bosters that such bale workes;   *boasters; evil*

It befell him full foul that them so first named!"

1395   Then the rich Romans returnes their bridles,   *turn back*

To their tentes in teen, telles their lordes   *grief*

How Sir Marshall de Mowne is on the molde leved,   *ground*

Forjousted at that journee for his grete japes. [2]

But there chases on our men chevalrous knightes,

1400   Five thousand folk upon fair steedes,

Fast to a forest over a fell water   *strong (i.e., swift)*

That filles fro the fallow se fifty mile large.   *is filled; pale sea; away*

There were Bretons enbushed and banerettes noble,   *in ambush; senior knights*

Of chevalry chef of the kinges chamber;

1405   Sees them chase our men and changen their horses   *redirect*

And chop down cheftaines that they most charged.

Then the enbushment of Bretons broke out at ones,   *ambush*

---

[1] *With great force, on a brown horse, he offers battle boldly*

[2] *Outjousted at that battle despite his great boasts*

	Brothly at banner all Bedvere knightes	*Boldly; Bedivere's*
	Arrested of the Romans that by the firth rides,	*wood*
1410	All the realest renkes that to Rome longes;	*belong*
	They ishe on the enmies and egerly strikes,	*rush*
	Erles of England, and "Arthur!" ascries;	*cry*
	Through brenyes and bright sheldes brestes they thirle,	*hauberks; pierce*
	Bretons of the boldest, with their bright swordes.	
1415	There was Romans over-ridden and rudely wounded,	
	Arrested as rebawdes with riotous knightes!	*low fellows*
	The Romans out of array removed at ones	*broke ranks*
	And rides away in a rout — for reddour it seemes!	*fear*
	To the Senatour Peter a sandesman is comen	*messenger*
1420	And said: "Sir, sekerly, your segges are surprised!"	*men; seized*
	Then ten thousand men he sembled at ones	
	And set sodenly on our segges by the salt strandes.	*suddenly; men*
	Then were Bretons abaist and greved a little,	*abashed*
	But yet the bannerettes bold and bachelers noble	*(see note to line 68)*
1425	Brekes that batail with brestes of steedes;	*Break; battalion*
	Sir Bois and his bold men much bale workes!	*pain*
	The Romanes redies them, arrayes them better,	*rally themselves*
	And all to-rushes our men with their reste horses,	*dash asunder; rested*
	Arrested of the richest of the Round Table,	
1430	Over-rides our rere-ward and grete rewth workes!	*rear guard; sorrow*
	Then the Bretons on the bente abides no lenger,	*field*
	But fled to the forest and the feld leved;	
	Sir Berille is borne down and Sir Bois taken,	
	The best of our bold men unblithely wounded;	
1435	But yet our stale on a strenghe stotais a little,	*company; stronghold pauses*
	All to-stonayed with the stokes of tho steren knightes,	*astonished; thrusts*
	Made sorrow for their soveraign that so there was nomen,	*taken*
	Besought God of succour, send when him liked!	
	Then comes Sir Idrus, armed up at all rightes,	*completely*
1440	With five hundreth men upon fair steedes,	
	Fraines fast at our folk freshly thereafter	*Asks; eagerly*
	Yif their frendes were fer that on the feld founded.	*went*
	Then says Sir Gawain, "So me God help,	

175

We have been chased today and chulled as hares,   *driven like hares*
1445   Rebuked with Romanes upon their rich steedes,
And we lurked under lee as lowrand wretches!   *shelter; lowering*
I look never on my lord the dayes of my life [1]
And we so litherly him help that him so well liked!"

[handwritten: Sir Gawain says they're not doing well enough]

Then the Bretons brothely broches their steedes   *boldly; spur*
1450   And boldly in batail upon the bente rides;
All the fers men before frekly ascries,   *fierce; boldly cry*
Ferkand in the forest to freshen themselven.   *Striding through*
The Romanes then redyly arrayes them better,
On row on a rowm feld rightes their wepens,   *broad; adjust*
1455   By the rich river and rewles the pople;   *arrange the troops*
And with reddour Sir Bois is in arrest holden.   *fear*

Now they sembled unsaught by the salt stremes;   *fiercely attacked*
Sadly these seker men settes their dintes,
With lovely launces on loft they lushen togederes,   *dash together*
1460   In Lorraine so lordly on lepand steedes.
There were gomes through-gird with grounden wepens   *pierced; sharpened*
Grisly gaspand with grouchand lates.   *gasping; angry expressions*
Grete lordes of Greece greved so high.
Swiftly with swordes they swappen thereafter,   *strike*
1465   Swappes down full sweperly sweltande knightes,   *swiftly dying*
That all sweltes on swarth that they over-swingen.   *die; ground; cut down*
So many sways in swogh, swoonand at ones —   *faint*
Sir Gawain the gracious full graithly he workes;
The gretest he greetes with grisly woundes;
1470   With Galuth he girdes down full galiard knightes,   *strikes; jolly*
For gref of the grete lord so grimly he strikes!
He rides forth really and redyly thereafter   *royally*
There this real renk was in arrest holden;   *To where; i.e., Bois*
He rives the rank steel, he rittes their brenyes,   *rips; hauberks*
1475   And reft them the rich man and rode to his strenghes.   *bereft; stronghold*
The Senatour Peter then persewed him after,   *pursued*

---

[1] *May I never look on my lord the rest of my life / If we serve him so poorly, we who once pleased him so well*

Through the press of the pople with his pris knightes,
Appertly for the prisoner proves his strenghes, *Openly; strength*
With prikers the proudest that to the press longes; *riders; company*
1480 Wrothly on the wrong hand Sir Wawain he strikes, *Angrily; left*
With a wepen of war unwinly him hittes; *unpleasantly*
The breny on the back half he bristes in sonder; *hauberk; breaks in two*
And yet he brought forth Sir Bois for all their bale bernes! [1]

Then the Bretons boldly braggen their trumpes, *blow; trumpets*
1485 And for bliss of Sir Bois was brought out of bondes,
Boldly in batail they bere down knightes;
With brandes of brown steel they brittened mailes; *shining; armor*
They steked steedes in stour with steelen wepens *stuck; battle; steel*
And all stewede with strenghe that stood them againes! *struck down*
1490 Sir Idrus fitz Ewain then "Arthur!" ascries, *cries*
Assembles on the senatour with sixteen knightes *Attacks*
Of the sekerest men that to our side longed.
Sodenly in a soppe they set in at ones, *small troop*
Foines fast at the fore-breste with flamand swordes *Strike; gleaming*
1495 And fightes fast at the front freshly thereafter, *eagerly*
Felles fele on the feld upon the ferrer side, *many; farther*
Fey on the fair feld by tho fresh strandes. *Dead*

But Sir Idrus fitz Ewain aunters himselven *risks*
And enters in only and egerly strikes, *alone*
1500 Seekes to the senatour and seses his bridle; *siezes*
Unsaughtly he said him these sittand wordes: *Hostilely; fitting*
"Yelde thee, sir, yapely, yif thou thy life yernes; *Yield; quickly; yearn for*
For giftes that thou give may thou yeme not thyselven, *save*
For, dredles, drech thou or drop any wiles, [2]
1505 Thou shall die this day through dint of my handes!"

"I assent," quod the senatour, "so me Crist help. *said*
So that I be safe brought before the king selven; *Providing that*
Ransoun me reasonabely, as I may over-reche, *reasonably; obtain*

---

[1] *Even so, he (Sir Gawain) rescued Sir Bois despite all their baleful knights!*

[2] *For, doubtless, if you delay or play any tricks*

After my rentes in Rome may redyly further."   *tribute; readily furnish*

1510   Then answers Sir Idrus with austeren wordes:
"Thou shall have condicioun as the king likes,   *conditions*
When thou comes to the kith there the court holdes,
In case his counsel be to keep thee no longer,
To be killed at his commaundement his knightes before."

1515   They led him forth in the rout and latched off his weedes,   *took; armor*
Left him with Lionel and Lowell his brother.
O-low in the land then, by the lithe strandes,   *Below; pleasant*
Sir Lucius lege-men lost are forever!
The Senatour Peter is prisoner taken!
1520   Of Perse and Port Jaffe full many pris knightes   *Persia; Jaffa (Joppa)*
And much pople withal perished themselven!
For press of the passage they plunged at ones! [1]
There might men see Romans rewfully wounded,
Over-ridden with renkes of the Round Table.
1525   In the raike of the furth they righten their brenyes [2]
That ran all on red blood redyly all over;
They raght in the rere-ward full riotous knightes [3]
For ransoun of red gold and real steedes;   *noble*
Redyly relayes and restes their horses,   *change horses*
1530   In route to the rich king they rode all at ones.   *company*

A knight kaires before, and to the king telles: *goes*
"Sir, here comes thy messengeres with mirthes fro the mountes;
They have been matched today with men of the marches,
Foremagled in the morass with marvelous knightes!   *Hacked to pieces; marsh*
1535   We have foughten, in faith, by yon fresh strandes,
With the frekest folk that to thy fo longes;   *boldest; belongs*
Fifty thousand on feld of fers men of armes
Within a furlong of way fey are beleved!
We have eschewed this check through chaunce of Our Lord   *escaped; defeat*

---

[1] *Because of the crowd at the ford they leaped into the water together*

[2] *On the path by the stream they adjust their hauberks*

[3] *They placed the riotous (Roman) knights in the rear guard (as prisoners)*

1540	Of tho chevalrous men that charged thy pople.	
	The chef chaunceller of Rome, a cheftain full noble,	
	Will ask the charter of pees, for charitee himselven;	
	And the Senatour Peter to prisoner is taken.	
	Of Perse and Port Jaffe paynimes ynow	*pagans*
1545	Comes prikand in the press with thy pris knightes,	*spurring; choice*
	With povertee in thy prisoun their paines to drie.	*suffer*
	I beseek you, sir, say what you likes,	
	Whether ye suffer them saught or soon delivered.	*grant; peace*
	Ye may have for the senatour sixty horse charged	*loaded*
1550	Of silver by Saterday full sekerly payed,	
	And for the chef chaunceller, the chevaler noble,	
	Charottes chockful charged with gold.	*Wagons; loaded*
	The remenaunt of the Romanes be in arrest holden,	*remnant*
	Til their rentes in Rome be rightwisly knowen.	*correctly*
1555	I beseek you, sir, certify yon lordes,	*make certain*
	Yif ye will send them over the se or keep them yourselven.	
	All your seker men, for sooth, sound are beleved,	
	Save Sir Ewain fitz Henry is in the side wounded."	
	"Crist be thanked," quod the king, "and his clere Moder,	*immaculate*
1560	That you comforted and helped by craft of Himselven.	
	Skillfully skomfiture He skiftes as Him likes.[1]	
	Is none so skathly may scape ne skew fro His handes;	
	Destainy and doughtiness of deedes of armes,	*Destiny*
	All is deemed and delt at Drightenes will!	*God's*
1565	I can thee thank for thy come; it comfortes us all!	*coming*
	Sir knight," says the conquerour, "so me Crist help,	
	I give thee for thy tithandes Toulouse the rich,	*tidings*
	The toll and the tachementes, tavernes and other,	*appurtenances*
	The town and the tenementes with towres so high,	
1570	That touches to the temporaltee, whiles my time lastes.[2]	
	But say to the senatour I send him these wordes:	
	There shall no silver him save but Ewain recover.	*unless*

---

[1] *God skillfully handles trouble as He pleases. / No one is so harmful that he can escape or slip away from His hands*

[2] *All that concerns temporal life is yours while I live*

	I had lever see him sink on the salt strandes	*rather*
	Than the segge were seke that is so sore wounded.	*man; sick*
1575	I shall dissever that sorte, so me Crist help,	*separate; company*
	And set them full solitary in sere kinges landes.	*various*
	Shall he never sound see his seinoures in Rome,	*lords*
	Ne sit in the assemblee in sight with his feres,	*comrades*
	For it comes to no king that conquerour is holden	*is becoming; considered*
1580	To comone with his captives for covetis of silver.	*bargain; covetousness*
	It come never of knighthed, know it if him like,	*knighthood*
	To carp of cosery when captives are taken;	*business*
	It ought to no prisoners to press no lordes	*belongs (i.e., is proper)*
	Ne come in presence of princes when parties are moved.	*business is discussed*
1585	Commaund yon constable, the castle that yemes,	*governs*
	That he be clenlich keeped and in close holden;	*confinement*
	He shall have maundement to-morn ere mid-day be rungen	*command*
	To what march they shall merk with maugree to lengen."	*go; spite*
	They convey this captive with clene men of armes	*excellent*
1590	And kend him to the constable, als the king biddes	*entrust; as*
	And senn to Arthur they ayer and egerly him touches	*go; tell*
	The answer of the Emperour, irous of deedes.	*angry*
	Then Sir Arthur, on erthe athelest of other	*noblest*
	At even, at his own borde avaunted his lordes:	*praised*
1595	"Me ought to honour them in erthe over all other thinges,	
	That thus in mine absence aunters themselven!	
	I shall them love whiles I live, so me Our Lord help	
	And give them landes full large where them best likes;	
	They shall not lose on this laik, yif me life happen,	*game; is granted*
1600	That thus are lamed for my love by these lithe strandes."	*wounded; pleasant*
	But in the clere dawing the dere king himselven	*dawn*
	Commaunded Sir Cador, with his dere knightes,	
	Sir Cleremus, Sir Cleremond, with clene men of armes,	
	Sir Clowdmur, Sir Cleges, to convey these lordes;	
1605	Sir Bois and Sir Berille, with banners displayed,	
	Sir Bawdwin, Sir Brian, and Sir Bedvere the rich,	
	Sir Raynald and Sir Richer, Rowlaunde childer,	
	To ride with the Romanes in route with their feres:	*comrades*
	"Prikes now privily to Paris the rich	*secretly*

180

1610	With Peter the prisoner and his pris knightes;	
	Beteche them the provost in presence of lordes	*Entrust them to*
	O pain and o peril that pendes there-to	*On the; appends*
	That they be wisely watched and in ward holden,	
	Warded of warantises with worshipful knightes;	*sworn guards*
1615	Wage him wight men and wonde for no silver;	*Hire; hesitate*
	I have warned that wye; beware yif him likes!"	

	Now bounes the Britons als the king biddes,	*prepare; as*
	Buskes their batailes, their banners displayes,[1]	
	Toward Chartres they chese, these chevalrous knightes,	*go*
1620	And in the Champain land full fair they escheved,	*succeeded*
	For the Emperour of might had ordained himselven	
	Sir Utolf and Sir Evander, two honourable kinges,	
	Erles of the Orient with austeren knightes,	*stern*
	Of the auntrousest men that to his host longed	*most adventurous*
1625	Sir Sextynour of Lyby and senatours many,	*Lybia*
	The king of Surry himself with Sarazens ynow;	*Syria*
	The senatour of Sutere with summes full huge	*Sutri*
	Was assigned to that court by sente of his peeres,	*assent*
	Trays toward Troys the tresoun to work,	*Goes; Troyes (in France)*
1630	To have betrapped with a trayn our traveland knightes,	*trick; travelling*
	That had perceived that Peter at Paris sholde leng	
	In prisoun with the provost his paines to drie.	*suffer*
	Forthy they busked them boun with banners displayed,	*made themselves ready*
	In the buscaile of his way, on blonkes full huge,	*bushes*
1635	Plantes them in the path with power arrayed	
	To pick up the prisoners fro our pris knightes.	

	Sir Cador of Cornwall commaundes his peeres,	
	Sir Clegis, Sir Cleremus, Sir Cleremond the noble:	
	"Here is the Close of Clime with cleves so high;	*cliffs*
1640	Lookes the countree be clere; the corners are large;	
	Discoveres now sekerly skrogges and other,	*Search; carefully shrubs*
	That no scathel in the skrogges scorn us hereafter;	*harmful person; shrubs*
	Look ye skift it so that us no scathe limpe,	*arrange; harm befall*

---

[1] *Make ready their battalions, display their banners*

181

For no scomfiture in skulkery is scomfit ever." [1]

1645	Now they hie to the holt, these harageous knightes,	*hasten; wood; violent*
	To herken of the high men to helpen these lordes,	*hear; noble*
	Findes them helmed hole and horsed on steedes,	*completely armed*
	Hovand on the high way by the holt hemmes.	*Waiting; wood's edges*
	With knightly countenaunce Sir Clegis himselven	
1650	Cries to the company and carpes these wordes:	
	"Is there any kidd knight, kaiser or other,	*renowned; peace officer*
	Will kithe for his kinges love craftes of armes?	*show*
	We are comen fro the king of this kith rich	*powerful country*
	That knowen is for conquerour, crownd in erthe;	
1655	His rich retinues here, all of the Round Table,	
	To ride with that real in rout when him likes.	
	We seek jousting of war, yif any will happen,	
	Of the jolliest men ajudged by lordes;	
	If here be any hathel man, erl or other,	*noble*
1660	That for the Emperour love wil aunter himselven."	

	And an erl then in anger answeres him soon:	
	"Me angers at Arthur and at his hathel bernes	*noble*
	That thus in his errour occupies these rewmes,	
	And outrayes the Emperour, his erthly lord!	*outrages*
1665	The array and the realtees of the Round Table	*royalty*
	Is with rancour rehersed in rewmes full many,	*told*
	Of our rentes of Rome such revel he holdes;	
	He shall give resoun full rathe, if us right happen,	*quickly*
	That many shall repent that in his rout rides,	
1670	For the reckless roy so rewles himselven!"	*Because; king*

	"A!" says Sir Clegis then, "so me Crist help!	
	I know by thy carping a counter thee seemes!	*talking; accountant*
	But be thou auditour or erl or Emperour thyselven,	*accountant*
	Upon Arthures behalf I answer thee soon,	
1675	The renk so real that rewles us all,	*man*
	The riotous men and the rich of the Round Table:	

---

[1] *No attack from ambush is ever defeated*

He has araised his account and redde all his rolles,   *drawn up; read; records*
For he will give a reckoning that rew shall after,   *rue*
That all the rich shall repent that to Rome longes   *powerful (ones)*
1680 Ere the rerage be requite of rentes that he claimes.   *debt be repaid*
We crave of your courtaisy three courses of war,
And claimes of knighthood, take keep to yourselven!
Ye do but trayn us today with troufeland wordes;   *trick; trifling*
Of such traveland men trechery me thinkes.   *travelling*
1685 Send out sadly certain knightes
Or say me sekerly sooth; forsake yif you likes."   *surrender*

Then says the King of Surry, "Als save me Our Lord,   *Syria; As*
Yif thou hufe all the day thou bes not delivered!   *delay; will be*
But thou sekerly ensure with certain knightes
1690 That thy cote and thy crest be knowen with lordes,   *coat of arms*
Of armes of auncestry enterd with landes."   *endowed*

"Sir King," says Sir Clegis, "full knightly thou askes;
I trow it be for cowardis thou carpes these wordes;   *believe; cowardice*
Mine armes are of auncestry envered with lordes,   *acknowledged*
1695 And has in banner been borne senn Sir Brut time;
At the citee of Troy that time was enseged,   *besieged*
Oft seen in assaut with certain kinghtes;   *assault*
Forthy Brut brought us and all our bold elders   *Therefore*
To Bretain the Brodder within ship-bordes."   *Great Britain; aboard ships*

1700 "Sir," says Sir Sextynour, "say what thee likes,
And we shall suffer thee, als us best seemes;
Look thy trumpes be trussed and troufle no lenger, [1]
For though thou tarry all the day, thee tides no better,   *betides*
For there shall never Roman that in my rout rides
1705 Be with rebawdes rebuked, whiles I in world regne!"   *low fellows*

Then Sir Clegis to the king a little enclined,   *bowed*
Kaires to Sir Cador and knightly him telles:
"We have founden in yon firth, flourished with leves,   *forest*

---

[1] *See that you pack up your trumpets and trifle no longer*

183

The flowr of the fairest folk that to thy fo longes,

1710 Fifty thousand of folk of fers men of armes, *fierce*

That fair are fewtered on front under yon free bowes; *prepared for battle*

They are enbushed on blonkes, with banners displayed, *in ambush*

In yon beechen wood, upon the way sides. *beech*

They have the furth for-set all of the fair water, *ford obstructed*

1715 That fayfully of force fight us behooves, *truly*

For thus us shapes today, shortly to tell; *it befalls us*

Whether we shoun or shew, shift as thee likes." [1]

"Nay," quod Cador, "so me Crist help,

It were shame that we sholde shoun for so little! *shun (battle)*

1720 Sir Launcelot shall never laugh, that with the king lenges,

That I sholde let my way for lede upon erthe; *give up; man*

I shall be dede and undone ere I here dreche *delay*

For drede of any dogges-son in yon dim shawes!" *dog's son; bushes*

Sir Cador then knightly comfortes his pople,

1725 And with corage keen he carpes these wordes: *heart*

"Think on the valiant prince that vesettes us ever *endows*

With landes and lordshippes where us best likes.

That has us ducherys delt and dubbed us knightes, *dukedoms*

Given us gersoms and gold and guerdons many, *gifts; rewards*

1730 Grayhoundes and grete horse and alkine games, *every sort of pleasure*

That gaines til any gome that under God lives; *profit any man*

Think on rich renown of the Round Table,

And let it never be reft us for Roman in erthe; *taken from*

Foyne you not faintly, ne frithes no wepens, *Duel; spare*

1735 But look ye fight faithfully, frekes yourselven;

I wolde be welled all quick and quartered in sonder, [2]

But I work my deed, whiles I in wrath lenge." *Unless*

Then this doughty duke dubbed his knightes:

Ioneke and Askanere, Aladuke and other,

1740 That eieres were of Essex and all those este marches, *heirs; eastern*

---

[1] *Whether we shun (battle) or show (fight), decide as you please*

[2] *I would be boiled alive and cut in quarters*

	Howell and Hardolf, happy in armes,	*fortunate*
	Sir Heryll and Sir Herygall, these haragous knightes.	*violent*
	Then the soveraign assigned certain lordes,	
	Sir Wawayne, Sir Uryelle, Sir Bedvere the rich,	
1745	Raynald and Richere, Rowlandes childer:	
	"Takes keep on this prince with your pris knightes,	*Take care of;* i.e., *Peter*
	And yif we in the stour withstanden the better,	*battle*
	Standes here in this stede and stirres no further;	*place*
	And yif the chaunce fall that we be over-charged,	
1750	Eschewes to some castle and cheves yourselven,	*Escape; save*
	Or ride to the rich king, if you roo happen,	*respite*
	And bid him come redyly to rescue his bernes."	

	And then the Bretons brothely enbraces their sheldes,	*boldly; strap on*
	Braides on bacenettes and buskes their launces;	*Draw on helmets*
1755	Thus he fittes his folk and to the feld rides,	*arranges*
	Five hundreth on a front fewtered at ones!	*readied spears*
	With trumpes they trine and trapped steedes,	*trumpets; go; caparisoned*
	With cornettes and clariouns and clergial notes;	*skillful*
	Shockes in with a shake and shuntes no longer,	*sudden movement; hold back*
1760	There shawes were sheen under the shire eves. [1]	
	And then the Romanes rout removes a little,	
	Raikes with a rere-ward those real knightes;	*Goes; rear guard*
	So raply they ride there that all the rout ringes	*quickly*
	Of rives and rank steel and rich gold mailes. [2]	

1765	Then shot out of the shaw sheltrones many,	*bushes troops*
	With sharp wepens of war shootand at ones.	
	The King of Lyby before the avauntward he ledes,	*Libya; vanguard*
	And all his lele lege-men all on loud ascries.	*loyal liegemen*
	Then this cruel king castes in fewter,	*readies his spear*
1770	Caught him a coverd horse, and his course holdes,	*armored*
	Beres to Sir Berille and brothely him hittes,	*stoutly*
	Through the golet and the gorger he hurtes him even.	*gullet; neckpiece*
	The gome and the grete horse at the ground ligges,	*man*

---

[1] *Where shrubs were bright under the shining eaves of the forest*

[2] *Of rivets and strong steel and rich gold chain mail*

And gretes graithely to God and gives Him the soul.   *cries*
1775 Thus is Berille the bold brought out of life,
And bides after the burial that him best likes.   *awaits the burial*

And then Sir Cador of Cornwall is careful in herte,   *sorrowful*
Because of his kinsman that thus is miscarried;
Umbeclappes the corse, and kisses him oft,   *Embraces*
1780 Gart keep him covert with his clere knightes.   *Commanded; protected*
Then laughs the Lyby king, and all on loud meles: *speaks*
"Yon lord is lighted! Me likes the better!   *fallen*
He shall not dere us today; the devil have his bones!"   *harm*

"Yon king," says Sir Cador, "carpes full large,
1785 Because he killed this keen — Crist have thy soul! —   *brave one*
He shall have corn-bote, so me Crist help!   *penance*
Ere I kaire of this coste, we shall encounter ones: *place*
So may the wind wheel turn, I quite him ere even,   *As does; repay*
Soothly himselven or some of his feres!"   *companions*

1790 Then Sir Cador the keen knightly he workes,
Cries, "A Cornwall!" and castes in fewter,   *readies his spear*
Girdes streke through the stour on a steed rich;   *Strikes straight; battle*
Many steren men he stirred by strenghe of him one;   *stern; struck*
When his spere was sprongen, he sped him full yerne,   *broken; eagerly*
1795 Swapped out with a sword that swiked him never,   *failed*
Wrought wayes full wide, and wounded knightes,
Workes in his wayfare full workand sides,   *Makes; painful*
And hewes of the hardiest halses in sonder,   *necks*
That all blendes with blood there his blonk runnes!   *horse*
1800 So many bernes the bold brought out of life,
Tittes tyrauntes down and temes their saddles,   *Knocks; empties*
And turnes out of the toil when him time thinkes!

Then the Lyby king cries full loud   *Libyan*
On Sir Cador the keen with cruel wordes:
1805 "Thou has worship won and wounded knightes!
Thou weenes for thy wightness the world is thine own!   *suppose; power*
I shall wait at thine hand, wye, by my trewth;   *man; word*
I have warned thee well, beware yif thee likes!"

	With cornus and clariouns these new-made knightes	*horns*
1810	Lithes unto the cry and castes in fewter,	*Listen; ready their spears*
	Ferkes in on a front on feraunt steedes, [1]	
	Felled at the first come fifty at ones;	
	Shot through the sheltrons and shivered launces,	*troops; split*
	Laid down in the lump lordly bernes.	*heap*
1815	And thus nobly our new men notes their strenghes!	*use*
	But new note is anon that noyes me sore:	*business; annoys*
	The King of Lyby has laght a steed that him liked,	*seized*
	And comes in lordly in liones of silver,	*with heraldic lions*
	Umbelappes the lump and lettes in sonder;	*Surrounds; group; drives*
1820	Many lede with his launce the life has he reved!	*taken*
	Thus he chases the childer of the kinges chamber,	
	And killes in the champaines chevalrous knightes;	*open fields*
	With a chasing spere he choppes down many!	*hunting spear*

	There was Sir Aladuke slain and Achinour wounded,	
1825	Sir Origge and Sir Ermyngall hewen all to peces!	*pieces*
	And there was Lewlin laght and Lewlins brother	*taken*
	With lordes of Lyby and led to their strenghes;	*stronghold*
	Ne had Sir Clegis comen and Clement the noble,	
	Our new men had gone to nought and many mo other.	*many others*

	Then Sir Cador the keen castes in fewter	*readies his spear*
1830	A cruel launce and a keen and to the king rides,	
	Hittes him high on the helm with his hard wepen,	
	That all the hot blood of him to his hand runnes!	
	The hethen harageous king upon the hethe ligges,	*heathen violent; heath*
1835	And of his hertly hurt heled he never.	*mortal; healed*
	Then Sir Cador the keen cries full loud:	
	"Thou has corn-bote, sir king, there God give thee sorrow;	*penance*
	Thou killed my cosin; my care is the less!	
	Kele thee now in the clay and comfort thyselven;	*Cool yourself*
1840	Thou scorned us long ere, with thy scornful wordes,	
	And now thou has cheved so, it is thine own scathe;	*fared; harm*

---

[1] *Ride on iron-gray steeds at the front rank (of the Romans)*

Hold at thou hent has; it harmes but little, [1]
For hething is home-hold, use it who-so will!"

	The King of Surry then is sorrowful in herte,	*Syria*
1845	For sake of his soveraign that thus was surprised;	*taken*
	Sembled his Sarazens and senatours many;	
	Unsaughtly they set then upon our sere knightes.	*Hostilely; various*
	Sir Cador of Cornwall he counters them soon	*encounters*
	With his kidd company clenlich arrayed;	*famous; splendidly*
1850	In the front of the firth, as the way forthes,	*forest; goes forth*
	Fifty thousand of folk was felled at ones.	
	There was at the assemblee certain knightes	
	Sore wounded soon upon sere halves.	*every side*
	The sekerest Sarazenes that to that sorte longed	*most dependable; company*
1855	Behind the saddles were set six foot large;	
	They sheerd in the sheltron shelded knightes;	*cut down; troop shielded*
	Shalkes they shot through shrinkand mailes;	*Men; wrinkled (plated)*
	Through brenyes browden brestes they thirled;	*armor braided; pierced*
	Bracers burnisht bristes in sonder;	*Arm guards; burst*
1860	Blasons bloody and blonkes they hewen,	*Bloody shields*
	With brandes of brown steel, brankand steedes!	*shining; prancing*
	The Bretons brothely brittenes so many	*quickly destroy*
	The bente and the brode feld all on blood runnes!	*earth*
	By then Sir Kayous the keen a capitain has wonnen;	*captured*
1865	Sir Clegis clinges in and clekes another;	*rushes; clutches*
	The Capitain of Cordewa, under the king selven,	*Cordova*
	That was key of the kith of all that coste rich	*country*
	Utolf and Evander Ioneke had nommen	*captured*
	With the Erl of Afrike and other grete lordes.	*Africa*
1870	The King of Surry the keen to Sir Cador is yelden,	*surrendered*
	The Seneschal of Sutere to Sagramour himselven.	*Sutri*
	When the chevalry saw their cheftaines were nomen,	*taken*
	To a chef forest they chosen their wayes,	*go*
	And feeled them so faint they fell in the greves,	*groves*
1875	In the feren of the firth for ferd of our pople.	*ferns; forest; fear*
	There might men see the rich ride in the shawes	*shrubs*

---

[1] *Keep what you have taken; it does little harm, / For scorn is internal, use it who will*

	To rip up the Romanes rudlich wounded,	*rudely*
	Shoutes after men harageous knightes,	*violent*
	By hundrethes they hewed down by the holt eves!	*edge of the wood*
1880	Thus our chevalrous men chases the pople;	
	To a castel they escheved the few that eschaped.	*achieved (got to); escaped*
	Then relies the renkes of the Round Table	*rally*
	For to riot the wood there the duke restes;	*ride through*
	Ransackes the rindes all, raght up their feres,	*woods; took; companions*
1885	That in the fighting before fey were beleved.	*left*
	Sir Cador gart charre them and cover them fair,[1]	
	Carried them to the king with his best knightes,	
	And passes unto Paris with prisoners himselven,	
	Betook them the provost, princes and other,	*entrusted them to*
1890	Tas a sope in the towr and tarries no longer	*Takes; meal*
	But turnes tite to the king and him with tonge telles:	*quickly; tongue*
	"Sir," says Sir Cador, "a case is befallen;	
	We have countered today in yon coste rich	*encountered; coast*
	With kinges and kaiseres cruel and noble,	
1895	And knightes and keen men clenlich arrayed!	
	They had at yon forest for-set us the wayes,	*blockaded*
	At the furth in the firth with fers men of armes;	*ford; forest*
	There fought we in faith and foined with speres	*duelled*
	On feld with thy fomen and felled them on live;	*alive (i.e., killed them)*
1900	The King of Lyby is laid and in the feld leved,	*laid low*
	And many of his lege-men that yore to him longed;	*formerly*
	Other lordes are laght of uncouthe ledes;	*taken; foreign countries*
	We have led them at lenge, to live whiles thee likes.	*to remain here*
	Sir Utolf and Sir Evander, these honourable knightes,	
1905	By an aunter of armes Ioneke has nomen,	*taken*
	With erles of Orient and austeren knightes,	
	Of auncestry the best men that to the host longed;	
	The Senatour Carous is caught with a knight,	
	The Capitain of Cornette that cruel is holden,	*Corneto*
1910	The Seneschal of Sutere, unsaught with these other,	*Sutri; distressed*
	The King of Surry himselven and Sarazenes ynow.	

---

[1] *Sir Cador commanded that they be put in wagons and covered with fair cloths*

But fey of ours in the feld are fourteen knightes.

I will not feyne ne forbere but faithfully tellen:　　*hold back; delay*

Sir Berille is one, a bannerette noble,

1915　Was killed at the first come with a king rich;

Sir Aladuke of Towell with his tender knightes,

Among the Turkes was tint and in time founden;　　*lost; found (dead)*

Good Sir Mawrelle of Mawnces and Mawrene his brother,

Sir Meneduke of Mentoche with marvelous knightes."

1920　　Then the worthy king writhes and weeped with his eyen,

Carpes to his cosin Sir Cador these wordes:

"Sir Cador, thy corage confoundes us all!　　*courage*

Cowardly thou castes out all my best knightes!

To put men in peril, it is no pris holden,　　*excellence*

1925　But the parties were purveyed and power arrayed;　　*prepared*

When thou were stedde on a strenghe thou sholde have with-stonden, [1]

But yif ye wolde all my steren stroy for the nones!"　　*strong men destroy*

　　"Sir," says Sir Cador, "ye know well yourselven;

Ye are king in this kith; carp what you likes!

1930　Shall never berne upbraid me that to thy borde longes,　　*table*

That I sholde blinn for their boste thy bidding to work!　　*cease; command*

When any stertes to stale, stuff them the better,　　*sets out; company; supply*

Or they will be stonayed and stroyed in yon strait landes.　　*astonished; destroyed*

I did my deligence today — I do me on lordes — [2]

1935　And in daunger of dede for diverse knightes,　　*death*

I have no grace to thy gree but such grete wordes;　　*reward*

Yif I heven my herte, my hap is no better."　　*speak my mind; fortune*

　　Though Sir Arthur was angered, he answers fair:

"Thou has doughtily done, Sir Duke, with thy handes,

1940　And has done thy dever with my dere knightes;　　*duty*

Forthy thou art deemed with dukes and erles

For one of the doughtiest that dubbed was ever!

There is none ischew of us on this erthe sprongen;　　*issue (child); sprung*

---

[1] *When you were placed in a stronghold, you should have endured*

[2] *I did my duty today — I put myself at the judgment of lords*

190

	Thou art apparent to be eier, or one of thy childer;	*heir*
1945	Thou art my sister son; forsake shall I never!	*sister's (Anna's)*
	Then gart he in his owen tent a table be set,	*commanded; own*
	And tryed in with trumpes traveled bernes,	*invited; trumpets; exhausted*
	Served them solemnly with selcouthe metes,	*rare foods*
	Swithe seemly in sight with silveren dishes.	*very*
1950	When the senatours herde say that it so happened,	*heard*
	They said to the Emperour: "Thy segges are surprised!	*warriors; taken*
	Sir Arthur, thine enmy, has outrayed thy lordes	*outraged*
	That rode for the rescue of yon rich knightes!	
	Thou dos but tinnes thy time and tourmentes thy pople;	*do; lose; torment*
1955	Thou art betrayed of thy men that most thou on traisted.	*by; trusted*
	That shall turn thee to teen and torfer forever!"	*pain; sorrow*
	Then the Emperour irous was, angerd at his herte	*irate*
	For our valiant bernes such prowesh had wonnen.	*prowess*
	With king and with kaiser to counsel they wend,	
1960	Soveraignes of Sarazens and senatours many.	
	Thus he sembles full soon certain lordes,	
	And in the assemblee then he says them these wordes:	*assembly*
	"My herte soothly is set, assent if you likes,	
	To seek into Sessoine with my seker knightes,	*Soissons*
1965	To fight with my fomen, if fortune me happen,	
	Yif I may find the freke within the four halves;	*sides*
	Or enter into Auguste aunters to seek,	*Autun (province in France)*
	And bide with my bold men within the burg rich,	
	Rest us and revel and riot ourselven,	
1970	Lende there in delite in lordshippes ynow,	*Remain; delight*
	To Sir Leo be comen with all his lele knightes,	*Until; loyal*
	With lordes of Lumbardy to let him the wayes."	*hinder*
	But our wise king is wary to waiten his renkes,	*look out for*
	And wisely by the woodes voides his host;	*withdraws*

1975	Gart felshen his fires flamand full high, [1]	
	Trussen full traistely and treunt there-after.	
	Sithen into Sessoine · he sought at the gainest,	*Soissons; went; quickest*
	And at the sours of the sun disseveres his knightes,	*rising; separates*
	For-set them the citee upon sere halves,	*Blockaded; all sides*
1980	Sodenly on eche halfe, with seven grete stales,	*Suddenly; each side; troops*
	Only in the vale a vaweward enbushes.	*vanguard lies in ambush*

Sir Valiant of Wales with valiant knightes
Before the kinges visage made such avowes
To vanquish by victory the Viscount of Rome;
1985   Forthy the king charges him, what chaunce so befall,   *appoints*
Cheftain of the check with chevalrous knightes,   *attack*
And sithen meles with mouth that he most traistes;   *to those that; trusts*
Demenes the middilward menskfully himselven,   *Leads; middle guard*
Fittes his footmen als him fair thinkes;   *Arranges*
1990   On front in the fore-breste the flowr of his knightes;   *first rank*
His archers on either half he ordained there-after   *side*
To shake in a sheltron to shoot when them likes;   *go; troop*
He arrayed in the rereward full real knightes
With renkes renowned of the Round Table,
1995   Sir Raynald, Sir Richere that rade was never,   *fearful*
The rich Duke of Rouen with riders ynow;
Sir Kayous, Sir Clegis, and clene men of armes, [2]
The king castes to keep by tho clere strandes;
Sir Lot and Sir Launcelot, these lordly knightes
2000   Shall lenge on his left hand with legiones ynow,
To move in the morn-while, if the mist happen;   *morning*
Sir Cador of Cornwall, and his keen knightes,
To keep at the karfuke, to close in thir other;   *watch; crossroads; these*
He plantes in such places princes and erles
2005   That no power sholde pass by no privee wayes.   *secret*

---

[1] *Commands that his fires be fed so that they flame very high / And (commands them) to pack up securely and march away thereafter*

[2] *Sir Kayous, Sir Clegis, and good men of arms / The king decides should keep watch by those shining strands.*

But the Emperour anon with honourable knightes
And erles enters the vale, aunters to seek,   *entry; add to*
And findes Sir Arthur with hostes arrayed,
And at his in-come, to eeken his sorrow,   *entry; add to*
2010 Our burlich bold king upon the bente hoves,   *strong; plain rides*
With his batail on-brode and banners displayed.   *battalions spread out*
He had the citee for-set upon sere halves,   *besieged; many sides*
Both the cleves and the cliffes with clene men of armes,   *gullies*
The moss and the morass with mountes so high   *bogs*
2015 With grete multitude of men to mar him in the wayes.   *harm*

When Sir Lucius sees, he says to his lordes:
"This traitour has treunt this tresoun to work!   *marched here; treason*
He has the citee for-set upon sere halves,   *blockaded*
All the cleves and the cliffes with clene men of armes!   *gullies*
2020 Here is no way, iwis, ne no wit else,   *advice*
But fight with our fomen, for flee may we never!"

Then this rich man rathe arrayes his bernes,   *swiftly*
Rewled his Romans and real knightes;
Buskes in the avauntward the Viscount of Rome;   *vanguard*
2025 Fro Viterbo to Venice these valiant knightes
Dresses up dredfully the dragon of gold,   *Raise*
With egles all over enamelled of sable;   *eagles; adorned*
Drawen dreghly the wine and drinken there-after,   *solemnly*
Dukes and douspeeres, dubbed knightes;
2030 For dauncesing of Dutch-men and dinning of pipes,   *Germans; sounding*
All dinned for din that in the dale hoved.   *resounded; noise; stood*
And then Sir Lucius on loud said lordlich wordes:
"Think on the much renown of your rich faders,
And the riotours of Rome that regned with lordes,   *ravagers*
2035 And the renkes over-ran, all that regned in erthe,
Ecroched all Cristendom by craftes of armes;   *Invaded*
In everich a viage the victory was holden   *each expedition*
Inset all the Sarazenes within seven winter,   *Overcame*
The part from Port Jaffe to Paradise gates!   *Jaffa*
2040 Though a rewm be rebel, we reck it but little;   *reckon*
It is resoun and right the renk be restrained!
Do dress we therefore, and bide we no longer,   *Let us prepare ourselves*

For dredles, withouten doubt, the day shall be oures!"   *surely*

When these wordes was said, the Welsh king himselven
2045 Was ware of this widerwin that warrayed his knightes;   *adversary; warred on*
Brothely in the vale with voice he ascries: *Quickly*
"Viscount of Valence, envious of deedes,
The vassalage of Viterbo today shall be revenged!
Unvanquisht fro this place void shall I never."   *leave*

2050 Then the viscount, valiant, with a voice noble
Avoided the avauntward, enveround his horse;   *Left; vanguard; turned*
He dressed in a derf sheld, endented with sable,   *strong; edged*
With a dragon engoushed, dredful to shew,   *swollen*
Devourand a dolphin with doleful lates,   *Devouring; expression*
2055 In sign that our soveraign sholde be destroyed,
And all done of dayes, with dintes of swordes,
For there is nought but dede there the dragon is raised!   *death*

Then the comlich king castes in fewter,
With a cruel launce coupes full even   *strikes exactly*
2060 Aboven the spayre a span, among the short ribbes, [1]
That the splent and the spleen on the spere lenges!   *piece of armor plate*
The blood sprent out and spredde as the horse springs,   *spurt; spread*
And he sproules full spakely, but spekes he no more!   *sprawls; swiftly*
And thus has Sir Valiant holden his avowes,
2065 And vanquisht the Viscount that victor was holden!

Then Sir Ewain fitz Urien full enkerly rides   *eagerly*
Anon to the Emperour his egle to touch;   *eagle*
Through his brode batail he buskes belive,   *hurries quickly*
Braides out his brand with a blithe cheer,   *Draws*
2070 Reversed it redily and away rides,
Ferkes in with the fowl in his fair handes,   *Goes; i.e., the eagle*
And fittes in freely on front with his feres.   *companions*

Now buskes Sir Launcelot and braides full even   *hurries; pulls*

---

[1] *Six inches above the waist, between the short ribs*

194

	To Sir Lucius the lord and lothly him hittes;	
2075	Through paunce and plates he perced the mailes	*stomach guard; pierced*
	That the proud pensel in his paunch lenges!	*pennon*
	The hed hailed out behind an half foot large,	*came*
	Through hawberk and haunch with the hard wepen;	
	The steed and the steren man strikes to the ground,	*(Launcelot) strikes*
2080	Strak down a standard and to his stale wendes!	*struck; company*

	"Me likes well," says Sir Lot, "yon lordes are delivered!	*fulfilled [their] vows*
	The lot lenges now on me, with leve of my lord;	
	Today shall my name be laid, and my life after,	*laid low*
	But some lepe fro the life that on yon land hoves!"	*leap; stand*

2085	Then strekes the steren and straines his bridle,[1]	
	Strikes into the stour on a steed rich,	*battle*
	Enjoined with a giaunt and jagged him through!	*Engaged; slashed*
	Jollily this gentle knight for-jousted another,	*outjousted*
	Wrought wayes full wide, warrayand knightes,	*attacking*
2090	And woundes all wathely that in the way standes!	*woefully*
	Fightes with all the frap a furlong of way,	*troop*
	Felled fele upon feld with his fair wepen,	*many*
	Vanquisht and has the victory of valiant knightes,	
	And all enverouned the vale and void when him liked.	*rode around; left*

2095	Then bowmen of Bretain brothely there-after	*quickly*
	Bekered with brigandes of fer in tho landes;[2]	
	With flones fletterd they flit full freshly thir frekes,	
	Fichen with fetheres through the fine mailes;	*Pierce; feathers*
	Such flytting is foul that so the flesh deres,	*contention; harms*
2100	That flow a ferrom in flankes of steedes.	*flew; from afar*
	Dartes the Dutch-men delten againes,	*Germans; dealt; in return*
	With derf dintes of dede dagges through sheldes;	*cut*
	Quarrels quaintly quappes through knightes[3]	

---

[1] *Then rushes the steadfast man and grips his bridle*

[2] *Fought with foot-soldiers (brigands) from afar in those lands; / With feathered arrows they very eagerly shoot those men*

[3] *Crossbow bolts skillfully whip through knights*

	With iron so wekerly that wink they never.	*swiftly*
2105	So they shrinken for shot of the sharp arrows,	
	That all the sheltron shunt and shuddered at ones;	*troops hung back*
	The rich steedes rependes and rashes on armes,	*buck; rush*
	The hole hundreth on hie upon hethe ligges;	*whole; hastily; heath*
	But yet the hatheliest on hie, hethen and other,	*most noble hastily*
2110	All hourshes over hede, harmes to work.	*rush*
	And all these giauntes before, engendered with fendes,	
	Joines on Sir Jonathal and gentle knightes,	*Attack*
	With clubbes of clene steel clanked in helmes,	
	Crashed down crestes and crashed braines,	
2115	Killed coursers and coverd steedes,	*armored*
	Chopped through chevalers on chalk-white steedes;	
	Was never steel ne steed might stand them againes,	
	But stonays and strikes down that in the stale hoves,	*astonish; troop*
	Til the conquerour come with his keen knightes.	
2120	With cruel countenaunce he cried full loud:	
	"I wend no Bretons wolde be bashed for so little,	*supposed; abashed*
	And for bare-legged boyes that on the bente hoves!"	*knaves; remain*
	He clekes out Caliburn, full clenlich burnisht,	*draws; Excalibur*
	Graithes him to Golopas, that greved him most,	
2125	Cuttes him even by the knees clenly in sonder;	
	"Come down," quod the king, "and carp to thy feres!	
	Thou art too high by the half, I hete thee in trewth!	*promise*
	Thou shall be handsomer in hie, with the help of my Lord!"	*hastily*
	With that steelen brand he stroke off his hed.	*struck*
2130	Sterenly in that stour he strikes another.	
	Thus he settes on seven with his seker knightes;	
	Whiles sixty were served so ne sesed they never;	*did not cease*
	And thus at this joining the giauntes are destroyed,	*encounter*
	And at that journee for-jousted with gentle knightes.	*outjousted*
2135	Then the Romanes and the renkes of the Round Table	
	Rewles them in array, rereward and other,	*Arrange*
	With wight wepenes of war they wroughten on helmes,	*worked*
	Rittes with rank steel full real mailes	*Rip*
	But they fit them fair, these frek bernes,	*ordered themselves; bold*
2140	Fewters in freely on feraunt steedes	*Fix lances; iron-gray*

Foines full felly with flishand speres, *Duel; fiercely; flashing*
Fretten off orfrayes fast upon sheldes; *Cut; gold ornaments; fastened*
So fele fey is in fight upon the feld leved
That ech a furth in the firth of red blood runnes. *every stream; forest*
2145 By that swiftely on swarth the swet is beleved, *By then; ground; lifeblood*
Swordes swangen in two, sweltand knightes *swung; dying*
Lies wide open welterand on walopand steedes; *rolling about; galloping*
Woundes of wale men workand sides, *choice; paining*
Faces fetteled unfair in feltered lockes, *enclosed; matted*
2150 All craysed, for-trodden with trapped steedes,[1]
The fairest on folde that figured was ever, *earth; created*
As fer as a furlong, a thousand at ones!

By then the Romanes were rebuked at little, *somewhat*
Withdrawes them drerily and dreches no lenger; *drearily; delay*
2155 Our prince with his power persewes them after, *pursues*
Prikes on the proudest with his pris knightes,
Sir Kayous, Sir Clegis, Sir Cleremond the noble,
Encounters them at the cliff with clene men of armes;
Fightes fast in the firth, frithes no wepen, *spares*
2160 Felled at the first come five hundreth at ones!
And when they fande them for-set with our fers knightes, *found; blockaded*
Few men again fele mot fich them better, *against many must pierce*
Fightes with all the frap, foines with speres, *troop, duel*
And fought with the frekkest that to Fraunce longes. *boldest*
2165 But Sir Kayous the keen castes in fewter,
Chases on a courser and to a king rides;
With a launce of Lettow he thirles his sides *Lithuania; pierces*
That the liver and the lunges on the launce lenges;
The shaft shuddered and shot in the shire berne, *shining armor*
2170 And sought throughout the sheld and in the shalk restes. *went; man*
But Kayous at the in-come was keeped unfair *entry*
With a coward knight of the kith rich;
At the turning that time the traitour him hit
In through the felettes and in the flank after *loins*
2175 That the bustous launce the bewelles entamed, *wild; bowels pierced*

---

[1] *All crushed, stamped to death by armored steeds*

That braste at the brawling and broke in the middes. *middle*
Sir Kayous knew well by that kidd wound *infamous*
That he was dede of the dint and done out of life;
Then he raikes in array and on row rides, *goes; at the rank*
2180 On this real renk his dede to revenge: *royal person*
"Keep thee, coward!" he calles him soon,
Cleves him with his clere brand clenlich in sonder:
"Had thou well delt thy dint with thy handes,
I had forgiven thee my dede, by Crist now of heven!" *death*

2185 He wendes to the wise king and winly him greetes: *pleasantly*
"I am wathely wounded, waresh mon I never; *woefully; recover may*
Work now thy worship, as the world askes, *requires*
And bring me to burial; bid I no more. *ask*
Greet well my lady the queen, yif thee world happen, *if you survive*
2190 And all the burlich birdes that to her bowr longes; *stately maids*
And my worthily wife, that wrathed me never, *worthy; angered*
Bid her for her worship work for my soul!"

The kinges confessour come with Crist in his handes, *i.e., the Host*
For to comfort the knight, kend him the wordes; *told; i.e., absolution*
2195 The knight covered on his knees with a kaunt herte, *arose to; stout*
And caught his Creatour that comfortes us all.
Then romes the rich king for rewth at his herte, *bellows*
Rides into rout his dede to revenge,
Pressed into the plump and with a prince meetes *crowd*
2200 That was eier of Egypt in those este marches, *heir; east*
Cleves him with Caliburn clenlich in sonder! *Excalibur*
He broches even through the berne and the saddle bristes,
And at the back of the blonk the bewelles entamed! *bowels pierced*
Manly in his malencoly he meetes another; *rage (melancholy)*
2205 The middle of that mighty that him much greved
He merkes through the mailes the middes in sonder, *slashes; middle*
That the middes of the man on the mount falles, *ground*
The tother half of the haunch on the horse leved; *other; remained*
Of that hurt, as I hope, heles he never! *suppose*
2210 He shot through the sheltrons with his sharp wepen, *troops*
Shalkes he shrede through and shrinked mailes; *Men; cut; wrinkled*
Banners he bore down, brittened sheldes; *destroyed*

198

Brothely with brown steel his brethe he there wrekes; *shining; anger*
Wrothely he writhes by wightness of strenghe, *Wrathfully*
2215 Woundes these widerwinnes, warrayed knightes *adversaries, attacked*
Threped through the thickes thriteen sithes, *Fought; crowds; times*
Thringes throly in the throng and chis even after! *Presses hard; pushes*

Then Sir Gawain the good with worshipful knightes
Wendes in the avauntward by tho wood hemmes, *vanguard; edges*
2220 Was ware of Sir Lucius on land there he hoves
With lordes and lege-men that to himself longed.
Then the Emperour enkerly askes him soon: *eagerly*
"What will thou, Wawain? Work for thy wepen? *do you want*
I wot by thy wavering thou wilnes after sorrow; *roving; want*
2225 I shall be wroken on thee, wretch for all thy grete wordes!" *avenged*

He laght out a long sword and lushed on fast, *took out; lashed*
And Sir Lionel in the land lordly him strikes,
Hittes him on the hed that the helm bristes,
Hurtes his herne-pan an hand-bred large! *skull; hand's breadth deep*
2230 Thus he layes on the lump and lordly them served, *crowd*
Wounded worthily worshipful knightes,
Fightes with Florent, that best is of swordes,
Til the fomand blood til his fist runnes! *foaming*

Then the Romans releved that ere were rebuked, *rallied*
2235 And all torattes our men with their reste horses; *scatter; rested*
For they see their cheftain be chauffed so sore, *bothered*
They chase and chop down our chevalrous knightes!
Sir Bedvere was borne through and his breste thirled *pierced*
With a burlich brand, brode at the hiltes;
2240 The real rank steel to his herte runnes, *noble stout sword*
And he rushes to the erthe; rewth is the more! *sorrow is the greater*

Then the conquerour took keep and come with his strenghes
To rescue the rich men of the Round Table,
To outraye the Emperour, yif aunter it shew, *outrage; chance*
2245 Even to the egle, and "Arthur!" ascries.
The Emperour then egerly at Arthur he strikes,
Awkward on the umbrere, and egerly him hittes; *Slantwise; visor*

199

The naked sword at the nose noyes him sore;	*annoys*
The blood of the bold king over the breste runnes,	
2250 Bebledde at the brode sheld and the bright mailes!	*Bloodied*
Our bold king bowes the blonk by the bright bridle,	*turns; horse*
With his burlich brand a buffet him reches	*blow; reaches to (gives)*
Through the breny and breste with his bright wepen;	*hauberk*
O slant down fro the slot he slittes him at ones!	*Aslant; base of throat*
2255 Thus endes the Emperour of Arthure handes,	*by*
And all his austeren host there-of were affrayed.	*afraid*

Now they ferk to the firth, a few that are leved,	
For ferdness of our folk, by the fresh strandes;	*fear*
The flowr of our fers men on feraunt steedes	*iron-grey*
2260 Followes frekly on the frekes that frayed was never.	*frightened*
Then the kidd conquerour cries full loud:	
"Cosin of Cornwall, take keep to thyselven	
That no capitain be keeped for none silver,	*preserved*
Ere Sir Kayous dede be cruelly venged!"	*death*

2265 "Nay," says Sir Cador, "so me Crist help!	
There ne is kaiser ne king that under Crist regnes	
That I ne shall kill cold-dede by craft of my handes!"	

There might men see cheftains on chalk-white steedes	
Chop down in the chase chevalry noble,	
2270 Romanes the richest and real kinges,	
Braste with rank steel their ribbes in sonder,	
Braines forbrusten through burnisht helmes,	*burst into pieces*
With brandes forbrittened on brode in the landes;	*battered to death; abroad*
They hewed down hethen men with hilted swordes,	
2275 By hole hundrethes on hie by the holt eves;	*hastily; edges of the wood*
There might no silver them save ne succour their lives,	*ransom*
Sowdan, ne Sarazen, ne senatour of Rome.	

Then releves the renkes of the Round Table,	*rally; warriors*
By the rich river that runnes so fair;	
2280 Lodges them lovely by tho lighte strandes,	*pleasant*
All on lowe in the land, those lordlich bernes.	*on the ground*
They kaire to the carriage and took what them likes,	*go*

200

Camels and cokadrisses and coffers full rich,   *cockatrices (crocodiles)*
Hackes and hackenays and horses of armes,   *Work horses*
2285 Housing and herberage of hethen kinges;   *lodgings*
Them drew out dromedaries of diverse lordes,
Moilles milk-white and marvelous bestes,   *Mules; beasts*
Olfendes and arrabys and olyfauntes noble   *Camels; Arabian horses; elephants*
That are of the Orient with honourable kinges.

2290   But Sir Arthur anon ayeres thereafter   *advances*
Even to the emperour with honourable kinges,
Laght him up full lovelyly with lordlich knightes,
And led him to the layer there the king ligges.   *resting place*
Then harawdes hiely at hest of the lordes,   *heralds quickly; command*
2295 Huntes up the haythemen that on height ligges,   *heathens*
The Sowdan of Surry and certain kinges,
Sixty of the chef senatours of Rome.
Then they buskes and bawmed thir burlich kinges,   *embalmed; these strong*
Sewed them in sendell sixty-fold after,   *fine linen*
2300 Lapped them in lede, less that they sholde   *Wrapped; lead*
Change or chauffe yif they might escheve [1]
Closed in kestes clene unto Rome,   *enclosed in chests*
With their banners aboven, their badges there-under,
In what countree they kaire, that knightes might know
2305 Ech king by his colours, in kith where he lenged.

          Anon on the second day, soon by the morn,   *immediately at dawn*
Two senatours there come and certain knightes,
Hoodless fro the hethe, ovre the holt-eves,   *wood's edge*
Bare-foot over the bente with brandes so rich,   *ground*
2310 Bowes to the bold king and biddes him the hiltes.   *offer*
Whether he will hang them or hedde or hold them on life,   *behead*
Kneeled before the conquerour in kirtels alone,   *gowns (i.e., without armor)*
With careful countenaunce they carped these wordes:
"Two senatours we are, thy subjettes of Rome,   *subjects*
2315 That has saved our life by these salt strandes,
Hid us in the high wood through the helping of Crist,

---

[1] *Spoil or rot before they could arrive*

201

	Beseekes thee of succour, as soveraign and lord;	*beseech*
	Graunt us life and limm with liberal herte,	*limb*
	For His love that thee lente this lordship in erthe!"	*granted*

2320	"I graunt," quod the good king, "through grace of myselven;	
	I give you life and limm and leve for to pass,	
	So ye do my message menskfully at Rome,	*Providing; honorably*
	That ilke charge that I you give here before my chef knightes."	

	"Yes," says the senatours, "that shall we ensure,	
2325	Sekerly by our trewthes, thy sayinges to fulfill;	*pledged words*
	We shall let for no lede that lives in erthe,	
	For pope ne for potestate ne prince so noble,	*potentate*
	That ne shall lely in land thy letteres pronounce,	
	For duke ne for douspeer, to die in the pain!"	

2330	Then the bannerettes of Bretain brought them to tents	
	There barbours were boun with basins on loft;	*barbers; ready*
	With warm water, iwis, they wet them full soon;	
	They shoven these shalkes shapely thereafter	*shaved; men; suitably*
	To reckon these Romanes recreant and yelden	*mark; surrendered*
2335	Forthy shove they them to shew for skomfit of Rome.	*shaved; discomfiture*
	They coupled the kestes on camelles belive,	*chests; quickly*
	On asses and arrabyes, these honourable kinges;	*Arabian horses*
	The Emperour for honour all by him one,	
	Even upon an olyfaunt, his egle out over;	*elephant*
2340	Bekend them the captives, the king did himselven,	*Entrusted them to*
	And all before his keen men carped these wordes:	
	"Here are the kestes," quod the king, "kaire over the mountes,	*chests*
	Mette full monee that ye have mikel yerned,	*Measured; money; much*
	The tax and the tribute of ten score winteres	
2345	That was teenfully tint in time of our elders;	*painfully lost*
	Say to the senatour the citee that yemes	*controls*
	That I send him the sum; assay how him likes!	
	But bid them never be so bold, whiles my blood regnes	*family*
	Eft for to brawl them for my brode landes,	*Again*
2350	Ne to ask tribute ne tax by nokin title,	*no kind of*
	But such tresure as this, whiles my time lastes."	

	Now they raik to Rome the rediest wayes	*quickest*
	Knelles in the Capitol and commouns assembles,	*Ring bells*
	Soveraignes and senatours the citee that yemes,	*rule*
2355	Bekend them the carriage, kestes and other,	*Gave; baggage, chests*
	Als the conquerour commaunde with cruel wordes:	
	"We have trustily travailed this tribute to fetch,	*worked*
	The tax and the trewage of foure score winteres,	*tribute*
	Of England, of Ireland and all thir out-iles,	*those; outer isles*
2360	That Arthur in the Occident occupies at ones.	
	He biddes you never be so bold whiles his blood regnes	
	To brawl you for Bretain ne his brode landes,	
	Ne ask him tribute ne tax by nokins title	*no kind of*
	But such tresure as this, whiles his time lastes.	
2365	We have foughten in Fraunce and us is foul happened,	
	And all our much fair folk fey are beleved;	
	Eschaped there ne chevalry ne cheftaines nother,	*escaped; neither*
	But chopped down in the chase, such chaunce is befallen!	
	We rede ye store you of stone and stuffen your walles;	
2370	You wakens wandreth and war; be ware if you likes!"	*awaken trouble*

	In the kalendes of May this case is befallen;	*first day*
	The roy real renowned with his Round Table	
	On the coste of Constantine by the clere strandes	*Cotentin*
	Has the Romanes rich rebuked for ever!	

2375	When he had foughten in Fraunce and the feld wonnen	
	And fersely his fomen felld out of life,	*felled*
	He bides for the burying of his bold knightes,	
	That in batail with brandes were brought out of life.	
	He buries at Bayonne Sir Bedwere the rich;	
2380	The corse of Kayous the keen at Came is beleved,	*Caen; left*
	Covered with a crystal clenly all over;	
	His fader conquered that kith knightly with handes.	
	Senn in Burgoine he badde to bury mo knightes,	*Burgundy; abode; more*
	Sir Berade and Bawdwyne, Sir Bedwar the rich,	
2385	Good Sir Cador at Came, as his kind askes.	*Caen; race requires*

| | Then Sir Arthur anon in the Auguste thereafter, | *Autumn* |
| | Enteres to Almaine with hostes arrayed, | *Germany* |

203

	Lenges at Lusheburgh to lechen his knightes,	*Luxembourg; heal*
	With his lele lege-men as lord in his owen;	*own (realm)*
2390	And on Cristofer day a counsel he holdes	*July 25*
	With kinges and kaisers, clerkes and other,	
	Commaundes them keenly to cast all their wittes	
	How he may conquer by craft the kith that he claimes;	
	But the conquerour keen, courtais and noble,	
2395	Carpes in the counsel these knightly wordes:	
	"Here is a knight in these cleves, enclosed with hilles,	*valleys*
	That I have covet to know because of his wordes,	*desire*
	That is Lorraine the lele, I keep not to laine.	*take care not to deceive*
	The lordship is lovely, as ledes me telles;	*men*
2400	I will that duchy devise and dele as me likes,	*divide; deal out*
	And senn dress with the duke, if destainy suffer;	*deal; destiny allow*
	The renk rebel has been unto my Round Table,	
	Redy ay with Romanes to riot my landes.	*to ravage*
	We shall reckon full rathe, if resoun so happen,	
2405	Who has right to that rent, by rich God of heven!	
	Then will I by Lumbardy, likand to shew,	*pleasing to see*
	Set law in the land that last shall ever,	
	The tyrauntes of Tuskan tempest a little,	*Tuscany; trouble*
	Talk with the temporal, whiles my time lastes;	*temporal lords (lay rulers)*
2410	I give my protection to all the pope landes,	
	My rich pensel of pees my pople to shew.	*pennant; peace*
	It is a folly to offend our fader under God	*father*
	Other Peter or Paul, tho postles of Rome;	*Either; apostles*
	If we spare the spiritual we speed but the better;	*succeed*
2415	Whiles we have for to speke, spill shall it never!"[1]	

	Now they speed at the spurres withouten speche more,	
	To the march of Meyes, these manlich knightes,	*region; Metz; manly*
	That is in Lorraine alosed as London is here,	*praised*
	Citee of that seinour that soveraign is holden.	*lord*
2420	The king ferkes forth on a fair steed	
	With Ferrer and Ferawnte and other four knightes;	
	About the citee tho seven they sought at the next,	*nearest (way)*

---

[1] *While I have power to speak, the Church's possessions shall never be harmed*

204

	To seek them a seker place to set with engines.	*secure; siege engines*
	Then they bended in burgh bowes of vise,	*town cross bows*
2425	Bekers at the bold king with bustous lates,	*Shoot; hostile expressions*
	Allblawsters at Arthur egerly shootes	*Arbalasters (crossbowmen)*
	For to hurt him or his horse with that hard wepen.	
	The king shunt for no shot ne no sheld askes,	*hangs back*
	But shews him sharply in his sheen weedes,	
2430	Lenges all at leisere and lookes on the walles	*leisure*
	Where they were lowest the ledes to assail.	

	"Sir," said Sir Ferrer, "a folly thou workes,	
	Thus naked in thy noblay to nighe to the walles,	*nobleness*
	Singly in thy surcote this citee to reche	*surcoat (i.e., without armor)*
2435	And shew thee within there to shend us all;	*to those within; shame*
	Hie us hastily henne or we mon foul happen,	*hence; must*
	For hit they thee or thy horse, it harmes for ever!"	

	"If thou be ferde," quod the king, "I rede thee ride utter,	*further back*
	Less that they rew thee with their round wepen.	*lest; harm*
2440	Thou art but a fauntekein, no ferly me thinkes!	*baby; wonder*
	Thou will be flayed for a fly that on thy flesh lightes!	
	I am nothing aghast, so me God help!	*afraid*
	Though such gadlinges be greved, it greves me but little;	*worthless men*
	They win no worship of me, but wastes their tackle;	*equipment*
2445	They shall want ere I wend, I wagen mine heved!	*lack (equipment); wager*
	Shall never harlot have happe, through help of my Lord,	*rascal; fortune*
	To kill a crownd king with crisom annointed!"	*holy oil*

	Then come the herbariours, harageous knightes,	*scouts; violent*
	The hole batailes on hie harraunt thereafter,	*in haste shouting*
2450	And our forreours fers upon fele halfes	*forragers; many sides*
	Come flyand before on feraunt steedes,	*iron-grey*
	Ferkand in array, thir real knightes,	*Going; these*
	The renkes renowned of the Round Table!	
	All the frek men of Fraunce followed thereafter,	
2455	Fair fitted on front and on the feld hoves.	
	Then the shalkes sharply shiftes their horses,	*men*
	To shewen them seemly in their sheen weedes;	
	Buskes in batail with banners displayed,	

205

	With brode sheldes enbraced and burlich helmes,	*on their arms; stately*
2460	With penouns and pensells of ilke prince armes,	*pennons; pennants*
	Apparelled with perry and precious stones;	*pearls*
	The launces with loraines and lemand sheldes,	*pennons; shining*
	Lightenand as the levening and lemand all over;	*Flashing; lightning; gleaming*
	Then the pris men prikes and proves their horses,	
2465	Satilles to the citee upon sere halves;	*Converge on; many*
	Enserches the suburbes sadly thereafter,	*Search; carefully*
	Discoveres of shot-men and skirmish a little,	*archers*
	Scares their skotifers and their scout-watches	*shield bearers; guards*
	Brittenes their barrers with their bright wepens,	*barriers*
2470	Bette down a barbican and the bridge winnes;	*Beat; main gate tower*
	Ne had the garnison been good at the grete gates,	*Had not; garrison*
	They had won that wonne by their owen strenghe!	*dwelling; own*

	Then with-drawes our men and dresses them better,	
	For drede of the draw-bridge dashed in-sonder; [1]	
2475	Hies to the herberage there the king hoves	*lodging*
	With his batail on high, horsed on steedes.	
	Then was the prince purveyed and their places nomen,	
	Pight paviliouns of pall and plattes in sege. [2]	
	Then lenge they lordly as them lef thought,	*as seemed good to them*
2480	Watches in ilke ward, as to the war falles,	
	Settes up sodenly certain engines.	*siege engines*

	On Sononday by the sun has a flethe yolden, [3]	
	The king calles on Florent, that flowr was of knightes:	*king [of Lorraine]*
	"The Fraunchmen enfeebleshes; ne ferly me thinkes!	*grow feeble; no wonder*
2485	They are unfonded folk in tho fair marches,	*untried (i.e., weakened)*
	For them wantes the flesh and food that them likes.	*is lacking to them*
	Here are forestes fair upon fele halves,	
	And thider fomen are fled with freelich bestes.	*noble beasts*
	Thou shall founde to the felle and forray the mountes:	*go; mountains; forage*
2490	Sir Ferawnte and Sir Floridas shall follow thy bridle.	

---

[1] *For fear of being dashed asunder by the draw bridge*

[2] *Pitched tents of silk and placed (themselves) in siege*

[3] *On Sunday by the time the sun gave out a flood of light*

Us moste with some fresh mete refresh our pople   *we must*
That are fed in the firth with the fruit of the erthe.
There shall wend to this viage Sir Gawain himselven,   *journey*
Warden full worshipful, and so him well seemes;
2495   Sir Wecharde, Sir Walter, these worshipful knightes,
With all the wisest men of the west marches,
Sir Clegis, Sir Claribald, Sir Cleremond the noble,
The Capitain of Cardiff, clenlich arrayed.
Go now, warn all the watch, Gawain and other,
2500   And wendes forth on your way withouten mo wordes."

    Now ferkes to the firth these fresh men of armes,
To the felle so fawe, these freshlich bernes,   *mountain; colorful; eager*
Through hoppes and hemland, hilles and other,   *valleys; borderland*
Holtes and hore woodes with heslin shawes,   *gray; hazel copses*
2505   Through morass and moss and mountes so high,
And in the misty morning on a mede falles,   *meadow*
Mowen and unmade, mainovred but little, [1]
In swathes sweppen down, full of sweet flowres;
There unbridels these bold and baites their horses.   *graze*
2510   To the gryging of the day that birdes gan sing   *dawning; did*
Whiles the sours of the sun, that sande is of Crist,   *rising; messenger*
That solaces all sinful that sight has in erthe.

    Then wendes out the warden, Sir Gawain himselven,
Als he that wise was and wight, wonders to seek;
2515   Then was he ware of a wye, wonder well armed,
Baitand on a water bank by the wood eves,   *Grazing his horse*
Busked in breny bright to behold,
Enbraced a brode sheld on a blonk rich,   *Holding on his arm; horse*
Withouten any berne, but a boy one   *servant*
2520   Hoves by him on a blonk and his spere holdes.
He bore gessenande in gold three grayhoundes of sable,   *couchant*
With chappes and chaines of chalk-white silver,   *jowls; collars*

---

[1] *(The hay) mown and unstacked, worked over but little, / In rows of cuttings swept down, full of sweet flowers*

A charbocle in the chef, changand of hewes, [1]
And a chef aunterous, challenge who likes.

2525	Sir Gawain gliftes on the gome with a glad will;	*looks; man*
	A grete spere from his groom he grippes in handes,	
	Girdes even over the streme on a steed rich	*Goes right*
	To that steren in stour on strenghe there he hoves, [2]	
	Egerly on English "Arthur!" he ascries.	
2530	The tother irously answers him soon	*other*
	On the lange of Lorraine with a loud steven	*language; voice*
	That ledes might listen the lenghe of a mile:	*hear; length*
	"Whider prikes thou, pilour, that proffers so large?	*spur; soldier*
	Here pickes thou no prey, proffer when thee likes,	
2535	But thou in this peril put of the better,	*Unless; i.e., fight better*
	Thou shall be my prisoner for all thy proud lates!"	*appearance*

	"Sir," says Sir Gawain, "so me God help,	
	Such glaverand gomes greves me but little!	*chattering*
	But if thou graithe thy gere thee will gref happen	*prepare; gear*
2540	Ere thou go of this greve, for all thy grete wordes!"	*from; grove*

	Then their launces they latchen, these lordlich bernes,	*seize*
	Laggen with long speres on liard steedes,	*lay on; gray*
	Coupen at aunter by craftes of armes	*Strike at random*
	Til both the cruel speres brusten at ones;	*break*
2545	Through sheldes they shot and sheered through mailes,	*cut*
	Both sheer through sholders a shaft-monde large.	*span (six inches) deep*
	Thus worthily these wyes wounded are bothen;	
	Ere they wreke them of wrath away will they never.	
	Then they raght in the rein and again rides,	*pulled*
2550	Redily these rathe men rushes out swordes,	*hasty*
	Hittes on helmes full hertilich dintes,	
	Hewes on hawberkes with full hard wepens!	
	Full stoutly they strike, thir steren knightes,	*these*

---

[1] *A carbuncle is in the chef (upper third of the shield), changing in colors, / And (he was) an adventurous chief, challenge him who will*

[2] *To that man, steadfast in battle, strongly he stands*

208

	Stokes at the stomach with steelen pointes,	*Thrust*
2555	Fighten and flourish with flamand swordes,	
	Til the flawes of fire flames on their helmes.	*gusts*

	Then Sir Gawain was greved and grouched full sore;	*angered*
	With Galuth his good sword grimly he strikes,	
	Clef the knightes sheld clenlich in sonder.	*Cleaved*
2560	Who lookes to the left side, when his horse launches,	
	With the light of the sun men might see his liver.	
	Then grones the gome for gref of his woundes,	*groans*
	And girdes at Sir Gawain as he by glentes,	*strikes; goes*
	And awkward egerly sore he him smites;	*slantwise*
2565	An alet enameld he oches in sonder,	*shoulder plate; hacks*
	Bristes the rerebrace with the brand rich,	*upper-arm plate*
	Carves off at the coutere with the clene edge	*elbow piece*
	Anentis the avawmbrace vailed with silver; [1]	
	Through a double vesture of velvet rich	
2570	With the venomous sword a vein has he touched	
	That voides so violently that all his wit changed;	*empties*
	The vesar, the aventail, his vestures rich	*visor, lower face-guard*
	With a valiant blood was verred all over.	*spotted*

	Then this tyraunt tite turnes the bridle,	*quickly*
2575	Talkes untenderly and says: "Thou art touched!	
	Us bus have a blood-band ere thy blee change! [2]	
	For all the barbours of Bretain shall not thy blood staunch,	*barbers (surgeons)*
	For he that is blemist with this brode brande blinne shall he never! [3]	

	"Ya," quod Sir Gawain, "thou greves me but little.	
2580	Thou weenes to glopin me with thy grete wordes;	*think to terrify*
	Thou trowes with thy talking that my herte talmes;	*suppose; falters*
	Thou betides torfer ere thou henne turn	*trouble; hence*
	But thou tell me tite and tarry no lenger	*quickly*
	What may staunch this blood that thus fast runnes."	

---

[1] *Near the lower arm plate, veiled with silver*

[2] *We must have a bandage, ere your color changes*

[3] *For he who is wounded with this broad sword shall never cease bleeding!*

2585   "Yis, I say thee soothly and seker thee my trewth,   *pledge my word to you*
        No surgeon in Salerne shall save thee the better,   *(see note)*
        With-thy that thou suffer me for sake of thy Crist   *Providing; allow*
        To shew shortly my shrift and shape me for mine end."   *confession; prepare*

        "Yis," quod Sir Gawain, "so me God help,
2590   I give thee grace and graunt, though thou have gref served, [1]
        With-thy thou say me sooth what thou here seekes,   *Providing*
        Thus singly and sulain all thyself one,   *alone*
        And what lay thou leves on — laine not the sooth —   *religion; believe; hide*
        And what legeaunce and land and where thou art lord."   *allegiance*

2595   "My name is Sir Priamus, a prince is my fader,   *father*
        Praised in his partyes with proved kinges;   *country; experienced*
        In Rome there he regnes he is rich holden;
        He has been rebel to Rome and ridden their landes,
        Warrayand wisely winters and yeres   *Waging war*
2600   By wit and by wisdom and by wight strenghe
        And by worshipful war his owen has he won.
        He is of Alexander blood, overling of kinges;   *overlord*
        The uncle of his aiele, Sir Ector of Troy.   *grandfather; Hector*
        And here is the kinreden that I am of come,   *family*
2605   Of Judas and Josue, these gentle knightes;   *Judas Maccabeus; Joshua*
        I am apparent his eier, and eldes of other;   *his heir apparent*
        Of Alexandere and Afrike and all tho out-landes   *Alexandria*
        I am in possession and plenerly sesed.   *fully in possession*
        In all the pris citees that to the port longes
2610   I shall have trewly the tresure and the landes
        And both tribute and tax whiles my time lastes.
        I was so hautain of herte whiles I at home lenged   *haughty*
        I held none my hip-height under heven rich;   *as tall as my hip*
        For-thy was I sent hider with seven score knightes
2615   To assay of this war by sente of my fader;   *experience; assent*
        And I am for surquidrie shamely surprised   *pride shamefully captured*
        And by aunter of armes outrayed for ever!   *disgraced*
        Now have I told thee the kin that I of come,

---

[1] *I give you grace and grant you your life, though you have deserved grief*

Will thou for knighthede ken me thy name?" *knighthood*

2620 "By Crist," quod Sir Gawain, "knight was I never!
With the kidd conquerour a knave of his chamber *servant*
Has wrought in his wardrope winters and yeres *wardrobe*
On his long armour that him best liked;
I poine all his paviliouns that to himselve pendes, *pitch; tents; belong*
2625 Dightes his doublettes for dukes and erles, *Put on*
Aketouns avenaunt for Arthur himselven *Padded jackets seemly*
That he has used in war all these eight winter!
He made me yomen at Yole and gave me grete giftes, *yeoman (free man); Yule*
An hundreth pound, and a horse, and harness full rich."

2630 "Yif I hap to my hele that hende for to serve [1]
I be holpen in haste, I hete thee for-sooth!
If his knaves be such, his knightes are noble!
There is no king under Crist may kempe with him one! *battle*
He will be Alexander eier that all the world louted, *bowed to*
2635 Abler than ever was Sir Ector of Troy!
Now for the crisom that thou caught that day thou was cristened, *holy oil*
Whether thou be knight or knave knowe now the sooth." *acknowledge*

"My name is Sir Gawain, I graunt thee for-sooth
Cosin to the conquerour, he knowes it himselven, *acknowledges*
2640 Kidd in his kalender a knight of his chamber, *records*
And rolled the richest of all the Round Table! *recorded as*
I am the douspeer and duke he dubbed with his handes
Daintily on a day before his dere knightes;
Grouch not, good sir, though me this grace happen; *Grudge*
2645 It is the gift of God; the gree is his owen!" *reward*

"Peter!" says Priamus, "now payes me better *[it] pleases*
Than I of Provence were prince and of Paris rich!

---

[1] *If I have the good luck, for my recovery, to serve that noble (Arthur), / I will be quickly cured, I tell thee truly*

For me were lever privily be priked to the herte[1]
Than ever any priker had such a prise wonnen.

2650	But here is herberd at hand in yon huge holtes,	*lodged; woods*
	Hole batailes on high, take heed if thee like!	
	The Duke of Lorraine the derf and his dere knightes,	*cruel*
	The doughtiest of Dolfinede and Dutch-men many,	*Dauphine (in France)*
	The lordes of Lumbardy that leders are holden,	*leaders*
2655	The garnison of Goddard gaylich arrayed,	*garrison; Mt. Goddard*
	The wyes of the Westfale, worshipful bernes,	*Westphalia*
	Of Sessoine and Suryland Sarazenes ynow;	*Saxony; Syria*
	They are numbered full nigh and named in rolles	
	Sixty thousand and ten, for sooth, of seker men of armes;	
2660	But if thou hie fro this hethe, it harmes us bothe,	*Unless*
	And but my hurtes be soon holpen, hole be I never!	*helped; whole (healthy)*
	Take heed to this hansemen, that he no horn blow,	*servant (henchman)*
	Or thou hiely in haste bes hewen all to peces,	*quickly; will be; pieces*
	For they are my retinues to ride where I will;	
2665	Is none redier renkes regnand in erthe;	
	Be thou raght with that rout, thou rides no further,	*If you are seized by*
	Ne thou bes never ransouned for riches in erthe!"	

	Sir Gawain went ere the wathe come where him best liked,	*trouble*
	With this worthilich wye that wounded was sore,	
2670	Merkes to the mountain there our men lenges	*Goes*
	Baitand their blonkes there on the brode mede,	*Grazing; mead*
	Lordes lenand low on lemand sheldes,	*leaning; gleaming*
	With loud laughters on loft for liking of birdes,	
	Or larkes, of linkwhites, that lovelich songen;	*linnets*
2675	And some was sleght on sleep with slight of the pople[2]	
	That sang in the sesoun in the sheen shawes,	*season; shrubs*
	So low in the laundes so likand notes.	*hills; pleasing*
	Then Sir Wicher was ware their warden was wounded	*aware*
	And went to him weepand and wringand his handes;	

---

[1] *I would rather be stabbed to the heart in private / Than to have an ordinary soldier win such a prize*

[2] *And some had fallen asleep because of the skillful singing of the creatures*

2680 Sir Wecharde, Sir Walter, these wise men of armes
     Had wonder of Sir Wawain and went him againes,   *toward*
     Met him in the mid-way and marvel them thought
     How he mastered that man, so mighty of strenghes.
     By all the welth of the world so wo was them never: *wealth*
2685 "For all our worship, iwis, away is in erthe!"

     "Greve you not," quod Gawain, "for Goddes love of heven,
     For this is but gosesomer and given on erles;   *gossamer; to be expected*
     Though my shoulder be shrede and my sheld thirled,   *cut; pierced*
     And the weld of mine arm workes a little,   *movement; hurts*
2690 This prisoner, Sir Priamus, that has perilous woundes,
     Says that he has salves shall soften us bothen."

     Then stertes to his stirrup sterenfull knightes,   *stern*
     And he lordly alightes and laght off his bridle,   *pulled*
     And let his burlich blonk baite on the flowres,   *graze*
2695 Braides off his bacenett and his rich weedes,   *Draws; helmet*
     Bounes to his brode sheld and bowes to the erthe;   *Leans on*
     In all the body of that bold is no blood leved!
     Then presses to Sir Priamus precious knightes,
     Avisely of his horse hentes him in armes   *Carefully off; take*
2700 His helm and his hawberk they taken off after,
     And hastely for his hurt all his herte changed;
     They laid him down in the laundes and laght off his weedes,   *lawn*
     And he lened him on long or how him best liked.   *leaned (stretched out)*
     A foil of fine gold they fande at his girdle,   *found*
2705 That is full of the flowr of the four welle
     That flowes out of Paradise when the flood rises,
     That much fruit of falles that feed shall us all;
     Be it frette on his flesh there sinews are entamed,   *rubbed; where; cut*
     The freke shall be fish-hole within four houres.   *fit as a fish*
2710 They uncover that corse with full clene handes,
     With clere water a knight clenses their woundes,
     Keled them kindly and comforted their hertes;   *Cooled*
     And when the carves were clene they cledde them again.   *wounds; clad*
     Barrel-ferrers they broched and brought them the wine,   *Wine casks; broke open*
2715 Both brede and brawn and bredes full rich;   *roast; lean meat; breads*
     When they had eten anon they armed after.   *eaten*

213

Then tho auntrend men *"As armes!"* ascries,   *those adventuring; To arms!*
With a clarioun clere thir knightes togeder   *trumpet; these*
Calles to counsel and of this case telles:
2720 "Yonder is a company of clene men of armes,
The keenest in contek that under Crist lenges;   *strife*
In yon oken wood an host are arrayed,   *oak*
Under-takand men of these oute-landes,   *Determined*
As says Sir Priamus, so help Saint Peter!
2725 Go men," quod Gawain, "and grope in your hertes   *search*
Who shall graithe to yon greve to yon grete lordes;   *wood*
If we get-less go home, the king will be greved   *empty-handed*
And say we are gadlinges, aghast for a little.   *worthless men*
We are with Sir Florent, as to-day falles,
2730 That is flowr of Fraunce, for he fled never;
He was chosen and charged in chamber of the king
Cheftain of this journee, with chevalry noble;
Whether he fight or he flee we shall follow after;
For all the fere of yon folk forsake shall I never!"   *fear*

2735 "Fader," says Sir Florent, "full fair ye it tell!   *Father (i.e., Sir)*
But I am but a fauntekin, unfraisted in armes;   *infant; untested*
If any folly befall the faut shall be ours   *fault*
And fremedly o Fraunce be flemed for ever!   *hostilely; chased*
Woundes not your worship, my wit is but simple,
2740 Ye are our warden, iwis; work as you likes."

"Ye are at the ferrest not passand five hundreth,   *(Priamus speaks); most*
And that is fully too few to fight with them all,
For harlottes and hansemen shall help but little;   *rascals; servants*
They will hie them henn for all their grete wordes!   *hence*
2745 I rede ye work after wit, as wise men of armes,   *according to*
And warpes wilily away, as worshipful knightes."   *go with wile*

"I graunt," quod Sir Gawain, "so me God help!
But here are some galiard gomes that of the gree serves,   *deserve a reward*
The cruelest knightes of the kinges chamber,
2750 That can carp with the cup knightly wordes;
We shall prove today who shall the prise win!"   *prize*

	Now forreours fers unto the firth rides	*foragers*
	And fanges a fair feld and on foot lightes,	*take*
	Prikes after the prey, as pris men of armes,	
2755	Florent and Floridas, with five score knightes,	
	Followed in the forest and on the way foundes,	
	Flingand a fast trot and on the folk drives.	*Dashing at*
	Then followes fast to our folk well a five hundreth	
	Of frek men to the firth upon fresh horses;	
2760	One Sir Feraunt before, upon a fair steed,	
	Was fostered in Famacoste; the fend was his fader;	*Famagusta (on Cyprus)*
	He flinges to Sir Florent and prestly he cries:	*quickly*
	"Why flees thou, false knight? The Fend have thy soul!"	
	Then Sir Florent was fain and in fewter castes,	*eager*
2765	On Fawnell of Frisland to Feraunt he rides,	*(his horse)*
	And raght in the rein on the steed rich,	*pulled*
	And rides toward the rout, restes he no lenger!	
	Full butt in the front he flishes him even,	*Smack-dab; forehead; pierces*
	And all disfigures his face with his fell wepen!	*cruel weapon*
2770	Through his bright bacenett his brain has he touched,	*helmet*
	And brusten his neck-bone that all his breth stopped!	*broke; breath*

	Then his cosin ascried and cried full loud:	
	"Thou has killed cold-dede the king of all knightes!	
	He has been fraisted on feld in fifteen rewmes;	*tested*
2775	He fand never no freke might fight with him one!	*found*
	Thou shall die for his dede, with my derf wepen,	
	And all the doughty for dole that in yon dale hoves!"	

	"Fy," says Sir Floridas, "thou fleryand wretch!	*sneering*
	Thou weenes for to flay us, floke-mouthed shrew!"	*twisted-mouthed*
2780	But Floridas with a sword, as he by glentes,	*glides*
	All the flesh of the flank he flappes in sonder	*strikes asunder*
	That all the filth of the freke and fele of his guttes	
	Followes his fole foot when he forth rides!	*horse's*

	Then rides a renk to rescue that berne;	*man; man*
2785	That was Raynald of the Rodes, and rebel to Crist,	*Rhodes*
	Perverted with paynims that Cristen persewes,	*pagans; persecute*
	Presses in proudly as the prey wendes,	

For he had in Prussland much prise wonnen;   *Prussia; praise (prize)*
For-thy in presence there he proffers so large.
2790 But then a renk, Sir Richere of the Round Table,
On a real steed rides him againes;
Through a round red sheld he rushed him soon
That the rosseld spere to his herte runnes!   *tempered*
The renk reeles about and rushes to the erthe,
2795 Rores full rudly but rode he no more!

Now all that is fere and unfey of these five hundreth   *unhurt; alive*
Falles on Sir Florent and five score knightes,
Betwix a plash and a flood, upon a flat land;   *marshy place*
Our folk fangen their feld and fought them againes;   *take*
2800 Then was loud upon loft "Lorraine!" ascried,
When ledes with long speres lashen togeders,   *rush*
And "Arthur!" on our side when them ought ailed.

Then Sir Florent and Floridas in fewter they cast,
Frushen on all the frap and bernes affrayed,   *Rush; company*
2805 Felles five at the front there they first entered
And, ere they ferk further, fele of these other;
Brenyes brouden they briste, brittened sheldes,   *braided*
Betes and beres down the best that them bides;
All that rewled in the rout they riden away,
2810 So rudly they rere, these real knightes!   *rudely; move*

When Sir Priamus, that prince, perceived their gamen,   *sport*
He had pitee in herte that he ne durste proffer;   *dared*
He went to Sir Gawain and says him these wordes:
"Thy pris men for thy prey put are all under;
2815 They are with Sarazenes over-set, mo than seven hundreth
Of the Sowdanes knightes, out of sere landes;
Wolde thou suffer me, sir, for sake of thy Crist   *allow me*
With a sop of thy men suppowel them ones."   *small troop; support*

"I grouch not," quod Gawain, "the gree is their owen;   *grudge; reward*
2820 They mon have guerdons full grete graunt of my lord;   *should; granted by*
But the frek men of Fraunce fraist themselven;   *But let; bold; test*
Frekes fought not their fill this fifteen winter!"

216

I will not stir with my stale half a steed lenghe,   *troop; length*
But they be stedde with more stuff than on yon stede hoves!"   *beset; place*

2825   Then Sir Gawain was ware, withouten the wood-hemmes,
Wyes of the Westfale, upon wight horses,   *Westphalia*
Walopand wodely as the way forthes,   *Galloping madly; goes forth*
With all the wepens, iwis, that to the war longes;
The erl Antele the old the avauntward he buskes,   *vanguard*
2830   Ayerand on either hand eight thousand knightes;   *Coming*
His pelours and pavisers passed all in number   *bowmen; shield bearers*
That ever any prince lede purveyed in erthe!   *princely*

Then the Duke of Lorraine dresses thereafter
With double of the Dutch-men that doughty were holden,   *double the number*
2835   Paynims of Prussland, prikers full noble,   *Pagans*
Come prikand before with Priamus knightes.
Then said the erl Antele to Algere his brother:
"Me angers ernestly at Arthures knightes,
Thus enkerly on an host aunters themselven!   *Who thus eagerly*
2840   They will be outrayed anon, ere undron ring,   *undern (9 a.m.)*
Thus foolily on a feld to fight with us all!   *foolishly*
But they be fesed, in fey, ferly me thinkes; [1]
Wolde they purpose take and pass on their wayes,
Prik home to their prince and their prey leve,
2845   They might lenghen their life and losen but little,   *lengthen; lose*
It wolde lighten my herte, so help me our Lord!"

"Sir," says Sir Algere, "they have little used
To be outrayed with host; me angers the more!
The fairest shall be full fey that in our flock rides,
2850   Als few as they ben, ere they the feld leve!"   *be*

Then good Gawain, gracious and noble,
All with glorious glee he gladdes his knightes:
"Glopins not, good men, for glitterand sheldes,   *Fear*
Though yon gadlinges be gay on yon grete horses!   *worthless men*

---

[1] *If they are not defeated, in faith, it would seem to me a great wonder*

2855	Bannerettes of Bretain, buskes up your hertes!	*buck up*
	Bes not baist of yon boyes ne of their bright weedes!	*Be; abashed by; knaves*
	We shall blenke their boste, for all their bold proffer,	*weaken; boast*
	Als buxom as bird is in bed to her lord!	*submissive; maid*
	Yif we fight today, the feld shall be ours,	
2860	The fekil fey shall fail and falssede be destroyed!	*false of faith; falsehood*
	Yon folk is on frontere, unfraisted them seemes;	*in front untested*
	They make faith and faye to the Fend selven!	*belief*
	We shall in this viage victores be holden	*engagement*
	And avaunted with voices of valiant bernes,	*praised by*
2865	Priased with princes in presence of lordes	
	And loved with ladies in diverse landes!	
	Ought never such honour none of our elders,	*Possessed*
	Unwine ne Absolon ne none of these other!	
	When we are most in distress Marie we mene	*pray to*
2870	That is our master's saine that he much traistes,	*saint; trusts*
	Meles of that milde queen that menskes us all;	*Speaks; dignifies*
	Who-so meles of that maid, miscarries he never!"	
	By these wordes were said they were not fer behind,	*By the time that*
	But the lenghe of a land and "Lorraine!" ascries;	*length of the field*
2875	Was never such a jousting at journee in erthe	
	In the vale of Josephate, as gestes us telles,	*tales*
	When Julius and Joatelle were judged to die,	
	As was when the rich men of the Round Table	
	Rushed into the rout on real steedes,	
2880	For so rathely they rush with rosseld speres	*swiftly; tempered*
	That the rascal was rade and ran to the greves,	*fearful; woods*
	And kaired to that court as cowardes for ever!	
	"Peter!" says Sir Gawain, "this gladdes mine herte,	*gladdens*
	That yon gadlinges are gone that made grete number!	*worthless fellows*
2885	I hope that these harlottes shall harm us but little,	*suppose; low fellows*
	For they will hide them in haste in yon holt eves;	
	They are fewer on feld than they were first numbered	
	By fourty thousand, in faith, for all their fair hostes."	
	But one Jolyan of Gene, a giaunt full huge,	
2890	Has joined on Sir Gerard, a justice of Wales;	*judge*

Through a jerownde sheld he jagges him through, *gyronny; stabs*
And a fine gesseraunt of gentle mailes; *coat of mail*
Jointer and gemous he jagges in sonder! *Joint; clasp*
On a jambe steed this journee he makes; *swift*
2895 Thus is the giaunt for-jouste, that erraunt Jew, *outjousted; wandering*
And Gerard is jocound and joyes him the more.

Then the genatours of Gene enjoines at ones *horse soldiers; Genoa*
And ferkes on the frontere well a five hundreth; *front rank*
A freke hight Sir Frederik with full fele other *named*
2900 Ferkes on a frush and freshlich ascries *charge; eagerly*
To fight with our forreours that on feld hoves; *foragers*
And then the real renkes of the Round Table
Rode forth full ernestly and rides them againes,
Melles with the middle-ward, but they were ill-matched; *Meddles; middle guard*
2905 Of such a grete multitude was marvel to here.
Senn at the assemblee the Sarazenes discoveres
The soveraign of Sessoine that salved was never; *saved*
Giauntes for-jousted with gentle knightes *outjousted by*
Through gesserauntes of Gene jagged to the herte! *hauberks; Genoa*
2910 They hew through helmes hautain bernes, *haughty*
That the hilted swordes to their hertes runnes!
Then the renkes renowned of the Round Table
Rives and rushes down renayed wretches; *renegade*
And thus they driven to the dede dukes and erles *death*
2915 All the dregh of the day, with dredful workes! *length*

Then Sir Priamus the prince, in presence of lordes,
Presses to his penoun and pertly it hentes, *pennon; openly*
Reverted it redily and away rides *reversed*
To the real rout of the Round Table;
2920 And hiely his retinue raikes him after, *quickly; rushes*
For they his resoun had redde on his sheld rich. *reason (intent); read*
Out of the sheltron they shed as sheep of a fold, *poured; from*
And steeres forth to the stour and stood by their lord.
Senn they sent to the duke and said him these wordes:
2925 "We have been thy soudeours these six yere and more; *mercenaries*
We forsake thee today by sert of our lord. *feudal service*
We sew to our soveraign in sere kinges landes; *follow*

219

Us defautes our fee of this four winteres.   *We lack our pay*

Thou art feeble and false and nought but fair wordes;

2930   Our wages are wered out and thy war ended;   *worn*

We may with worship wend whither us likes!

I rede thou trete of a trewe and troufle no lenger,   *truce; trifle*

Or thou shall tinne of thy tale ten thousand ere even."   *lose; number (tally)*

"*Fy a diables!*" said the duke, "the Devil have your bones!"   *Devil take you*

2935   The daunger of yon dogges drede shall I never!

We shall dele this day, by deedes of armes,   *bargain for*

My dede and my duchery and my dere knightes;   *dukedom*

Such soudeours as ye I set but at little,   *mercenaries; reckon*

That sodenly in defaut forsakes their lord!"   *despite obligation*

2940   The duke dresses in his sheld and dreches no lenger,   *delays*

Drawes him a dromedary with dredful knightes;

Graithes to Sir Gawain with full grete number   *Confronts*

Of gomes of Gernaide that grevous are holden.   *Granada*

Those fresh horsed men to the front rides,

2945   Felles of our forreours by fourty at ones!   *foragers*

They had foughten before with a five hundreth;

It was no ferly, in faith, though they faint waxen.   *wonder; grow faint*

Then Sir Gawain was greved and grippes his spere,

And girdes in again with galiard knightes,

2950   Meetes the Marches of Meyes and melles him through,   *Marquis of Metz; pierces*

As man of this middle-erthe that most had greved!

But one Chastelayne, a child of the kinges chamber,   *i.e., young man*

Was ward to Sir Wawain of the west marches,

Chases to Sir Cheldrik, a cheftain noble;

2955   With a chasing-spere he shockes him through!   *hunting spear; drives*

This check him escheved by chaunces of armes.   *defeat; achieved*

So they chase that child eschape may he never;   *escape*

But one Swyan of Swecy, with a sword edge,   *Sweden*

The swyers swire-bone he swappes in sonder!   *young noble's neck bone*

2960   He swoonand died and on the swarth lenged,   *turf*

Sweltes even swiftly   and swank he no more!   *Dies; worked*

Then Sir Gawain gretes with his gray eyen;   *weeps*

The guite was a good man, beginnand of armes.   *youth*

220

	For the chery child so his cheer changed	*dear*
2965	That the chilland water on his cheekes runned!	
	"Wo is me," quod Gawain, "that I ne witten had!	*known*
	I shall wage for that wye all that I weld,	*spend*
	But I be wroken on that wye that thus has him wounded!"	*avenged*
	He dresses him drerily and to the duke rides,	
2970	But one Sir Dolphin the derf dight him againes,	*cruel confronted*
	And Sir Gawain him gird with a grim launce	
	That the grounden spere glode to his herte!	*glided*
	And egerly he hent out and hurt another,	*pulled*
	An hethen knight, Hardolf, happy in armes;	*fortunate*
2975	Slyly in at the slot slittes him through	*base of throat*
	That the slidand spere of his hand slippes!	
	There is slain in that slope by sleghte of his handes	*hillside by skill*
	Sixty slongen in a slade of sleghe men of armes!	*slung; ditch; skillful*
	Though Sir Gawain were wo, he waites him by	
2980	And was ware of that wye that the child wounded,	
	And with a sword swiftly he swappes him through,	
	That he swiftly swelt and on the erthe swoones!	
	And then he raikes to the rout and rushes on helmes,	
	Rich hawberkes he rent and rased sheldes;	*destroyed*
2985	Rides on a randoun and his raik holdes;	*swiftly; course*
	Throughout the rereward he holdes wayes,	
	And there raght in the rein, this real the rich,	*powerful nobleman*
	And rides into the rout of the Round Table.	*i.e., back to*
	Then our chevalrous men changen their horses,	
2990	Chases and choppes down cheftaines noble,	
	Hittes full hertely on helmes and sheldes,	
	Hurtes and hewes down hethen knightes!	
	Kettle-hattes they cleve even to the shoulders;	I.e., *kettle-shaped helmets*
	Was never such a clamour of capitaines in erthe!	
2995	There was kinges sonnes caught, courtais and noble,	
	And knightes of the countree that knowen was rich;	
	Lordes of Lorraine and Lumbardy bothen	
	Laght was and led in with our lele knightes.	*Seized*
	Those that chased that day their chaunce was better;	
3000	Such a check at a chase escheved them never!	*victory; achieved*

When Sir Florent by fight had the feld wonnen
He ferkes in before with five score knightes;
Their preyes and their prisoneres passes on after,
With pelours and pavisers and pris men of armes;   *bowmen; shield bearers*
3005 Then goodly Sir Gawain guides his knightes,
Gos in at the gainest, as guides him telles,   *goes; quickest way*
For gref of a garnison of full grete lordes   *fear; troop*
Sholde not grip up his gere ne such gram work;   *booty; mischief*
For-thy they stood at the straightes and with his stale hoved,   *pass*
3010 Til his preyes were past the path that he dredes.

When they the citee might see that the king seged
(Soothly the same day was with assaut wonnen),   *assault*
An heraud hies before at heste of the lordes,   *herald; behest*
Home at the herberage, out of the high landes,   *to; lodgings*
3015 Turnes tite to the tent and to the king telles   *quickly*
All the tale soothly and how they had sped:
"All thy forreours are fere that forrayed withouten,   *foragers; safe*
Sir Florent and Sir Floridas and all thy fers knightes;
They have forrayed and foughten with full grete number
3020 And fele of thy fo-men has brought out of life!
Our worshipful warden is well escheved,   *has well succeeded*
For he has won today worship for ever;
He has Dolphin slain and the duke taken!   *Dauphin*
Many doughty is dede by dint of his handes!
3025 He has prisoners pris, princes and erles,
Of the richest blood that regnes in erthe;
All thy chevalrous men fair are escheved,
But a child, Chastelain, mischaunce has befallen."

"Hautain," says the king, "heraud, by Crist,   *Valiant man; herald*
3030 Thou has heled mine herte, I hete thee for-sooth!   *healed; promise*
I give thee in Hampton a hundreth pound large!"   *(see note)*

The king then to assaut he sembles his knightes   *assault*
With somercastel and sowe upon sere halves,   *moveable towers; shelters*
Shiftes his skotiferes and scales the walles,   *Moves about; shield bearers*
3035 And ech watch has his ward with wise men of armes.   *division; guard*
Then boldly they busk and bendes engines   *catapults*

222

Paises in pillotes and proves their castes.   *Heave; pellets; try*
Ministeres and masondewes they mall to the erthe, [1]
Churches and chapels chalk-white blaunched,   *painted*
3040 Stone steeples full stiff in the street ligges,
Chambers with chimnees and many chef inns,   *chimneys*
Paised and pelled down plastered walles;   *Demolished; struck*
The pine of the pople was pitee for to here!   *pain*

Then the duchess her dight with damesels rich,
3045 The countess of Crasine with her clere maidens,
Kneeles down in the kirnelles there the king hoved,   *battlements*
On a covered horse comlyly arrayed.   *armored*
They knew him by countenaunce and cried full loud:
"King crowned of kind, take keep to these wordes!   *by right; heed*
3050 We beseek you, sir, as soveraign and lord,
That ye save us today, for sake of your Crist!
Send us some succour and saughte with the pople,   *make peace*
Ere the citee be sodenly with assaut wonnen!"   *assault*

He veres his vesar with a vout noble,   *turns up; visor; expression*
3055 With visage virtuous, this valiant berne,
Meles to her mildly with full meek wordes:
"Shall none misdo you, madame, that to me longes;
I give you charter of pees, and your chef maidens,
The childer and the chaste men, the chevalrous knightes;   *i.e., priests*
3060 The duke is in daunger; dredes it but little!   *doubt*
He shall be deemed full well, dout you nought elles."   *fear*

Then sent he on ech a side to certain lordes
For to leve the assaut; the citee was yolden   *yielded*
(With the erle eldest son he sent him the keyes)
3065 And sesed the same night, by sent of the lordes.   *seized; assent*
The duke to Dover is dight and all his dere knightes,
To dwell in daunger and dole the dayes of his life.

There fled at the ferrer gate folk withouten number,   *farther*

---

[1] *Monasteries and hospitals they hammer to earth*

For ferd of Sir Florent and his fers knightes;   *fear*
3070 Voides the citee and to the wood runnes
With vitail and vessel, and vesture so rich;   *victuals; precious vessels*
They busk up a banner aboven the brode gates.
Of Sir Florent, in fay, so fain was he never!   *happy*
The knighte hoves on a hill, beheld the walles,
3075 And said: "I see by yon sign the citee is oures!"
Sir Arthur enters anon with hostes arrayed,
Even at the undron ettles to lenge.   *undern (9 a.m.); intends*
In eche levere on loud the king did cry   *division*
On pain of life and limm and lesing of landes   *limb; loss*
3080 That no lele lege-man that to him longed,
Sholde lie by no ladies, ne by no lele maidens,
Ne by no burgess wife, better ne worse
Ne no bernes misbid that to the burgh longed.   *harm what*

When the king Arthur had lely conquered
3085 And the castel covered of the kith rich,
All the cruel and keen, by craftes of armes,
Capitains and constables, knew him for lord.   *acknowledged*
He devised and delt to diverse lordes   *divided*
A dower for the duchess and her dere childer;   *widow's estate*
3090 Wrought wardenes by wit to weld all the landes   *rule*
That he had wonnen of war through his wise knightes.
Thus in Lorraine he lenges as lord in his owen,
Settes lawes in the land as him lef thought,
And on Lammas day to Lucerne he wendes,   *August 1*
3095 Lenges there at leisere with liking ynow.   *leisure; pleasure*
There his galleys were graithed, a full grete number,   *prepared*
All glitterand as glass, under green hilles,
With cabanes covered for kinges annointed   *cabins*
With clothes of clere gold for knightes and other;
3100 Soon stowed their stuff and stabled their horses,
Strekes streke over the streme into the strait landes.   *Strikes straight; narrow*

Now he moves his might with mirthes of herte
Over mountes so high, those marvelous wayes,
Gos in by Goddard, the garret he winnes,   *Mt. Goddard; watch tower*
3105 Graithes the garnison grisly woundes!   *Deals; garrison*

224

When he was passed the height, then the king hoves
With his hole batail beholdand about,
Lookand on Lumbardy and on loud meles:
"In yon likand land lord be I think!" [1]

3110   Then they kaire to Combe with kinges annointed,   *Como*
        That was kidd of the coste, key of all other.   *i.e., of Lake Como*
        Sir Florent and Sir Floridas then foundes before
        With freke men of Fraunce well a five hundreth;
        To the citee unseen they sought at the gainest,   *quickest way*
3115   And set an enbushment, als themselve likes,   *ambush*
        Then ishewes out of that citee, full soon by the morn;   *issue*
        Sleyly discoverers skiftes their horses;   *Slyly scouts manage*
        Then skiftes these scowerers and skippes on hilles,   *shift; searchers*
        Discoverers for skulkers that they no scathe limpen. [2]
3120   Poverall and pastorelles passed on after   *Poor people; shepherds*
        With porkes to pasture at the pris gates;   *hogs*
        Boyes in the suburbes bourden full high   *Servants; jest*
        At a bore singlere that to the bente runnes.   *wild boar*

        Then brekes our bushment and the bridge winnes,   *breaks out; ambush*
3125   Braides into the burgh with banners displayed,   *Rush*
        Stekes and stabbes through that them again-standes;   *Stick; withstand*
        Four streetes, ere they stint, they stroyed forever!

        Now is the conquerour in Combe and his court holdes   *Como*
        Within the kidd castel with kinges annointed,
3130   Recounseles the commons that to the kith longes,   *Advises*
        Comfortes the care-full with knightly wordes,
        Made a capitain keen a knight of his owen;
        But all the countree and he full soon were accorded.

        The Sire of Milan herde say the citee was wonnen,
3135   And send to Arthur certain lordes,
        Grete summes of gold, sixty horses charged,   *laden*

---

[1] *I intend to be lord of that pleasing land!*

[2] *Scout for those hiding so that no harm may befall them*

225

	Besought him as soveraign to succour the pople,	
	And said he wolde soothly be subjet forever,	*subject*
	And make him service and suite for his sere landes;	*feudal homage*
3140	For Plesaunce, for Pawnce, and for Pownte Tremble,	*(see note)*
	For Pise and for Pavy he proffers full large	*Pisa; Pavia*
	Both purpure and pall and precious stones,	*purple dye; silk*
	Palfreyes for any prince and proved steedes	
	And ilk a yere for Milan a melion of gold,	*million*
3145	Meekly at Martinmas to menske with his hordes,[1]	
	And ever, withouten asking, he and his eiers	
	Be hommagers to Arthur whiles his life lastes.	
	The king by his counsel a condeth him sendes,	*safe conduct*
	And he is comen to Combe and knew him as lord.	*Como; acknowledged*

	Into Tuskane he turnes when thus wel timed,	
3150		
	Takes townes full tite with towres full high;	
	Walles he welt down, wounded knightes,	*knocked*
	Towres he turnes, and tourmentes the pople,	*overturns*
	Wrought widowes full wlonk wrotherayle singen,	*fair misery to sing*
3155	Oft werye and weep and wringen their handes;	*curse*
	And all he wastes with war there he away rides;	
	Their welthes and their wonninges wandreth he wrought!	*dwellings; sadness*

	Thus they springen and sprede and spares but little,	*spread*
	Spoiles dispiteously and spilles their vines,	*Plunder pitilessly; destroy*
3160	Spendes unsparely that spared was long,	*without stinting; saved*
	Speedes them to Spolett with speres ynow!	*Spoletto*
	Fro Spain into Spruysland the word of him springes	*Prussia*
	And spekings of his spenses; despite is full huge.	*talk; spending; bitterness*
	Toward Viterbo this valiant aveeres the reines;	*turns*
3165	Avisely in that vale he vitailes his bernes,	*Shrewdly; victuals*
	With Vernage and other wine and venison baken	*white wine; baked*
	And on the Viscounte landes he vises to lenge.	*Viscount's; determines*
	Vertely the avauntward voides their horses	*Quickly*
	In the Vertenonne vale the vines i-monges;	*among*
3170	There sujournes this soveraign with solace in herte,	

---

[1] *Meekly on St. Martin's Day (November 11) to pay homage with his treasures*

To see when the Senatours sent any wordes,
Revel with rich wine, riotes himselven,   *carouse*
This roy with his real men of the Round Table,   *king*
With mirthes and melody and manykin gamnes;   *many sorts of pleasures*
3175   Was never merrier men made on this erthe!

     But on a Saterday at noon, a seven-night there-after,
The cunningest Cardinal that to the court longed
Kneeles to the conquerour and carpes these wordes,
Prayes him for the pees and proffers full large
3180   To have pitee of the Pope, that put was at-under   *at a disadvantage*
Besought him of suraunce for sake of the Lord   *a truce*
But a seven-night day to they were all sembled   *a week from today; until*
And they sholde sekerly him see the Sononday there-after   *Sunday*
In the citee of Rome, as soveraign and lord,
3185   And crown him kindly with crismed handes   *anointed*
With his sceptre and swerde, as soveraign and lord.
Of this undertaking hostage are comen,   *agreement*
Of eiers full avenaunt, eight score children,   *pleasant*
In togges of tars full richly attired,   *Chinese silk*
3190   And betook them the king and his clere knightes.   *gave them to*

     When they had treted their trewe, with trumping thereafter   *discussed; truce*
They trine unto a tent where tables were raised;   *go*
The king himselven is set and certain lordes
Under a sylure of silk, saught at the bordes.   *canopy; reconciled*
3195   All the senatours are set sere by them one,   *each by himself*
Served solemnly with selcouthe metes.
The king, mighty of mirth, with his mild wordes,
Rehetes the Romanes at his rich table,   *Cheers*
Comfortes the Cardinal, so knightly himselven,
3200   And this roy real, as romaunce us telles,
Reverences the Romans in his rich table.
The taught men and the cunning, when them time thought,
Tas their leve at the king and turned again;   *Take*
To the citee that night they sought at the gainest,
3205   And thus the hostage of Rome with Arthur is leved.

     Then this roy real reherses these wordes: *rehearses (tells)*

227

"Now we may revel and rest, for Rome is our owen!

Make our hostage at ese, these avenaunt children,   *ease; pleasant*

And look ye honden them all that in mine host lenges,   *guard*

3210   The Emperour of Almaine and all these este marches;

We shall be overling of all that on erthe lenges!

We will by the Cross-days encroch these landes   *Sept. 13–14; invade*

And at the Cristenmass day be crowned there-after,

Regne in my realtees and hold my Round Table,

3215   With the rentes of Rome, as me best likes;

Senn graithe over the grete se with good men of armes

To revenge the Renk that on the Rood died!"   *Cross*

Then this comlich king as cronicles telles,

Bounes brothly to bed with a blithe herte;

3220   Off he slinges with sleght and slakes his girdle, [1]

And for slewth of slomour on a sleep falles.   *sloth; slumber*

But by one after midnight all his mood changed;   *1:00 a.m.*

He mette in the morn-while full marvelous dremes;   *dreamed; morning; dreams*

And when his dredful dreme was driven to the ende,

3225   The king dares for doute, die as he sholde,   *cowers in fear*

Sendes after philosophers, and his affray telles: *terror*

"Senn I was formed, in faith, so ferd was I never!

For-thy ransackes redily and rede me my swevenes,   *search; interpret; dreams*

And I shall redily and right rehersen the sooth.   *rehearse (tell)*

3230   "Me thought I was in a wood, willed mine one   *wandered by myself*

That I ne wiste no way whider that I sholde,   *knew; whither; should go*

For wolves and wild swine and wicked bestes

Walked in that wastern wathes to seek,   *waste place prey*

There lions full lothly licked their tuskes   *loathly*

3235   All for lapping of blood of my lele knightes!

Through that forest I fled there flowres were high,

For to fele me for ferd of tho foul thinges,   *hide; fear*

Merked to a medow with mountaines enclosed   *meadow*

The merriest of middle-erthe that men might behold.

3240   The close was in compass casten all about   *enclosed place; extent covered*

---

[1] *He throws himself quickly on the bed and loosens his belt*

228

With clover and clerewort cledde even over; *small grass clad*
The vale was enveround with vines of silver, *encircled*
All with grapes of gold, greter were never,
Enhorild with arbory and alkins trees, *Surrounded; groves; all kinds of*
3245 Erberes full honest, and herdes there-under; *Gardens*
All fruites foddemed was that flourished in erthe, *produced*
Fair frithed in fraunk upon the free bowes; [1]
Was there no danking of dew that ought dere sholde;
With the drought of the day all dry were the flowres.

3250 "Then descendes in the dale, down fro the cloudes,
A duchess dereworthily dight in diapered weedes, *expensively; patterned*
In a surcote of silk full selcouthly hewed, *surcoat; rarely*
All with loyotour overlaid low to the hemmes *otter fur*
And with ladily lappes the lenghe of a yard, *ladylike lappets*
3255 And all redily reversed with rebanes of gold, *trimmed; ribbons*
With brouches and besauntes and other bright stones; *brooches; medallions*
Her back and her breste was broched all over, *adorned*
With kell and with coronal clenlich arrayed, *hairnet; diadem*
And that so comly of colour one knowen was never. *complexion*

3260 "About sho whirled a wheel with her white handes,
Overwhelm all quaintly the wheel, as sho sholde; *Turned skillfully*
The rowel was red gold with real stones, *wheel*
Railed with riches and rubies ynow; *Adorned*
The spekes was splented all with speltes of silver, *spokes; plated; bars*
3265 The space of a spere-lenghe springand full fair; *spear length*
There-on was a chair of chalk-white silver
And checkered with charbocle changing of hewes *carbuncle*
Upon the compass there cleved kinges on row, *outer edge; clung*
With crowns of clere gold that cracked in sonder;
3270 Six was of that settle full sodenlich fallen, *seat*
Ilk a segge by himself and said these wordes: *warrior*
'That ever I regned on this roo me rewes it ever! *wheel*
Was never roy so rich that regned in erthe! *king*

---

[1] *Beautifully enclosed upon the noble boughs; / There was no moisture that could harm anything*

	When I rode in my rout rought I nought elles	*I thought of*
3275	But rivaye and revel and raunson the pople!	*to hunt*
	And thus I drive forth my dayes whiles I drie might,	*endure*
	And therefore derflich I am damned for ever!'	*direly*

	"The last was a little man that laid was beneth;	*beneath*
	His leskes lay all lene and lothlich to shew,	*loins; lean*
3280	His lockes liard and long the lenghe of a yard,	*gray*
	His lire and his ligham lamed full sore,	*face; body crippled*
	The tone eye of the berne was brighter than silver	*The one*
	The other was yellower than the yolk of a nay.	*an egg*

	"'I was lord,' quod the lede, 'landes ynow,	
3285	And all ledes me louted that lenged in erthe.	*bowed to me*
	And now is left me no lap my ligham to hele	*rag; body to cover*
	But lightly now am I lost, leve eche man the sooth.'	*quickly; believe*

	"The second sir, forsooth, that sewed them after	*followed*
	Was sekerer to my sight and sadder in armes;	*stronger; more determined*
3290	Oft he sighed unsound and said these wordes:	
	'On yon see have I sitten als soveraign and lord,	*throne*
	And ladies me loved to lap in their armes,	*fold*
	And now my lordshippes are lost and laid for ever!'	

	"The third thoroughly was thro and thick in the shoulders,	*stout*
3295	A thro man to thret of there thirty were gadered;	*threaten*
	His diadem was dropped down, dubbed with stones,	*adorned*
	Endented all with diamaundes and dight for the nones;	*Adorned; diamonds*
	'I was dredde in my dayes,' he said, 'in diverse rewmes,	*dreaded*
	And now damned to the dede, and dole is the more!'	

3300	"The fourt was a fair man and forcy in armes,	*fourth; forceful*
	The fairest of figure that formed was ever.	
	'I was frek in my faith,' he said, 'whiles I on folde regned,	*bold; earth*
	Famous in fer landes and flowr of all kinges;	
	Now is my face defaded and foul is me happened,	*withered*
3305	For I am fallen fro fer and frendles beleved.'	

	"The fift was a fairer man than fele of these other,	*fifth*

230

A forcy man and a fers, with fomand lippes;   *forceful; foaming*
He fanged fast on the feleighes and folded his armes   *gripped; rim*
But yet he failed and fell a fifty foot large;
3310   But yet he sprang and sprent and spradden his armes,   *leaped; spread*
And on the spere-lenghe spekes he spekes these wordes: *spokes*
'I was in Surry a Sire and set by mine one
As soveraign and seinyour of sere kinges landes;   *lord*
Now of my solace I am full sodenly fallen
3315   And for sake of my sin yon sete is me rewed.'   *yon seat is denied me*

"The sixt had a sawter seemlich bounden   *sixth; psalter; bound*
With a surepel of silk sewed full fair,   *surplice (cover); sewn*
A harp and a hand-sling with hard flint-stones;
What harmes he has hent he hallowes full soon: *suffered; announces*
3320   'I was deemed in my dayes,' he said, 'of deedes of armes
One of the doughtiest that dwelled in erthe;
But I was marred on molde in my most strenghes   *injured*
With this maiden so mild that moves us all.'

"Two kinges were climband and claverand on high,   *clambering*
3325   The erest of the compass they covet full yerne.   *top; wheel; eagerly*
'This chair of charbocle,' they said, 'we challenge hereafter,   *carbuncle*
As two of the chefest chosen in erthe.'

"The childer were chalk-white, cheekes and other,
But the chair aboven cheved they never.   *achieved*
3330   The furthermost was freely with a front large   *noble; forehead*
The fairest of fisnamy that formed was ever,   *physiognomy*
And he was busked in a blee of a blew noble   *dressed; color; blue*
With flourdelys of gold flourished all over;   *fleur-de-lis (lilies)*
The tother was cledde in a cote all of clene silver,   *The other; clad*
3335   With a comlich cross corven of gold;   *carved*
Four crosselettes crafty by the cross restes   *little crosses*
And thereby knew I the king, that cristened him seemed.

"Then I went to that wlonk and winly her greetes,   *bright (one); graciously*
And sho said: 'Welcome, iwis, well art thou founden;   *come*
3340   Thou ought to worship my will, and thou well couthe,   *knew how*
Of all the valiant men that ever was in erthe,

231

For all thy worship in war by me has thou wonnen;
I have been frendly, freke, and fremmed til other.   *strange (hostile) to others*
That thou has founden, in faith, and fele of thy bernes,
3345   For I felled down Sir Frolle with froward knightes;   *defeated; hostile*
For-thy the fruits of Fraunce are freely thine owen.
Thou shall the chair escheve, I chese thee myselven,   *achieve*
Before all the cheftaines chosen in this erthe.'

"Sho lift me up lightly with her lene handes   *lean*
3350   And set me softly in the see, the septer me reched;   *throne; sceptre; gave*
Craftily with a comb sho kembed mine heved,   *combed*
That the crispand krok to my crown raught;   *curling lock; reached*
Dressed on me a diadem that dight was full fair,
And senn proffers me a pome pight full of fair stones,   *orb set*
3355   Enameld with azure, the erthe there-on depainted,
Circled with the salt se upon sere halves,   *all sides*
In sign that I soothly was soveraign in erthe.

"Then brought sho me a brand with full bright hiltes   *sword*
And bade me braundish the blade: 'The brand is mine owen;
3360   Many swain with the swing has the swet leved,   *lifeblood left*
For whiles thou swank with the sword it swiked thee never.'   *labored; failed*

"Then raikes sho with roo and rest when her liked,   *quiet*
To the rindes of the wood, richer was never;   *trees*
Was no pomerie so pight of princes in erthe,   *orchard*
3365   Ne none apparel so proud but paradise one.
Sho bade the bowes sholde bow down and bring to my handes   *boughs*
Of the best that they bore on braunches so high;
Then they helded to her hest, all holly at ones,   *bowed; command*
The highest of ech a hirst, I hete you forsooth.   *grove; promise*
3370   Sho bade me frith not the fruit, but fonde whiles me liked: *spare; try*
'Fonde of the finest, thou freelich berne,   *Try; noble*
And reche to the ripest and riot thyselven.   *reach; enjoy*
Rest, thou real roy, for Rome is thine owen,
And I shall redily roll the roo at the gainest   *wheel*
3375   And reche thee the rich wine in rinsed cuppes.'

"Then sho went to the well by the wood eves,

232

That all welled of wine and wonderlich runnes,
Caught up a cup-full and covered it fair;
Sho bade me derelich draw and drink to herselven;   *dearly take a draught*
3380 And thus sho led me about the lenghe of an hour,
With all liking and love that any lede sholde.   *should want*

  "But at the mid-day full even all her mood changed,
And made much menace with marvelous wordes.
When I cried upon her, she cast down her browes:
3385 'King, thou carpes for nought, by Crist that me made!
For thou shall lose this laik and thy life after;   *pleasure*
Thou has lived in delite and lordshippes ynow!'   *delight*

  "About sho whirles the wheel and whirles me under,
Til all my quarters that while were quasht all to peces,   *time; crushed*
3390 And with that chair my chin was chopped in sonder;
And I have shivered for chele senn me this chaunce happened.   *chill*
Thus wakened I, iwis, all wery fordremed,   *wearied from dreaming*
And now wot thou my wo; worde as thee likes."   *speak*

  "Freke," says the philosopher, "thy fortune is passed,   *Bold warrior*
3395 For thou shall find her thy fo; fraist when thee likes!
Thou art at the highest, I hete thee forsooth;   *promise*
Challenge now when thou will, thou cheves no more!
Thou has shed much blood and shalkes destroyed,   *men*
Sakeles, in surquidrie, in sere kinges landes;   *Innocent; pride*
3400 Shrive thee of thy shame and shape for thine end.   *Confess; prepare*
Thou has a shewing, Sir King, take keep yif thee like,   *revelation*
For thou shall fersly fall within five winters.
Found abbeyes in Fraunce, the fruites are thine owen,
For Frolle and for Feraunt and for thir fers knightes
3405 That thou fremedly in Fraunce has fey beleved. [1]
Take keep yet of other kinges, and cast in thine herte,   *consider*
That were conquerours kidd and crowned in erthe.

  "The eldest was Alexander that all the world louted,   *bowed to*

---

[1] *Whom you unkindly (as a stranger) left dead in France.*

The tother Ector of Troy, the chevalrous gome;   *other*

3410   The third Julius Cesar, that giaunt was holden,
In eche journee gentle, ajudged with lordes.
The fourth was Sir Judas, a jouster full noble,
The masterful Macabee, the mightiest of strenghes;
The fift was Josue, that jolly man of armes,   *fifth*

3415   That in Jerusalem host full much joy limped;   *befell*
The sixt was David the dere, deemed with kinges   *sixth*
One of the doughtiest that dubbed was ever,
For he slew with a sling by sleight of his handes   *skill*
Golias the grete gome, grimmest in erthe;   *Goliath*

3420   Senn endited in his dayes all the dere psalmes   *composed*
That in the sawter are set with selcouthe wordes.   *psalter*

"The tone climand king, I know it forsooth,   *The one*
Shall Karolus be called, the kinge son of Fraunce;   *Charlemagne; king's*
He shall be cruel and keen and conquerour holden,

3425   Cover by conquest contrees ynow;   *Obtain*
He shall encroch the crown that Crist bore himselven,   *capture*
And that lifelich launce that lepe to His herte   *strong*
When He was crucified on cross, and all the keen nailes
Knightly he shall conquer to Cristen men handes.   *i.e., for*

3430   "The tother shall be Godfray, that God shall revenge   *The other*
On the Good Friday with galiard knightes;   *jolly*
He shall of Lorraine be lord by leve of his fader
And senn in Jerusalem much joy happen,
For he shall cover the cross by craftes of armes   *recover*

3435   And senn be crowned king with crisom annointed.   *holy oil*
Shall no dukes in his day such destainy happen,   *destiny*
Ne such mischief drie when trewth shall be tried.   *suffer; proved*

"For-thy Fortune thee fetches to fulfill the number,
Als ninde of the noblest named in erthe;   *ninth of the Worthies*

3440   This shall in romaunce be redde with real knightes,
Reckoned and renownd with riotous kinges,
And deemed on Doomesday for deedes of armes,
For the doughtiest that ever was dwelland in erthe;
So many clerkes and kinges shall carp of your deedes

3445   And keep your conquestes in cronicle for ever.

      "But the wolves in the wood and the wild bestes
      Are some wicked men that werrayes thy rewmes,   *attack*
      Is entered in thine absence to werray thy pople,
      And alienes and hostes of uncouthe landes.   *foreign*
3450   Thou gettes tidandes, I trow, within ten dayes,   i.e., *will get*
      That some torfer is tidde senn thou fro home turned.   *trouble has happened*
      I rede thou reckon and reherse unresonable deedes   *tell (i.e., confess)*
      Ere thee repentes full rathe all thy rewth workes.   *quickly; sad*
      Man, amend thy mood, ere thou mishappen,   *have misfortune*
3455   And meekly ask mercy for meed of thy soul."   *reward*

      Then rises the rich king and raght on his weedes,
      A red acton of rose, the richest of flowres,   *quilted jacket*
      A pesan and a paunson and a pris girdle; [1]
      And on he hentes a hood of scarlet full rich,   *draws*
3460   A pavis pillion-hat that pight was full fair   *large cloth hat*
      With perry of the Orient and precious stones;   *pearls*
      His gloves gaylich gilt and graven by the hemmes   *decorated*
      With graines of rubies full gracious to shew.   *small stones*
      His bede greyhound and his brand and no berne else *[He takes] his hunting*
3465   And bounes over a brode mede with brethe at his herte. *meadow; anger*
      Forth he stalkes a sty by tho still eves,   *path*
      Stotays at a high street, studyand him one. [2]

      At the sours of the sun he sees there comand,   *rising*
      Raikand to Rome-ward the rediest wayes,   *Going; quickest*
3470   A renk in a round clok with right rowme clothes [3]
      With hat and with high shoon homely and round;   *shoes; comfortable*
      With flat farthinges the freke was flourished all over *coins; adorned*
      Many shreddes and shragges at his skirtes hanges   *scalloped edges*

---

[1] *An armor neckpiece, a stomach guard, and an excellent belt*
[2] *Pauses at a main road, thinking by himself*
[3] *A man in a full-cut cloak and very roomy clothes*

235

With scrip and with slawin and scallopes ynow[1]

3475   Both pike and palm, als pilgrim him sholde;

The gome graithly him grette and bade good morwen;   *greeted; morning*

The king, lordly himself, of langage of Rome,   *language; i.e., Italian*

Of Latin corrumped all, full lovely him menes: *corrupted; speaks*

"Wheder wilnes thou, wye, walkand thine one?   *Whither seek*

3480   Whiles this world is o war, a wathe I it hold;   *at war; danger*

Here is an enmy with host, under yon vines;   *enemy*

And they see thee, forsooth, sorrow thee betides;

But if thou have condeth of the king selven,   *safe-conduct*

Knaves will kill thee and keep at thou haves,   *what*

3485   And if thou hold the high way, they hent thee also,   *take*

But if thou hastily have help of his hende knightes."

Then carpes Sir Craddok to the king selven:

"I shall forgive him my dede, so me God help,   *death*

Any gome under God that on this ground walkes!

3490   Let the keenest come that to the king longes,

I shall encounter him as knight, so Crist have my soul!

For thou may not reche me ne arrest thyselven,   *seize; stop (me)*

Though thou be richly arrayed in full rich weedes;

I will not wonde for no war to wend where me likes   *hesitate*

3495   Ne for no wye of this world that wrought is on erthe!

But I will pass in pilgrimage this pas to Rome   *way*

To purchase me pardon of the Pope selven,

And of the paines of Purgatory be plenerly assoilled;   *fully forgiven*

Then shall I seek sekerly my soveraign lord,

3500   Sir Arthur of England, that avenaunt berne!   *seemly*

For he is in this empire, as hathel men me telles,   *noble*

Hostayand in this Orient with awful knightes."   *Warring; awesome*

"Fro whethen come thou, keen man," quod the king then,   *whence*

"That knowes King Arthur and his knightes also?

3505   Was thou ever in his court whiles he in kith lenged?

Thou carpes so kindly it comfortes mine herte!

---

[1] *With wallet and with pilgrim's mantle and many scallop shells, / Both staff and palm branch, as if he were a pilgrim*

Well wele has thou went and wisely thou seekes,   *nobly*
For thou art Breton berne, as by thy brode speche."   *British; plain*

"Me ought to know the king; he is my kidd lord,
3510   And I called in his court a knight of his chamber;
Sir Craddok was I called in his court rich,
Keeper of Caerlion, under the king selven;
Now I am chased out of kith, with care at my herte,
And that castel is caught with uncouthe ledes."   *captured; foreign men*

3515   Then the comlich king caught him in armes,
Cast off his kettle-hat and kissed him full soon,
Said: "Welcome, Sir Craddok, so Crist mot me help!
Dere cosin of kind, thou coldes mine herte!   *blood relative*
How fares it in Bretain with all my bold bernes?
3520   Are they brittened or brint or brought out of life?   *burned*
Ken thou me kindly what case is befallen;   *Tell*
I keep no credens to crave; I know thee for trew." [1]

"Sir, thy warden is wicked and wild of his deedes,   *i.e., Mordred*
For he wandreth has wrought senn thou away passed.   *misery; since*
3525   He has castels encroched and crownd himselven,   *captured*
Caught in all the rentes of the Round Table;
He devised the rewm and delt as him likes;   *divided*
Dubbed of the Denmarkes dukes and erles,   *i.e., Danes*
Disservered them sonderwise, and citees destroyed;   *Scattered; everywhere*
3530   Of Sarazenes and Sessoines upon sere halves   *Saxons; both sides*
He has sembled a sorte of selcouthe bernes,   *foreign*
Soveraignes of Surgenale and soudeours many   *South Wales; mercenaries*
Of Peghtes and paynims and proved knightes   *Picts; pagans*
Of Ireland and Argyle, outlawed bernes;
3535   All tho laddes are knightes that long to the mountes,
And leding and lordship has all, als themselve likes;   *command*
And there is Sir Childrik a cheftain holden,
That ilke chevalrous man, he charges thy pople;   *burdens*
They rob thy religious and ravish thy nunnes   *monks*

---

[1] *I need ask for no credentials; I know you are true*

237

3540	And redy rides with his rout to raunson the poor;	*rob*
	Fro Humber to Hawyk he holdes his owen,	*(see note)*
	And all the countree of Kent by covenant entailled,	*in his possession*
	The comlich castles that to the crown longed,	
	The holtes and the hore wood and the hard bankes,	*hoar (gray)*
3545	All that Hengest and Hors hent in their time;	*held*
	At Southampton on the se is seven score shippes,	
	Fraught full of fers folk, out of fer landes,	*Filled*
	For to fight with thy frap when thou them assailes.	*company*
	But yet a word, witterly, thou wot not the worst!	*certainly*
3550	He has wedded Waynor and her his wife holdes,	
	And wonnes in the wild boundes of the west marches,	*dwells*
	And has wrought her with child, as witness telles!	
	Of all the wyes of this world, wo mot him worthe,	*men; woe be to him*
	Als warden unworthy women to yeme!	*preserve*
3555	Thus has Sir Mordred marred us all!	*injured*
	For-thy I merked over these mountes to mene thee the sooth."	*came; tell*
	Then the burlich king, for brethe at his herte	
	And for this booteless bale all his blee changed;	*without remedy; color*
	"By the Rood," says the roy, "I shall it revenge!	
3560	Him shall repent full rathe all his rewth workes!"	*quickly; calamitous*
	All weepand for wo he went to his tentes;	
	Unwinly this wise king he wakenes his bernes,	*Unhappily*
	Cleped in a clarioun kinges and other,	*Called with a trumpet*
	Calles them to counsel and of this case telles:	
3565	"I am with tresoun betrayed, for all my trew deedes!	
	And all my travail is tint, me tides no better!	*labor; destroyed*
	Him shall torfer betide this tresoun has wrought,	*trouble; i.e., who this*
	And I may traistely him take, as I am trew lord!	*can surely*
	This is Mordred, the man that I most traisted,	
3570	Has my castels encroched and crownd himselven	
	With rentes and riches of the Round Table;	
	He made all his retinues of renayed wretches,	*renegade*
	And devised my rewm to diverse lordes,	*divided*
	To soudeours and Sarazenes out of sere landes!	
3575	He has wedded Waynor and her to wife holdes,	
	And a child is y-shaped, the chaunce is no better!	
	They have sembled on the se seven score shippes,	

	Full of ferrom folk to fight with mine one!	*foreign*
	For-thy to Bretain the Brode buske us behooves, [1]	
3580	For to britten the berne that has this bale raised.	*break; grief*
	There shall no freke men fare but all on fresh horses	
	That are fraisted in fight and flowr of my knightes.	*proven*
	Sir Howell and Sir Hardolf here shall beleve	*remain*
	To be lordes of the ledes that here to me longes;	
3585	Lookes into Lumbardy that there no lede change, [2]	
	And tenderly to Tuskane take tent als I bid;	*attention*
	Receive the rentes of Rome when they are reckoned;	
	Take sesin the same day that last was assigned,	*possession*
	Or elles all the hostage withouten the walles	
3590	Be hanged high upon height all holly at ones."	

	Now bounes the bold king with his best knightes,	
	Gars trome and trusse and trines forth after, [3]	
	Turnes through Tuskane, tarries but little;	
	Lights not in Lumbardy but when the light failed;	
3595	Merkes over the mountaines full marvelous wayes,	*Marches*
	Ayers through Almaine even at the gainest	
	Ferkes even into Flandresh with his fers knightes.	*Hastens; Flanders*
	Within fifteen dayes his fleet is assembled,	
	And then he shope him to ship and shounes no lenger,	*prepared himself; delays*
3600	Sheeres with a sharp wind over the shire waters;	*Cuts; translucent*
	By the roche with ropes he rides on anker.	*rocks; anchor*
	There the false men fleted and on flood lenged,	*floated*
	With chef chaines of charre chocked togeders, [4]	
	Charged even chock-full of chevalrous knightes,	
3605	And in the hinter on height, helmes and crestes;	*rear*
	Hatches with hethen men heled were there-under,	
	Proudlich pourtrayed with painted clothes,	*painted; on*
	Ech a pece by pece prikked til other,	*sewed*
	Dubbed with dagswainnes doubled they seem;	*Adorned; heavy cloth*

---

[1] *Therefore to Great Britain it behooves us to hasten*

[2] *See that in Lombardy no man change his allegiance*

[3] *Sends forth troops and baggage and goes forth thereafter*

[4] *Linked together with great wagon chains*

3610	And thus the derf Denmarkes had dight all their shippes,	*Danes*
	That no dint of no dart dere them sholde.	*harm*
	Then the roy and the renkes of the Round Table	
	All realy in red arrayes his shippes;	
	That day ducheries he delt and dubbed knightes,	
3615	Dresses dromoundes and dragges and drawen up stones;	*galleys; barges*
	The top-castels he stuffed with toiles, as him liked;	*slings*
	Bendes bowes of vise brothly there-after;	*crossbows; fiercely*
	Toloures tently tackle they righten,	*Haulers carefully*
	Brasen hedes full brode busked on flones,	*Bronze; missiles*
3620	Graithes for garnisons, gomes arrayes,	*garrisons*
	Grim godes of steel, gives of iron;	*goads; fetters*
	Stighteles steren on steren with stiff men of armes;	*Supplies; stern (ship)*
	Many lovelich launce upon loft standes,	
	Ledes on leburd, lordes and other,	*lee (sea side of ship)*
3625	Pight pavis on port, painted sheldes, [1]	
	On hinder hurdace on height helmed knightes.	*rear barrier*
	Thus they shiften for shottes on those shire strandes,	*maneuver; shooting*
	Ilke shalk in his shroud, full sheen were their weedes.	*garment*
	The bold king is in a barge and about rowes,	
3630	All bare-hevede for besy with beveren lockes, [2]	
	And a berne with his brand and an helm beten,	*adorned (beaten)*
	Menged with a mauntelet of mailes of silver,	*Adorned; little mantle*
	Compast with a coronal and covered full rich;	*Encircled; diadem; decorated*
	Kaires to ech a cogge to comfort his knightes;	*Travels; ship*
3635	To Clegis and Cleremond he cries on loud:	
	"O Gawain! O Galyran! These good mens bodies!"	
	To Lot and to Lionel full lovely he meles,	
	And to Sir Launcelot de Lake lordlich wordes:	
	"Let us cover the kith, the coste is our own,	*reclaim*
3640	And gar them brothelich blenk, all yon blood-houndes!	*make; violently blanch*
	Britten them within borde and brin them there-after!	*aboard; burn*
	Hew down hertily yon hethen tikes!	*dogs*

---

[1] *Arranged wooden shields on the left (port), painted shields*

[2] *All bareheaded because of business, with beaver-colored locks*

They are harlotes half, I hete you mine hand!"[1]

	Then he coveres his cogge and catches on anker,	*returns to; ship; anchor*
3645	Caught his comlich helm with the clere mailes;	
	Buskes banners on brode, beten of gules,	*Raises; adorned with red*
	With crowns of clere gold clenlich arrayed;	
	But there was chosen in the chef a chalk-white maiden,[2]	
	And a child in her arm that Chef is of heven;	
3650	Withouten changing in chase these were the chef armes	*noble*
	Of Arthur the avenaunt, whiles he in erthe lenged.	*worthy*
	Then the mariners meles and masters of shippes;	*get to work*
	Merrily ich a mate menes til other;	*each; speaks*
	Of their termes they talk, how they were tidd,[3]	
3655	Towen trussel on trete, trussen up sailes,	*Drag bundles on trestles*
	Bete bonnetes on brode, bettred hatches;	*Set small sails; battened*
	Braundisht brown steel, bragged in trumpes;	*blew in trumpets*
	Standes stiff on the stamin, steeres on after,	*stalwartly on the prow*
	Streken over the streme, there striving beginnes.	*Strike*
3660	Fro the waggand wind out of the west rises,	*When; swaying*
	Brothly bessomes with birr in bernes sailes,	*Suddenly sweeps; force*
	Wether bringes on borde burlich cogges,[4]	
	Whiles the biling and the beme bristes in sonder;	
	So stoutly the fore-stern on the stam hittes	*stern; prow*
3665	That stockes of the steer-borde strikes in peces!	*planks; starboard side*
	By then cogge upon cogge, crayers and other,	*ship; small ships*
	Castes crepers on-cross, als to the craft longes;	*grappling hooks across*
	Then was hed-ropes hewen, that held up the mastes;	
	There was contek full keen and cracking of shippes!	*strife*
3670	Grete cogges of kemp crashes in sonder!	*war*
	Many cabane cleved, cables destroyed,	*cabins*
	Knightes and keen men killed the bernes!	

---

[1] *They are on the rascal's side, I swear by my hand*

[2] *But there was placed in the chef (upper third of shield) a chalk-white maiden*

[3] *They talk in their jargon about what has happened*

[4] *Weather (wind) brings stout ships against planks (of other ships), / So that the bilge and the beam burst apart*

Kidd castels were corven, with all their keen wepen,   *Proven; carved*
Castels full comlich that coloured were fair!
3675   Up ties edgeling they ochen there-after;   *mast-stays; edgewise; hack*
With the swing of the sword sways the mastes,
Over-falles in the first frekes and other;   *i.e., first blow*
Many freke in the fore-ship fey is beleved!
Then brothly they beker with bustous tackle;   *fight; powerful equipment*
3680   Brushes boldly on borde brenyed knightes, [1]
Out of botes on borde, was busked with stones,
Bete down of the best, bristes the hatches;
Some gomes through-gird with godes of iron,   *pierced; goads*
Gomes gaylich cledde englaimes wepenes;   *Men; clad make slimy*
3685   Archers of England full egerly shootes,
Hittes through the hard steel full hertly dintes!   *Strikes; mortal*
Soon ochen in holly the hethen knightes,   *completely cut down*
Hurt through the hard steel, hele they never!   *heal*
Then they fall to the fight, foines with speres,   *duel*
3690   All the frekkest on front that to the fight longes,   *front rank*
And ilkon freshly fraistes their strenghes,   *each one*
War to fight in the fleet with their fell wepenes.   *to fight the battle*
Thus they delt that day, thir dubbed knightes,
Til all the Danes were dede and in the deep throwen!
3695   Then Bretons brothly with brandes they hewen;
Lepes in upon loft lordlich bernes;   *through the air*
When ledes of out-landes lepen in waters,
All our lordes on loud laughen at ones!

By then speres were sprongen, spalded shippes,   *broken; split*
3700   Spanioles speedily sprented over-bordes;   *Spaniards; leaped overboard*
All the keen men of kemp, knightes and other,   *battle*
Killed are cold-dede and casten over-bordes;
Their swyers swiftly has the swet leved;   *young men; lifeblood*
Hethen hevand on hatch in thir hawe rises,   *heaving; these gray waves*
3705   Sinkand in the salt se seven hundreth at ones!
Then Sir Gawain the good, he has the gree wonnen,   *prize*

---

[1] *Armored knights rush boldly on board, / (Coming) out of small boats on board, (and) were pelted with stones*

	And all the cogges grete he gave to his knightes.	
	Sir Garin, Sir Griswold, and other grete lordes;	
	Gart Galuth, a good gome, gird off their hedes!	i.e., *the captives'*
3710	Thus of the false fleet upon the flood happened,	
	And thus these ferin folk fey are beleved!	*foreign*

	Yet is the traitour on land with tried knightes,	
	And all trumped they trip on trapped steedes	*accompanied with trumpets*
	Shews them under sheld on the shire bankes;	
3715	He ne shuntes for no shame but shewes full high!	*shows himself*
	Sir Arthur and Gawain avyed them bothen	*set out*
	To sixty thousand of men that in their sight hoved.	
	By this the folk was felled, then was the flood passed; [1]	
	Then was it silke a slowde in slackes full huge	
3720	That let the king for to land in the low water.	
	For-thy he lenged on laye for lesing of horses,	
	To look of his lege-men and of his lele knightes,	
	Yif any were lamed or lost, live yif they sholde.	

	Then Sir Gawain the good a galley he takes	
3725	And glides up at a gole with good men of armes;	*small bay (gully)*
	When he grounded, for gref he girdes in the water	*ran aground; leaps*
	That to the girdle he goes in all his gilt weedes,	
	Shootes up upon the sand in sight of the lordes,	*Rushes*
	Singly with his soppe, my sorrow is the more!	*Alone; small troop*
3730	With banners of his badges, best of his armes,	*heraldic devices*
	He braides up on the bank in his bright weedes;	
	He biddes his banneour: "Busk thou belive	*banner bearer; Go quickly*
	To yon brode batail that on yon bank hoves,	
	And I ensure you soothe I shall you sew after;	*follow*
3735	Look ye blenk for no brand ne for no bright wepen,	*blanch*
	But beres down of the best and bring them o-dawe!	*out of daylight*
	Bes not abaist of their boste, abide on the erthe;	*Be; abashed*
	Ye have my banneres borne in batailes full huge;	

---

[1] *By the time the battle was finished the high tide had passed; / Then was the water near the shore such a slush in very large pools / That the king could not land in the low water. / Therefore, he remained on the deep water for fear of losing his horses*

We shall fell yon false, the fend have their soules!

3740   Fightes fast with the frap, the feld shall be oures!   *company*

May I that traitour over-take, torfer him tides   *If I can; woe*

That this tresoun has timbered to my trew lord!   *built for*

Of such a engendure full little joy happens,   *engendering*

And that shall in this journee be judged full even!"

3745   Now they seek over the sand, this soppe at the gainest,   *small troop*

Sembles on the soudeours and settes their dintes;   *Attack; set on*

Through the sheldes so sheen shalkes they touch

With shaftes shivered short of those sheen launces;   *broken*

Derf dintes they delt with daggand speres;   *piercing*

3750   On the dank of the dew many dede ligges,

Dukes and douspeeres and dubbed knightes;

The doughtiest of Danemark undone are forever!

Thus those renkes in rewth rittes their brenyes   *rip*

And reches of the richest unrecken dintes,   *give; countless*

3755   There they throng in the thick and thrustes to the erthe

Of the throest men three hundreth at ones!

But Sir Gawain for gref might not again-stand,   *withstand*

Umbegrippes a spere and to a gome runnes,   *Grasps*

That bore of gules full gay with goutes of silver;   *arms of red; droplets*

3760   He girdes him in at the gorge with his grim launce   *throat*

That the grounden glaive graithes in sonder;   *point*

With that bustous blade he bounes him to die!   *prepares himself*

The King of Gotheland it was, a good man of armes.   *Gothland (South Sweden)*

Their avauntward then all voides there-after,   *vanguard*

3765   Als vanquist verrayly with valiant bernes;   *vanquished; verily*

Meetes with middle-ward that Mordred ledes;   *middle guard*

Our men merkes them to, as them mishappened,   *advance toward*

For had Sir Gawain the grace to hold the green hill,

He had worship, iwis, wonnen forever!

3770   But then Sir Gawain, iwis, he waites him well

To wreke on this warlaw that this war moved,   *warlock*

And merkes to Sir Mordred among all his bernes,

With the Montagues and other grete lordes.

Then Sir Gawain was greved and with a grete will

3775   Fewters a fair spere and freshly ascries:

"False fostered fode, the fend have thy bones!   *creature; fiend*
Fy on thee, felon, and thy false workes!
Thou shall be dede and undone for thy derf deedes,
Or I shall die this day, if destainy worthe!"   *if it be my destiny*

3780   Then his enmy with host of outlawed bernes
        All enangles about our excellent knightes   *Surrounds*
        That the traitour by tresoun had tried himselven;   *experienced*
        Dukes of Danemark he dightes full soon,   *marshals*
        And leders of Lettow with legions ynow,   *Lithuania*
3785   Umbelapped our men with launces full keen,   *Surrounded*
        Soudeours and Sarazenes out of sere landes,
        Sixty thousand men, seemlyly arrayed,
        Sekerly assembles there on seven score knightes,
        Sodenly in dischaite by tho salt strandes.   *deceit*
3790   Then Sir Gawain grette with his grey eyen   *wept*
        For gref of his good men that he guide sholde.
        He wiste that they wounded were and wery for-foughten,   *exhausted with fighting*
        And what for wonder and wo, all his wit failed.
        And then sighand he said with syland teres: *flowing tears*
3795   "We are with Sarazenes beset upon sere halves!
        I sigh not for myself, so help our Lord,
        But for to see us surprised my sorrow is the more!   *captured*
        Bes doughty today, yon dukes shall be yours!   *Be*
        For dere Drighten this day dredes no wepen.
3800   We shall end this day als excellent knightes,
        Ayer to endless joy with angeles unwemmed;   *Go; spotless*
        Though we have unwittyly wasted ourselven,   *unwisely*
        We shall work all well in the worship of Crist!
        We shall for yon Sarazenes, I seker you my trewth,   *pledge*
3805   Soupe with our Saviour solemnly in heven,   *Dine*
        In presence of that Precious, Prince of all other,
        With prophetes and patriarkes and apostles full noble,
        Before His freelich face that formed us all!
        Yonder to yon yaldsones! He that yeldes him ever   *whore sons*
3810   Whiles he is quick and in quert, unquelled with handes,   *alive; sound health*
        Be he never mo saved, ne succoured with Crist,
        But Satanase his soul mowe sink into Hell!"   *may*

245

	Then grimly Sir Gawain grippes his wepen;	
	Again that grete batail he graithes him soon,	
3815	Radly of his rich sword he rightes the chaines;	*Quickly; cuts*
	In he shockes his sheld, shuntes he no lenger,	*pushes; hangs back*
	But all unwise, wodewise, he went at the gainest,	*madly*
	Woundes of those widerwinnes with wrakful dintes;	*enemies; wrathful*
	All welles full of blood there he away passes;	
3820	And though him were full wo, he wondes but little,	*hesitates*
	But wrekes at his worship the wrath of his lord!	
	He stickes steedes in stour and sterenfull knightes,	*pierces; stern*
	That steren men in the stirrupes stone-dede they ligge!	
	He rives the rank steel, he rittes the mailes;	*cleaves; rips*
3825	There might no renk him arrest; his resoun was passed!	
	He fell in a frensy for fersness of herte;	*frenzy*
	He fightes and felles down that him before standes!	
	Fell never fey man such fortune in erthe!	*Befell; a fated man*
	Into the hole batail hedlings he runnes	*headlong*
3830	And hurtes of the hardiest that on the erthe lenges;	
	Letand as a lion he launches them through,	*Acting like; stabs*
	Lordes and leders that on the land hoves.	*stand*
	Yet Sir Wawain for wo wondes but little,	*hesitates*
	But woundes of those widerwinnes with wonderful dintes,	*enemies*
3835	Als he that wolde wilfully wasten himselven,	
	And for wondsome and will all his wit failed,	*fierceness; wilfulness*
	That wode als a wild beste he went at the gainest;	*crazy*
	All wallowed on blood there he away passed;	
	Ich a wye may be ware by wreke of another! [1]	
3840	Then he moves to Sir Mordred among all his knightes,	
	And met him in the mid-sheld and malles him through,	*hammers*
	But the shalk for the sharp he shuntes a little;	*hangs back*
	He share him on the short ribbes a shaftmond large.	*cut; six inches deep*
	The shaft shuddered and shot in the shire berne	*dashed; shining*
3845	That the sheddand blood over his shank runnes	*leg*
	And shewed on his shin-bawde that was shire burnisht!	*shin plate; brightly*
	And so they shift and shove he shot to the erthe,	*as; fell precipitously*

---

[1] *Each man may be warned by vengeance wreaked on another*

	With the lush of the launce he light on his shoulders	*blow; i.e., Mordred*
	An acre-lenghe on a laund full lothly wounded.	*full length; hillock*
3850	Then Gawain gird to the gome and on the grouf falles;	*leaps; on his face*
	All his gref was graithed; his grace was no better!	*destined*
	He shockes out a short knife shethed with silver	*draws; sheathed*
	And sholde have slotted him in but no slit happened;	*stabbed*
	His hand slipped and slode o-slant on the mailes	*slid; aslant*
3855	And the tother slely slinges him under;	*the other; slyly hurls*
	With a trenchand knife the traitour him hittes	*cutting*
	Through the helm and the hed on high on the brain;	
	And thus Sir Gawain is gone, the good man of armes,	
	Withouten rescue of renk, and rew is the more!	*pity*
3860	Thus Sir Gawain is gone that guied many other;	*guided*
	Fro Gower to Gernesay, all the grete lordes	*Guernsey*
	Of Glamour, of Galys land, these galiard knightes	*Glamorgan; Wales*
	For glent of glopining glad be they never!	*sight of horror*
	King Frederik of Fres faithly there-after	*Frisia; faithfully*
3865	Fraines at the false man of our fers knight:	*Inquires of*
	"Knew thou ever this knight in thy kith rich?	
	Of what kind he was comen beknow now the sooth;	*family*
	What gome was he, this with the gay armes,	
	With this griffon of gold, that is on grouf fallen?	*on his face*
3870	He has gretly greved us, so me God help,	
	Gird down our good men and greved us sore!	*Struck*
	He was the sterenest in stour that ever steel wered,	*wore*
	For he stonayed our stale and stroyed for ever!"	*troop*
	Then Sir Mordred with mouth meles full fair:	
3875	"He was makless on molde, man, by my trewth.	*matchless*
	This was Sir Gawain the good, the gladdest of other,	
	And the graciousest gome that under God lived,	
	Man hardiest of hand, happiest in armes,	*most fortunate*
	And the hendest in hall under heven-rich,	*the kingdom of heaven*
3880	And the lordliest in leding whiles he live might,	*leadership*
	For he was lion alosed in landes ynow;	*praised as*
	Had thou knowen him, Sir King, in kithe there he lenged,	
	His cunning, his knighthood, his kindly workes,	
	His doing, his doughtiness, his deedes of armes,	

3885   Thou wolde have dole for his dede the dayes of thy life."   *grieved*

     Yet that traitour als tite teres let he fall,   *at once*
     Turnes him forth tite and talkes no more,   *quickly*
     Went weepand away and weryes the stounde   *curses the time*
     That ever his werdes were wrought such wandreth to work!   *fates; misery*
3890   When he thought on this thing it thirled his herte;   *pierced*
     For sake of his sib-blood sighand he rides;   *kinship*
     When that renayed renk remembered himselven   *renegade*
     Of reverence and riotes of the Round Table,
     He romed and repent him of all his rewth workes,   *moaned; foul deeds*
3895   Rode away with his rout, restes he no lenger,
     For rade of our rich king, rive that he sholde.   *fear; arrive; might*

     Then kaires he to Cornwall, care-full in herte,   *goes*
     Because of his kinsman that on the coste ligges;
     He tarries trembland ay, tidandes to herken.
3900   Then the traitour treunted the Tuesday there-after,   *set forth*
     Trines in with a trayn tresoun to work,   *Goes; trick*
     And by the Tamber that tide his tentes he reres,   *the River Tamar*
     And then in a mett-while a messanger he sendes   *short time*
     And wrote unto Waynor how the world changed
3905   And what comlich coste the king was arrived,
     On flood foughten with his fleet and felled them o life;   *from*
     Bade her ferken o-fer and flee with her childer   *hasten afar*
     Whiles he might wile him away and win to her speche,[1]
     Ayer into Ireland, into those oute-mountes,   *outer mountains*
3910   And wonne there in wilderness within tho waste landes.   *live; deserted*

     Then sho yermes and yeyes at York in her chamber,   *cries; sobs*
     Grones full grisly with gretand teres,   *weeping*
     Passes out of the palais with all her pris maidens,
     Toward Chester in a charre they chese her the wayes,   *carriage*
3915   Dight her even for to die with dole at her herte;
     Sho kaires to Caerlion and caught her a veil,   *i.e., became a nun*
     Askes there the habit in honour of Crist   *nun's garment*

---

[1] *Until he could get away by stealth and come to speak to her*

And all for falshed and fraud and fere of her lord!   *falsehood; fear; husband*

But when our wise king wiste that Gawain was landed,
3920   He al to-writhes for wo, and wringand his handes,   *writhes violently*
Gars launch his botes upon a low water,   *Gives orders to*
Landes als a lion with lordlich knightes,
Slippes in the sloppes o-slant to the girdle,   *pools; aslant*
Swalters up swiftly with his sword drawen,   *Splashes*
3925   Bounes his batail and banners displayes,
Buskes over the brode sand with brethe at his herte,
Ferkes frely on feld there the fey ligges;
Of the traitours men on trapped steedes,
Ten thousand were tint, the trewth to account,   *slain*
3930   And, certain, on our side seven score knightes,
In suite with their soveraign unsound are beleved.   *Together; not whole (dead)*

The king comly overcast knightes and other,   *turned over*
Erles of Afrike and Estriche bernes,   *Austrian*
Of Argyle and Orkney the Irish kinges,
3935   The noblest of Norway, numbers full huge,
Dukes and Danemarkes and dubbed knightes;
And the Guthede king in the gay armes   *Gothic*
Lies gronand on the ground and gird through even.
The rich king ransackes with rewth at his herte   *searches*
3940   And up rippes the renkes of all the Round Table,   *pulls*
Sees them all in a soppe in suite by them one   *little group; together*
With the Sarazenes unsound encircled about,   *not whole (i.e., dead)*
And Sir Gawain the good in his gay armes,
Umbegripped the gers and on grouf fallen,   *Clutched; grass; face down*
3945   His banners braiden down, beten of gules,   *adorned with red*
His brand and his brode sheld all bloody berunnen.   *run over*
Was never our seemlich king so sorrowful in herte,
Ne that sank him so sad but that sight one. [1]

Then gliftes the good king and glopins in herte,   *stares; is terror-struck*
3950   Grones full grislich with gretande teres,   *weeping*

---

[1] *Nor was there anything that sank him so sad as that sight alone*

	Kneeles down to the corse and caught it in armes,	*corpse*
	Castes up his umbrere and kisses him soon,	*visor*
	Lookes on his eye-liddes that locked were fair,	
	His lippes like to the lede and his lire fallowed.	*lead; complexion pale*
3955	Then the crownd king cries full loud:	
	"Dere cosin of kind in care am I leved,	*blood relative*
	For now my worship is went and my war ended!	
	Here is the hope of my hele, my happing in armes,	*well-being; good fortune*
	My herte and my hardiness holly on him lenged!	
3960	My counsel, my comfort, that keeped mine herte!	
	Of all knightes the king that under Crist lived!	
	Thou was worthy to be king, though I the crown bare!	
	My wele and my worship of all this world rich	*wealth*
	Was wonnen through Sir Gawain and through his wit one!	*only*
3965	"Alas," said Sir Arthur, "now eekes my sorrow!	*increases*
	I am utterly undone in mine owen landes!	
	A doutous, derf dede, thou dwelles too long!	*fearful cruel death*
	Why drawes thou so on dregh? Thou drownes mine herte!"	*delay; so long*
	Then sweltes the sweet king and in swoon falles,	*faints*
3970	Swafres up swiftly and sweetly him kisses	*Staggers*
	Til his burlich berde was bloody berunnen,	*covered with blood*
	Als he had bestes brittened and brought out of life;	*beasts*
	Ne had Sir Ewain comen and other grete lordes,	
	His bold herte had bristen for bale at that stounde!	*time*
3975	"Blinn," says these bold men, "thou blunders thyselven!	*stop; harm*
	This is bootless bale, for better bes it never!	*without remedy; will be*
	It is no worship, iwis, to wring thine handes;	
	To weep als a woman it is no wit holden!	
	Be knightly of countenaunce, als a king sholde,	
3980	And leve such clamour, for Cristes love of heven!"	
	"For blood," says the bold king, "blinn shall I never	*cease*
	Ere my brain to-brist or my breste other!	*shatter; either*
	Was never sorrow so soft that sank to my herte;	
	It is full sib to myself; my sorrow is the more.	*closely related*
3985	Was never so sorrowful a sight seen with mine eyen!	
	He is sakless surprised for sin of mine one!"	*innocent*

250

Down kneeles the king and cries full loud,
With care-full countenaunce he carpes these wordes:
"O rightwise rich God, this rewth thou behold,   *righteous*
3990 This real red blood run upon erthe!
It were worthy to be shrede and shrined in gold,   *clothed; enshrined*
For it is sakless of sin, so help me our Lord!"   *innocent*

Down kneeles the king with care at his herte,
Caught it up kindly with his clene handes,
3995 Cast it in a kettle-hat and coverd it fair,
And kaires forth with the corse in kithe there he lenges.

"Here I make mine avow," quod the king then,
"To Messie and to Mary, the mild Queen of heven: *Messiah*
I shall never rivaye ne ratches uncouple,   *hunt; hounds unleash*
4000 At roe ne rein-dere that runnes upon erthe,   *reindeer*
Never greyhound let glide, ne gossehawk let fly   *goshawk*
Ne never fowl see felled that flighes with wing,   *flies*
Faucon ne formel upon fist handle   *Falcon; female hawk*
Ne yet with gerefaucon rejoice me in erthe,   *gerfalcon*
4005 Ne regne in my royaltees, ne hold my Round Table,
Til thy dede, my dere, be duly revenged!   *death; beloved*
But ever droop and dare whiles my life lastes,   *lie still*
Til Drighten and derf dede have done what them likes!" *the Lord; cruel death*

Then caught they up the corse with care at their hertes,
4010 Carried it on a courser with the king selven;
The way unto Winchester they went at the gainest,   *by the shortest route*
Wery and wandsomly with wounded knightes;   *sorrowfully*
There come the prior of the place and professed monkes,
A-pas in procession, and with the prince meetes,   *Quickly*
4015 And he betook them the corse of the knight noble: *entrusted to*
"Lookes it be clenly keeped," he said, "and in the kirk holden;   *church*
Don for him diriges, as to the dede falles,   *Do; befits*
Mensked with masses for meed of the soul;   *Honored; reward*
Look it want no wax, ne no worship elles,   *See that; lack; candles*
4020 And that the body be baumed and on erthe holden;   *embalmed*
Yif thou keep thy covent, encroch any worship   *promise claim; reward*
At my coming again, yif Crist will it thole;   *allow*

Abide of the burying til they be brought under   *Wait for*
That has wrought us this wo and this war moved."

4025   Then says Sir Wichere the wye, a wise man of armes:
"I rede ye warily wend and workes the best,
Sujourn in this citee and semble thy bernes,
And bide with thy bold men in the burgh rich;
Get out knightes of countrees that castels holdes, [1]
4030   And out of garrisons grete good men of armes,
For we are faithly too few to fight with them all
That we see in his sorte upon the se bankes.   *saw*

With cruel countenaunce then the king carpes these wordes:
"I pray thee care not, sir knight, ne cast thou no dredes!   *imagine*
4035   Had I no segge but myself one under sun,
And I may him see with sight or on him set handes,
I shall even among his men malle him to dede,   *hammer*
Ere I of the stede stir half a steed lenghe!   *place*
I shall strike him in his stour and stroy him forever,
4040   And there-to make I mine avow devotly to Crist   *devoutly*
And to his moder Mary, the mild Queen of heven!
I shall never sujourn sound, ne saught at mine herte,   *nor have peace*
In citee ne in suburb set upon erthe,
Ne yet slomour ne sleep with my slow eyen,   *slumber; heavy*
4045   Til he be slain that him slogh, if any sleight happen,   *slew; chance*
But ever persew the paganes that my pople destroyed   *pursue*
Whiles I may pare them and pinne in place there me likes."   *hurt; imprison*

There durst no renk him arrest of all the Round Table,   *stop*
Ne none pay that prince with plesand wordes,   *pacify; pleasing*
4050   Ne none of his lege-men look him in the eyen,
So lordly he lookes for loss of his knightes!
Then drawes he to Dorset and dreches no lenger,   *hesitates*
Dref-ful, dredless, with droopand teres,   *Sorrowful doubtless*
Kaires into Cornwall with care at his herte;   *Proceeds*
4055   The trace of the traitour he trines full even,   *follows*

---

[1] *Get knights who hold your castles from their countries*

And turnes in by the Trentis the traitour to seek,   *River Trent*
Findes him in a forest   the Friday there-after;
The king lightes on foot and freshly ascries,
And with his freelich folk he has the feld nomen!   *taken*

4060   Now isshewes his enmy under the wood eves   *issues out*
With hostes of alienes full horrible to shew!
Sir Mordred the Malbranche, with his much pople,   *Ill-begotten*
Foundes out of the forest upon fele halves,   *Comes*
In seven grete batailes seemlich arrayed,
4065   Sixty thousand men — the sight was full huge —
All fightand folk of the fer landes,
Fair fitted on front by tho fresh strandes.   *arranged*
And all Arthurs host was amed with knightes   *reckoned by*
But eighteen hundreth of all, enterd in rolles.
4070   This was a match un-mete, but mightes of Crist,   *unequal save for*
To melle with that multitude in those main landes.   *fight*

          Then the royal roy of the Round Table
Rides on a rich steed, arrayes his bernes,
Buskes his avauntward, als him best likes;
4075   Sir Ewain and Sir Errak, and other grete lordes
Demenes the middle-ward menskfully there-after,   *Command*
With Merrak and Meneduke, mighty of strenghes;
Idrous and Alymer, thir avenaunt children,
Ayers with Arthur with seven-score of knightes;   *Proceed*
4080   He rewles the rereward redyly there-after,
The rekenest redy men of the Round Table;   *most active*
And thus he fittes his folk and freshly ascries,
And senn comfortes his men with knightlich wordes:
"I beseek you, sirs, for sake of our Lord,
4085   That ye do well today and dredes no wepen!
Fightes fersly now and fendes yourselven,   *defend*
Felles down yon fey folk, the feld shall be ours!   *fated*
They are Sarazenes, yon sorte, unsound mot they worthe!   *may they be*
Set on them sadly for sake of our Lord!
4090   Yif us be destained to die today on this erthe,   *destined*
We shall be heved unto heven ere we be half cold!   *lifted*
Look ye let for no lede lordly to work;

253

Layes yon laddes low by the laike end;   *end of the game*
Take no tent unto me, ne tale of me recke;   *Pay no attention; believe*
4095   Bes busy on my banners with your bright wepens,   *Be; around*
That they be strenghely stuffed with steren knightes   *strongly provided*
And holden lordly on-loft ledes to shew;
Yif any renk them arase, rescue them soon;   *is captured by them*
Workes now my worship; today my war endes!
4100   Ye wot my wele and my wo; workes as you likes!
Crist comly with crown comfort you all
For the kindest creatures that ever king led!
I give you all my blessing with a blithe will,
And all Bretons bold, blithe mot ye worthe!"   *may you be glad*

4105   They pipe up at prime time, approches them ner,   *9 a.m.; approach; nearer*
Pris men and preste proves their strenghes;   *Choice; ready*
Bremly the brethe-men bragges in trumpes,   *Boldly; buglers; blow*
In coronettes comlyly, when knightes assembles;   *horns*
And then jollyly enjoines these gentle knightes;   *join battle*
4110   A jollier journee ajudged was never,
When Bretones boldly enbraces their sheldes,   *put on (their arms)*
And Cristen encrossed them and castes in fewter!   *Christians; crossed themselves*

Then Sir Arthur host his enmy escries,   *sees*
And in they shock their sheldes, shuntes no lenger,   *thrust; delay*
4115   Shot to the sheltrones and shoutes full high;   *troops*
Through sheldes full sheen shalkes they touch!
Redily those rydde men of the Round Table   *fierce*
With real rank steel rittes their mailes;   *rip*
Brenyes brouden they brist and burnisht helmes,   *woven*
4120   Hewes hethen men down, halses in sonder!   *necks*
Fightand with fine steel the fey blood runnes;
Of the frekkest on front un-fers are beleved.   *unfierce (i.e., defeated)*
Hethenes of Argyle and Irish kinges
Enverounes our avauntward with venomous bernes,   *Surrounds*
4125   Peghtes and paynimes with perilous wepens,   *Picts*
With speres dispitously despoiles our knightes   *pitilessly*
And hewed down the hendest with hertly dintes!   *mortal blows*
Through the hole batail they holden their wayes;
Thus fersly they fight upon sere halves,   *various sides*

254

4130 That of the bold Bretons much blood spilles;
     There durst none rescue them for riches in erthe,   *dared*
     The steren were there so stedde and stuffed with other;   *beset; hard-pressed*
     He durst not stir a step, but stood for himselven,   *i.e., Arthur*
     Til three stales were stroyed by strenghe of him one!   *detachments*

4135   "Idrous," quod Arthur, "ayer thee behooves!
     I see Sir Ewain over-set with Sarazenes keen!
     Redy thee for rescues, array thee soon!
     Hie thee with hardy men in help of thy fader!
     Set in on the side and succour yon lordes!
4140 But they be succoured and sound, unsaught be I ever!"   *safe; troubled*

     Idrous him answers ernestly there-after:
     "He is my fader, in faith, forsake shall I never —
     He has me fostered and fed and my fair brethern —
     But I forsake this gate, so me God help,   *going (to his aid)*
4145 And soothly all sibreden but thyself one.   *kinship*
     I broke never his bidding for berne on life,   *command*
     But ever buxom as beste blithely to work.   *(was) obedient as a beast*
     He commaund me kindly with knightly wordes,
     That I sholde lely on thee lenge, and on no lede elles;
4150 I shall his commaundment hold, if Crist will me thole!   *allow*
     He is elder than I, and end shall we bothen;
     He shall ferk before, and I shall come after;
     Yif him be destained to die today on this erthe,   *destined*
     Crist, comly with crown, take keep to his soul!"

4155   Then romes the rich king with rewth at his herte,   *cries; grief*
     Heves his handes on height and to the Heven lookes: *Lifts*
     "Why then ne had Drighten destained at His dere will[1]
     That He had deemed me today to die for you all?   *ordered*
     That had I lever than be lord all my life-time
4160 Of all that Alexander ought whiles he in erthe lenged!"

     Sir Ewain and Sir Errak, these excellent bernes,

---

[1] *Why did the Lord not destine (me to die) at His dear will*

255

Enters in on the host and egerly strikes;

The hethenes of Orkney and Irish kinges

They gobone of the gretest with grounden swordes,   I.e., *Ewain and Errak; chop*

4165   Hewes on those hulkes with their hard wepens,

Layed down those ledes with lothly dintes;   *Laid*

Shoulders and sheldes they shrede to the haunches,

And middles through mailes they merken in sonder!   *midriffs; cut*

Such honour never ought none erthly kinges

4170   At their ending day but Arthur himselven!

    So the drought of the day dryed their hertes

That both drinkless they die; dole was the more!

Now melles our middle-ward and mengen togeder.   *attacks; mingles*

Sir Mordred the Malbranche with his much pople,   *Ill-begotten; great army*

4175   He had hid him behind within these holt eves,

With hole batail on hethe, harm is the more!   *whole battalion; heath*

He had seen the contek all clene to the end,   *conflict*

How our chevalry cheved by chaunces of armes;   *fared*

He wiste our folk was for-foughten that there was fey leved; *outfought; left dead*

4180   To encounter the king he castes him soon,   *plans*

But the cherles chicken had changed his armes;   *churlish offspring*

He had soothly forsaken the sauturour engreled,   *saltire engrailed*

And laght up three lions all of white silver,   *taken*

Passand in purpure of perry full rich, [1]

4185   For the king sholde not know the cautelous wretch.   *cunning*

Because of his cowardice he cast off his attire;   *heraldic device*

But the comlich king knew him full swithe,

Carpes to Sir Cador these kindly wordes:

"I see the traitour come yonder trinand full yerne;   *going*

4190   Yon lad with the lions is like to himselven;

Him shall torfer betide, may I touch ones,   *woe; if I can*

For all his tresoun and trayn, als I am trew lord!   *trickery*

Today Clarent and Caliburn shall kithe them togeders   *Excalibur; make known*

Whilk is keener of carfe or harder of edge!   *Which; carving*

4195   Fraist shall we fine steel upon fine weedes.   *Test*

It was my darling dainteous and full dere holden,   (i.e., *the sword Clarent); dainty*

---

[1] *Passant (shown from the side, walking) on a purple background of very rich jewels*

Keeped for encrownmentes of kinges annointed;   *coronations*
On dayes when I dubbed dukes and erles
It was burlich borne by the bright hiltes;
4200   I durst never dere it in deedes of armes   *harm*
But ever keeped clene because of myselven.
For I see Clarent uncledde that crown is of swordes,   *i.e., drawn*
My wardrope at Walingford I wot is destroyed.   *wardrobe*
Wiste no wye of wonne but Waynor herselven;   *Knew; the dwelling place*
4205   Sho had the keeping herself of that kidd wepen,
Of coffers enclosed that to the crown longed,
With ringes and relickes and the regale of Fraunce   *regalia*
That was founden on Sir Frolle when he was fey leved."   *left dead*

Then Sir Marrak in malencoly meetes him soon,   *melancholy*
4210   With a malled mace mightyly him strikes;   *hammered*
The bordour of his bacenett he bristes in sonder,   *border; helmet*
That the shire red blood over his breny runnes!
The berne blenkes for bale and all his blee changes,   *blanches; complexion*
But yet he bides as a bore and bremly he strikes!   *boar; fiercely*
4215   He braides out a brand bright als ever any silver   *I.e., Mordred*
That was Sir Arthur owen, and Utere his faders,
In the wardrope at Walingford was wont to be keeped;   *wardrobe*
Therewith the derf dog such dintes he reched   *impudent*
The tother withdrew on dregh and drust do none other   *other; back*
4220   For Sir Marrak was man marred in elde,   *weakened by age*
And Sir Mordred was mighty and in his most strenghes;
Come none within the compass, knight ne none other,
Within the swing of sword, that he ne the swet leved.   *lifeblood left*

That perceives our prince and presses to fast,   *i.e., to battle*
4225   Strikes into the stour by strenghe of his handes,   *melee*
Meetes with Sir Mordred; he meles unfair: *speaks gruffly*
"Turn, traitour untrew, thee tides no better;
By grete God, thou shall die with dint of my handes!
Thee shall rescue no renk ne riches in erthe!"

4230   The king with Caliburn knightly him strikes;
The cantel of his clere sheld he carves in sonder,   *cornerpiece*
Into the shoulder of the shalk a shaftmonde large   *six inches deep*

257

That the shire red blood shewed on the mailes!
He shuddered and shrinkes and shuntes but little,

4235 But shockes in sharply in his sheen weedes;
The felon with the fine sword freshly he strikes,
The felettes of the ferrer side he flashes in sonder,   *loins; farther*
Through jupon and gesseraunt of gentle mailes,   *gipon (tunic); hauberk*
The freke fiched in the flesh an half-foot large;   *pierced*

4240 That derf dint was his dede, and dole was the more   *hideous blow*
That ever that doughty sholde die but at Drightens will!

Yet with Caliburn his sword full knightly he strikes,
Castes in his clere sheld and coveres him full fair,
Swappes off the sword hand, als he by glentes —   *goes*

4245 An inch fro the elbow he oched it in sonder   *chopped*
That he swoones on the swarth and on swim falles —   *turf; swoon*
Through bracer of brown steel and the bright mailes,   *armguard*
That the hilt and the hand upon the hethe ligges.

Then freshlich the freke the fente up-reres,   *Arthur; vent raises*

4250 Broches him in with the brand to the bright hiltes,
And he brawles on the brand and bounes for to die.   *struggles*
"In faye," said the fey king, "sore me for-thinkes   *I sorely repent*
That ever such a false thef so fair an end haves."   *thief*

When they had finisht this fight, then was the feld wonnen,

4255 And the false folk in the feld fey are beleved!
Til a forest they fled and fell in the greves,   *groves*
And fers fightand folk followes them after,
Huntes and hewes down the hethen tikes,   *heathen dogs*
Murtheres in the mountaines Sir Mordred knightes;   *Murder*

4260 There chaped never no child, cheftain ne other,   *escaped*
But choppes them down in the chase; it charges but little!   *troubles*

But when Sir Arthur anon Sir Ewain he findes,
And Errak the avenaunt and other grete lordes,   *comely*
He caught up Sir Cador with care at his herte,

4265 Sir Clegis, Sir Cleremond, these clere men of armes,
Sir Lot and Sir Lionel, Sir Launcelot and Lowes,
Marrak and Meneduke, that mighty were ever;

With langour in the land there he layes them togeder,
Looked on their lighames, and with a loud steven,   *bodies; voice*
4270 Als lede that list not live and lost had his mirthes —   *man; desired*
Then he stotays for mad and all his strenghe failes,   *staggers; dizziness*
Lookes up to the lift and all his lire changes,   *sky; face*
Down he sways full swithe, and in a swoon falles,
Up he coveres on knees and cries full often —
4275 "King, comly with crown, in care am I leved!
All my lordship low in land is laid under,
That me has given guerdones, by grace of Himselven,   *rewards*
Maintained my manhed by might of their handes,   *manhood*
Made me manly on molde and master in erthe,
4280 In a teenful time this torfer was rered,   *painful; mischief; raised*
That for a traitour has tint all my trew lordes!   *destroyed*
Here restes the rich blood of the Round Table,
Rebuked with a rebaud, and rewth is the more!   *scoundrel*
I may helpless on hethe house by mine one,
4285 Als a woful widow that wantes her berne!   *children*
I may werye and weep and wring mine handes,   *curse*
For my wit and my worship away is forever!
Of all lordshippes I take leve to mine end!
Here is the Bretones blood brought out of life,
4290 And now in this journee all my joy endes!"

Then relies the renks of all the Round Table;   *rally*
To the real roy they ride them all;
Then assembles full soon seven score knightes
In sight to their soveraign that was unsound leved;
4295 Then kneeles the crowned king and cries on loud:
"I thank thee, God, of thy grace, with a good will,
That gave us vertue and wit to venquish these bernes,
And us has graunted the gree of these grete lordes!   *victory over*
He sent us never no shame ne shenship in erthe   *disgrace*
4300 But ever yet the over-hand of all other kinges;   *i.e., upper hand*
We have no leisere now these lordes to seek,   *leisure*
For yon lothly lad me lamed so sore!   *i.e., Mordred*

259

Graith us to Glashenbury; us gaines none other; [1]   *peace; search (treat)*
There we may rest us with roo and ransack our woundes.

4305 Of this dere day work the Drighten be lowed,   *costly; praised*
That us has detained and deemed to die in our owen."   *i.e., own land*

Then they hold at his hest holly at ones,   *command*
And graithes to Glashenbury the gate at the gainest;   *Glastonbury; way*
Entres the Ile of Avalon and Arthur he lightes,   *Isle*

4310 Merkes to a manor there, for might he no further;   *for he could go*
A surgen of Salerne enserches his woundes;   *surgeon; treats*
The king sees by assay that sound bes he never,   *examination; will be*
And soon to his seker men he said these wordes: *true*
"Do call me a confessor with Crist in his armes;   *i.e., the Eucharist*

4315 I will be houseld in haste what hap so betides.   *given the Sacrament*
Constantine my cosin he shall the crown bere,
Als becomes him of kind, if Crist will him thole!   *allow*
Berne, for my benison, thou bury yon lordes   *blessing*
That in batail with brandes are brought out of life,

4320 And sithen merk manly to Mordred children,   *pursue manfully*
That they be slely slain and slongen in waters;   *wisely; slung*
Let no wicked weed wax ne writhe on this erthe;   *grow nor flourish*
I warn, for thy worship, work als I bid!
I forgive all gref, for Cristes love of heven!

4325 If Waynor have well wrought, well her betide!"

He said *"In manus"* with main on molde where he ligges,   *"Into Your hands"*
And thus passes his spirit and spekes he no more!

The baronage of Bretain then, bishoppes and other,
Graithes them to Glashenbury with glopinand hertes   *Glastonbury; dismayed*

4330 To bury there the bold king and bring to the erthe
With all worhsip and welth that any wye sholde.   *person should have*
Throly belles they ring and *Requiem* singes,   *Loudly*
Dos masses and matins with mornand notes;   *do*
Religious reveste in their rich copes,   *Monastics dressed*

4335 Pontificalles and prelates in precious weedes,   *Bishops*

---

[1] *Let us go to Glastonbury, nothing else avails*

Dukes and douspeeres in their dole-cotes,   *mourning garments*
Countesses kneeland and claspand their handes,
Ladies languishand and lowrand to shew;   *frowning*
All was busked in black, birdes and other,   *dressed; women*
4340 That shewed at the sepulture with syland teres;   *sepulcher; flowing*
Was never so sorrowful a sight seen in their time!

Thus endes King Arthur, as auctors allege,   *authorities tell*
That was of Ectores blude, the kinge son of Troy   *Hector's blood*
And of Sir Priamous, the prince, praised in erthe;   *Priam*
4345 Fro thethen brought the Bretons all his bold elders   *thence (i.e., Troy)*
Into Bretain the brode, as the Brut telles.

Hic jacet Arthurus, rex quondam rexque futurus.
   (Here lies Arthur, king once and king to be.)
Here endes Morte Arthure, written by Robert of Thornton
R. Thornton dictus qui scripsit sit benedictus. Amen.
   (May the said R. Thornton, who wrote this, be blessed. Amen.)

261

Alliterative Morte Arthure

The following abbreviations are used in these notes to indicate editorial attribution:

Ba: Mary Macleod Banks, ed. *An Alliterative Poem of the Fourteenth Century*. London, New York: Longmans, Green and Co., 1900.

Be: Larry D. Benson, ed. *King Arthur's Death*. Indianapolis and New York: Bobbs-Merrill Company, Inc., 1974.

Bj: Erik Bjorkman, ed. *Morte Arthure*. Alt- und mittelenglische Texte, 9. Heidelberg and New York: Carl Winters, 1915.

Br: Edmund Brock, ed. *Morte Arthure or The Death of Arthur*. EETS o.s. 8. London, New York, Toronto: Oxford University Press, New Edition, 1871; reprinted 1961.

F: the present editor

GV: E. V. Gordon and Eugene Vinaver. "New Light on the Text of the Alliterative *Morte Arthure*." *Medium Aevum* 6 (1937), 81-98.

H: Mary Hamel, ed. *Morte Arthure: A Critical Edition*. Garland Medieval Texts, 9. New York and London: Garland Publishing, Inc., 1984.

K: Valerie Krishna, ed. *The Alliterative Morte Arthure*. New York: Burt Franklin and Company, Inc., 1976.

OED: Oxford English Dictionary

OL: J. L. N. O'Loughlin. "The Middle English Alliterative *Morte Arthure*." *Medium Aevum* 4 (1935), 153-168.

1   *Himselven*. On the prominence of reflexive formulas in the poem (*himselven, him likes*, etc.) as indicators of the will and willfulness, see Peck, pp. 158 ff.

29   *Uter*. Uther Pendragon, Arthur's father.

32   Scotland and England were often at war in the fourteenth century, hence *scathel* ("harmful") Scotland.

37   *Grace*. The MS reading. Most editors emend to *Grece* (Greece) but *Grace* (Grasse) makes more geographical sense. Grasse is a small city in southern

France, north of Cannes, which was an episcopal see from 1244 to 1790. K retains *Grace*.

41   *Vienne.* Ackerman suggests Vienna, though K thinks, rather, that it must refer to a town north of Valence or a district in Poitier.

42   *Overgne* (Ba, Be, K, H). I.e., Auvergne. MS: *Eruge.*

47   I.e., the whole extent of Denmark.

61   *Caerlion.* One of Arthur's principal cities where, according to the chronicles, he often spent Pentecost. K suggests that the reference to the city's "curious walles" may derive from Giraldus' description of the city: "[Caerleon] was of undoubted antiquity, and handsomely built of masonry, with courses of bricks, by the Romans. Many vestiges of its former splendour may yet be seen; immense palaces . . . a tower of prodigious size, remarkable hot baths, relics of temples, and theatres, all enclosed within fine walls, parts of which remain standing. You will find on all sides, both within and without the circuit of the walls, subterraneous buildings, aqueducts, underground passages; and what I think worthy of notice, stoves contrived with wonderful art, to transmit the heat insensibly through narrow tubes passing up the side walls" (p. 164).

64   *Carlisle.* Here, Arthur's new city, located on the Scottish border; another favorite site for Arthur's festivities, according to Froissant. The Middle English romance *Sir Gawain and the Carl of Carlisle* suggests the city's foundation at a place where courtesy turned monstrosity to civility.

66   *douspeeres.* Originally Charlemagne's twelve peers, but here simply "high noblemen."

68   A *bannerette* was a senior knight entitled to bear his own banner; a *bacheler* ranked somewhat lower and was either a newly made knight or a young man about to be knighted.

77   *West Marches.* The territories bordering Wales.

79   The bread is the first course (since the other food was heaped upon it), and the first course is the traditional time for the arrival of a messenger. Compare *Sir Gawain and the Green Knight*, lines 116-132.

86 *Lucius Iberius:* "The Emperor Lucius was apparently invented by Geoffrey of Monmouth [*History of the Kings of Britain*], who calls him Lucius Tiberius. . . . The attempt at a reconquest of Britain by the Romans in the sixth century also derives from Geoffrey" (K, p. 165).

92 *Lamass Day:* a harvest festival formerly celebrated on August 1.

95 Prime was "the first hour of the day, beginning at six-o'clock throughout the year or at the varying times of sunrise" (*OED*).

105 The Romans held title to Britain on the basis of Caesar's conquest, as recorded in chronicles based ultimately on Book V of Geoffrey of Monmouth's *History of the Kings of Britain*.

108 *route.* "Ambigious: either 'snore' (OE *hrutan*), an expression of Lucius's angry contempt, or more neutrally 'go, travel' (OF *router*), a contrast rather than a parallel to *ryste* (rest)" (H, p. 257).

134 *There is* (Br, Be, K). MS: *thare.*

142 *crowned was* (Bj, Be, K). MS: *corounde.*

168 Chambers with chimneys are heated rooms, a luxury at this time. See note to line 61.

176ff. The elaborate feast that follows might actually have been served at a royal household of the late fourteenth century. Menus for royal feasts are printed in *Two Fifteenth-Century Cooking Books*, ed. Austin, EETS o.s. 91 (London, 1888; reprinted 1964). See H's extensive notes on the dishes and feast practices of the later fourteenth century (pp. 259–63).

178 *togges* (OL, Be). MS: *togers.* H reads *toges;* Br and K follow MS.

186 *whom.* MS: *whame.* Bj, Be, and H emend to *when* or *whan,* but I have followed Br and K in retaining MS sense.

200 *Crete.* The poet regularly identifies wines by their place of origin. The universality of Arthur's wine cellar is impressive.

213   The virtues (powers) of precious stones were commonplace in the Middle Ages. See *English Medieval Lapidaries*, eds. Evans and Serjeantson, EETS o.s. 190 (London, 1932; reprinted 1960).

233   *Waynor* and *Gaynor* for Guinevere are used interchangeably as are *Gawain* and *Wawain* for Gawain.

234   *Sir Owglitreth.* Sir Owghtreth of Turry is evidently one of Arthur's vassals. *Turry* perhaps is Turin, Italy. J. L. N. O'Loughlin, "The Middle English Alliterative *Morte Arthure,"Medium Aevum* 4 (1935), 159, suggests that he is one of Lucius' ambassadors, who out of courtesy is assigned with Gawain to accompany the Queen.

245   *Giauntes Towr.* Since giants occupied Britain before the arrival of Brutus, this tower is, presumably, a "prehistoric" edifice.

256   *deffuse.* Be and H emend to *disuse*, but I have followed Br and K in retaining MS.

277   In Book III of Geoffrey's *History* we are told that, long before Caesar came to Britain, Belinus and Brennius conquered and ravaged Rome. This is, of course, not historical.

      "Baldwin the Third is unknown; perhaps he was invented for the sake of alliteration" (K, p. 169).

282   According to Geoffrey (Book V, chapter 6) Constantine was the son of a Roman Senator and a British Princess, and he succeeded to the kingship of Britain. Then he overthrew the Emperor Maxentius and became Emperor. According to legend, his mother, Helen, discovered the True Cross. Arthur claims kinship with Constantine because of his supposed British mother. Constantine actually did proclaim himself Caesar while in York, but he was never king of Britain and not of British descent.

288   *King Aungers.* Robert W. Ackerman, *An Index of Arthurian Names in Middle English* (Stanford: Stanford University Press, 1952), p. 20, identifies King Aungers as Geoffrey of Monmouth's Auguselus, a king of Scotland, son of Bryadens, grandson of Igerne, and brother of Lot and Urien. He was, like Lot, an enemy of Arthur who later became an ally.

297   The *vernacle* (the relic of Veronica) is the handkerchief with which St. Veronica wiped the face of Christ on His way to the Crucifixion. Miraculously, the image of His face was preserved on the handkerchief, which still survives. The cult of Veronica was especially strong in the fourteenth century. Pope John XXII granted an indulgence of ten thousand days for a prayer to the Veronica, and its legend had an important part in the popular romances about Titus and Vespasian.

301   *eldes*. Bj and Be emend to *monthes,* but I have followed Br, K, and H in retaining MS. It probably means "of two generations".

304   *Berne of Britain the Little*. King Hoel of Brittany.

305   *beseekes*. MS; *besekys*. Bj and Be emend to *congee beseekes*, but I have followed Br, K, and H in adhering to the MS reading.

320   *The Welsh king*. Perhaps Sir Valiant (line 2064).

334   *Of Wyghte and*. GV and Be emend to *of wightest;* H emends to *of wyghte men*, but I have followed Br and K in retaining MS.

337   *Sir Ewain fitz Urien*. Iwain son of Urien and Morgan le Fay.

352   *Petersand* (Petrasanta, i.e., the Vatican); *Pis* (Pisa); *Pount Tremble* (Pontremoli).

368–70   "Lancelot, the great hero of the Vulgate tradition, was unknown in the earlier chronicles. In introducing him as one of the 'lesse men' among Arthur's retainers, the poet gives his audience a clear signal: this poem will *not* be concerned with the issues and themes of that tradition" (H, p. 268).

369   *love*. H reads *lone* and translates the line "I praise God for this contribution" (H, p. 268).

375   *Genivers* (Genoese): "The notorious giants from Genoa in Lucius' army may derive from the Genoan mercenaries who fought with France against Edward III at Crecy and other important battles" (K, p. 170).

391   *renkes*. Not *rankes* (men) but *renkes* (paths) from OF *renc*.

415   *Epiphany*. From the Greek for "appearance" or "manifestation," it is the feast on January 6, commemorating the coming of the Magi to see the child Jesus and symbolizing the "manifestation" of the newborn savior to the whole world (*OED*).

450   *Watling Street*. The old Roman road leading from the southern coast by way of London to Cardigan in Wales.

451   *nyghes* (Ba, K). MS: *nyghttes*. "The appearance of *nyghte* in the same line is very likely the source of the scribal error" (K, p. 171).

458   *lette*. Bj, Be, and H emend to *lefe*, but I have followed Br and K in retaining MS.

471   *sixteen* (Bj, Be, K, H). MS: *sex sum of six*. "Either 'part of a company of six' or 'along with a company of six'. . . . In either case the number given [in the MS] is inconsistent with that of line 81, where the Senator arrives with a company of sixteen" (K, p. 171).

482   *Catrik*. A town in Yorkshire, identified with the Roman cataractonium.

490   Sandwich is the port from which the Romans will take ship. One of the "cinque ports," Sandwich is the site of the Church of St. Peter where curfew, now ceremonial, was rung.

497   *Mount Goddard*. One of the principal passes through the French Alps into Italy.

513   *sandes*. Bj, Be, and H emend to *sandesman*, but I have followed Br and K in retaining MS.

515   *wye* (OL, Be, K, H). MS: *waye*. Br's emendation.

572   *Ambyganye* and *Orcage* are apparently in the East. H emends to *Arcage*, the OF spelling of Arcadia. *Ambyganye*, she suggests, could be Albania.

575   *Irritane* (Hyrcania) and *Elamet* (Elam) are not islands but countries in Asia.

587   *Bayous.* Be emends to *boyes*; H emends to *barons*, but I have followed Br and K in retaining MS. This is an odd location in the context, but the suggested emendations are not persuasive. *Bayonne* (Beune) is in southwestern France.

588   Prester John was thought to be a Christian ruler living somewhere in the Orient. In *The Travels of Sir John Mandeville* (a famous fourteenth century book of fictitious travels, presented as a true account), Prester John is said to be the Emperor of India, allied by marriage to the great Khan of China. The legend was probably based on reports of Christian communities which actually did exist in the East. Pamphile is a region of Asia Minor.

604–05 *Prussland* (Prussia) and *Lettow* (Lithuania) were still pagan in the fourteenth century.

625   The octave of St. Hillary's day would be a week after January 24.

628–29 *Constantine* (the Peninsula of Cotentin) and *Barflete* (Barfleur) are on the coast of Normandy.

656   Arthur's concern for the protection of his game is not surprising in a century when (as shown by *Sir Gawain and the Green Knight*) hunting was of great importance to the aristocracy.

674   *wordles.* MS: *werdez.* Bj, K, H read *wer[l]de?*.

716   *Sways* (Bj, Be). MS: *Twys.*

734   *Hackes.* MS: *Hukes.* K emends to *Hekes.* H follows MS on grounds that *hukes* are outergarments or possibly "caparisons for horses" (*MED, s.v.*); she finds Bj's emendation *hackes* to be redundant if paired with *hackeneys.*

769   Be, following GV, supplies a supposed missing line after 769: *His tail was totattered with tonges ful huge*; K notes but does not accept the insertion. H accepts. I have followed K.

771   Be, following GV, supplies a supposed missing line after 771: *And his clawes were enclosed with clene gold*; K does not note. H accepts. I have not included the line.

785   *at.* Be notes MS *at,* but prints *it.* I have retained the MS reading as do Br and K. H deletes the word, explaining that the scribe miscopied the following *to* which he then corrected by writing *to* but failed to cross out the *at.*

      Rapped, H suggests, means "barked," not dashed to earth, which is inconsistent with the flying posture.

804   *thring.* MS: *brynge.* Holthausen's emendation, followed by Bj, Be, and K. H suggests *breen,* meaning "frighten, terrify." See her note discussing the problem. Br follows MS.

808   *seven science.* The seven liberal arts (grammar, rhetoric, logic, which were the *trivium,* and arithmetic, geometry, astronomy, music, which were the *quadrivium*); these were the basis of Medieval education.

812   Second half of 812 appears in the MS as the second half of 813 and vice versa (Bj, Be). K and H disagree, but I have followed Be.

821   *tattered* (Bj, Be, K, H). MS: *taschesesede.* Br: *tachesesede.*

841   *Templar.* A member of the Knights Templar, a military order founded c. 1118 for the protection of the Holy Sepulchre and pilgrims visiting the Holy Land. The order was suppressed in 1312.

848   *countree of Constantine.* The country around Cotentin, a peninsula on the coast of Normandy.

880   The promontory is Mont-Saint-Michel, on which, according to this story, Arthur founds the famous monastery to commemorate his victory. See also line 899.

905   *jupon.* A gipon is a sleeveless cloth garment worn over the armor; Arthur's is *jagged in shredes* — with fashionable scallopings at the edges. *Jerodine* is apparently a kind of cloth (perhaps gabardine).

910   *enarmed.* Bj and Be emend to *enamelled,* but I have followed Br, K, and H in retaining MS.

946   *them.* MS: *thus.* Br, K, and H retain MS.

964   *Wade*. A figure in German legend and a now-lost English romance.

1028   *piment*. Wine mixed with honey and spices.

1041   *source* (Bj, Be). MS: *sowre*. Br and K retain MS. H emends to *sowþe*.

1083   *eyen-holes* (Bj, Be). MS: *hole eyghn*. Br, K, and H retain MS.

1123   *genitals* (Bj, Br, Be, K, H). MS: *genitates*.

1142   *buskes*.   Bj and Be emend to *wild buskes*, but I have followed Br and K in retaining MS.

1175   A reference to the giant Pitho, whom Arthur slew "in Aravio Montem" (in the mount of Araby), the Aran mountains in Wales. The story is from Geoffrey of Monmouth, *History of the Kings of Britain*, Book X.

1225   *Castel Blank* is unique in this poem.

1231   *mene-while*. GV, Be, and H emend to *mete-while*, but I have followed Br and K in retaining MS even though the emendation is plausible.

1248   *frayes* (Bj, Be, K). MS: *fraisez*. Br and H retain MS.

1263   *Sir Bois*. Earl of Oxford. "The name Bos (Boso de Vado Boum in Geoffrey [of Monmouth] was probably invented by Geoffrey as a pun on *bos* and Oxford" (Ackerman, p. 38).

1264   *Sir Berille*. Perhaps Borel, Earl of Mans, who fights on Arthur's side and is given Le Mans.

1265   *Sir Grime*. Bj emends to Geryn of Chartres, one of Arthur's vassals who appears at this point in the chronicles and also in line 3708. Grime is not known elsewhere.

1281   *with* (Bj, Be, K, H). MS: *that with*. Br follows MS.

1302   *worthy* (Bj, Be, K). MS: *worthethy*. Br and H retain MS.

1334   Appears in MS as line 1330 (Bj, Be, H).

1364   *sable* (Bj, Be, K, H). MS: *salle.* Br follows MS.

1378   *unabaist all.* Bj and Be emend to *all unabaist,* but I have followed Br, K, and H
in retaining MS word order and have punctuated to make the grammatical
relation clear.

1402–02 The perilous water that falls from the sea fifty miles away apparently refers to
a tidal estuary (n.b. *salt strandes* in line 1422).

1405   I agree with H that *changen* should be taken as a hunting metaphor: to
"change" attention from prey to prey.

1408   *all* (Bj, Be). MS: *and*; *Bedvere* (Be, H). MS: *Bedwyne.* Br and K retain both MS
readings. Perhaps a miswriting of *Baldwin,* who appears in lines 1606 and
2384.

1427   *redies.* Be emends to *relies,* but I have followed Br, K, and H in retaining MS.

1436   *stokes.* Br and Be emend to *strokes,* but K notes that emendation is unneces-
sary, citing *OED stoke* sb2 (p. 182). H follows MS too.

1466-67 Appear in MS in reverse order (Be). I have followed K, H in retaining MS
order.

1503   *not* (Bj, Be). MS: *now.* Br, K, and H follow MS.

1558   *Sir Ewain fitz Henry.* Probably Sir Ewain fitz Urien, as in line 337. Ackerman
notes that he is given both names in Layamon's *Brut* as well (p. 248).

1567   *tithandes* (Bj, Be, H). MS: *thy?andez.* Br and K retain MS spelling, as a variant
of *tydandis.*

1622   *Sir Evander.* King of Syria and one of Lucius's vassals.

1638   *Sir Clegis, Sir Cleremus, Sir Cleremond.* Sir Clegis is a knight of the Round
Table. Either Sir Cleremus and Sir Cleremond might allude to Clarrus of

Clere Mounte who appears in other romances aiding Launcelot in his war against Arthur. Here the pair fill out the alliterative quatrain.

1653 *kith* (Bj, Be, K, H). MS: *lythe*. Br retains MS but glosses: "Read *Kythe*."

1681 Clegis challenges the Romans to a formal tournament, with three courses of war (that is, three jousts with the lance) and the claims of knighthood (the winner to take the horse and arms of the loser.)

1683 Clegis' insult, like the King of Syria's, is part of the formal "flyting."

1688 *hufe*. Bj and Be emend to *leng*, but I have followed Br, K, and H in retaining MS. The charge that Clegis is trying to delay things is only a *pro forma* insult. More significant is the King of Syria's inquiry about Clegis' ancestry, since it would be beneath his dignity to joust with any but the highest noble.

1690 *crest* (Bj, Be, H). MS: *breste* (Br, K).

1695 *Sir Brut*. The legendary founder of Britain. According to Geoffrey of Monmouth he was the great-grandson of Aeneas of Troy.

1698 *Forthy* (Be). MS: *ffro the*.

    Brut (Bj, Be, H). MS: *Borghte* (Br, K).

1732 *on*. Bj, Be, and H emend to *on the*, but I have followed Br and K in retaining MS.

1744 *Wawayne*. Bj, Be, and H emend to *Bawdwyne*, but I have followed Br and K in retaining MS.

1745 *Rowlaundes* (Bj, Be, H). MS: *and Rowlandez* (Br, K).

1768 *all on loud* (Bj, Be). MS: *o laundone* (Br, K, H).

1786 *corn-bote*. Literally a fine paid in grain.

1797 *in his* (Bj, Be, K). MS: *his ine* (Br). H argues that MS reads *in his*.

1855   I.e., the Saracens are six feet from the waist up.

1866   *Cordewa*. Be and H emend to *Cornett*, but I have followed Br and K in retaining MS.

1878   *men*. Bj, Be, and H emend to *hethen men*, but I have followed K in retaining MS.

1904   *Utolf* (Bj, Be, K, H). MS: *Vtere* (Br). Uther, Arthur's father, is dead. Utolfe appears in lines 1622 and 1868, along with Evander, as knights on the Roman side.

1908   *Carous* (K, H). MS: *Barous*. Br emends to *Barouns*.

1911   *Sarazenes ynow* (Bj, Be, K). MS: *sarazenes*.

1912   *are* (Bj, Be, H). MS: *a* (Br, K).

1930   *never berne* (Bj, Be). MS: *never* (Br, K, H).

1938   *Though* (Be). MS: *Thofe* (Br, K, H).

1979   *them*. Bj and Be emend to *then*, but I have followed Br, K, and H in retaining MS.

1980   *halfe*. Bj and Be emend to *side*, but I have followed Br, K, and H in retaining MS.

1982   *Wales* (Bj, Be, H). MS: *Vyleris* (Br, K).

2016   *sees*. Bj and Be emend to *him sees*, but I have followed Br, K, and H in retaining MS.

2047   The knights of the Round Table fulfill the vows they made; the King of Wales fulfills the vow he made in lines 330-32.

2066   *Ewain fitz Urien* (Bj, Be, K, H). MS: *Ewayne sir Fytz Vriene* (Br). Ewain fitz Urien fulfills the vow he made in lines 357-63.

2073   Lancelot had vowed (lines 372-77) to strike down the emperor himself, and accordingly he now strikes him down and leaves a spear stuck in his belly. The emperor evidently recovers very quickly, for he is soon back in battle.

2081   Lot had vowed to be the first to ride through the Roman ranks (lines 386-94), which he now does. When Lot has accomplished this, the vows are all fulfilled and the battle proper begins.

2108   *hethe* (Bj, Be, K). MS: *heyghe* (Br,H).

2112   *Jonathal* (OL, Be, H, K). MS: *Ienitall* (Br). Jonathal appears in a corresponding passage in Geoffrey of Monmouth.

2123   *Caliburn* is used for *Excalibur* by Geoffrey of Monmouth.

2151   *on folde* (Bj, Be, K). MS: *fygured folde* (Br). H emends to *faireste-fygured felde*.

2157   *Sir Cleremond the noble* (Bj, K). MS: *with clene mene of armes* (Br). Be, H have *Sir Bedvere the rich,* but *Cleremond the noble* is as familiar a formula and improves the alliteration.

2180   *real renk* (Bj, Be, H). MS: *reall* (K). Br reads *ryalle.* The addition of *renk* so much improves both rhythm and alliteration that a scribal omission seems likely.

2181   *he* (K). MS: *and* (Br, H).

2198   *into.* Bj, Be, and H emend to *into the,* but I have followed Br and K in retaining MS.

2217   *chis.* Bj, Be, and H emend to *thriches,* but I have followed Br and K in retaining MS.

2250   *at.* Bj, Be, and H emend to *all,* but I have followed Br and K in retaining MS.

2280   *lighte.* Bj and Be emend to *lithe,* but I have followed Br, K, and H in retaining MS.

2283   *cokadrisses* (Be, K, H). MS: *sekadrisses* (Br).

2286   *dromedaries of* (Bj, Be, H). MS: *of dromondaries* (Br).

2288   *Olfendes* (Bj, Be, K). MS: *elfaydes* (Br, H).

2305   *he lenged* (Br, Be, K, H). MS: *lengede.* The *colours* are the heraldic devices on the banners set above the caskets.

2328   *ne.* Bj, Be, and H emend to *we ne,* but I have followed Br and K in retaining MS.

2343   *full monee.* Bj and Be emend to *full of the monee,* but I have followed Br and K in retaining MS.

2358   Br, Bj, Be, and H all emend MS *fowre* to *ten.* "However, though the messenger is presumably referring in 2358 to the tribute that Arthur's court owed and had not paid for four score winters, Arthur in 2344 is referring to something else — the tribute from Rome to his own kingdom that was lost in his ancestors' days" (K, 187).

2384   *Sir Bedwar the rich.* Apparently not the same knight as *Sir Bedwere the rich* who was buried in line 2379. See Bj, p. 158, and K, pp. 187–88, on defects in lines 2371–85.

2386   *the Auguste.* OL, Be, and H emend to *Auguste,* but I have followed Br and K in retaining MS.

2390   *Cristofer day.* St. Christopher's day, July 25. St. Christopher has since been decanonized.

2398   *Lorraine the lele.* Bj and Be emend to *of Lorraine the lege,* but I have followed Br, K, and H in retaining MS.

2403   *to* (K). MS: *and.*

2408   *Tuskan* (Ba, Be, K, H). MS: *Turkayne* (Br).

2418   *is in* (Bj, Be, K, H). MS: *es* (Br).

2419   *Citee* (Br, Be, K, H). MS: *Pety.*

2424   Br, Be, and H note MS *beneyde: bended* (Bj). K emends to *bendyde*.

2438   *ferde*. Bj and Be emend to *rade*, but I have followed K and H in retaining MS.

2478   *plattes*. Bj and Be emend to *plantes*, but I have followed K in retaining MS.

2495   *Wecharde*. Be emends to *Wicher*, but I have followed K in retaining MS.

2519   *withouten any berne* (Bj, Be, K, H). MS: *with birenne ony borne*.

2521   *gessenande*. Be and H emend to *glessenand*, but I have followed K. Instead of glistening in gold the sable (black) grayhounds are lying couchant.

2522   *and* (Bj, Be, K, H). MS: *a* (Br).

2531   *the lange* (Bj, Be, H). MS: *a launde* (Br, K).

2568   *vailed* (K). MS: *vrayllede* (Br). Bj and Be emend to *railed*.

2586   *Salerne*. Salerno. The University of Salerno was famous in the Middle Ages for its medical school.

2588   Be follows GV suggestion to insert two lines to follow 2588: *That I might be cristened, with crisom annointed, / Become meek for my misdeeds for meed of my soul.*

2594   *legeaunce and land* (OL, Be). MS: *legyaunce* (Br, K). H emends to *undir what legyaunce*.

2648   It would be dishonorable for Priamus to be defeated by an ordinary soldier. Gawain is such a great knight that even to be defeated by him is an honor that Priamus would prize even if no one were to learn of it.

2663   Be, following GV, inserts the following after 2663: *For here hoves at thy hand an hundreth good knightes.* H agrees, but I have followed Br and K in omitting the line.

2664   *For they are*. Be emends to *they are*, but I have followed Br, K, and H in retaining MS.

2675   *slight* (Bj, Be, K). MS: *slaughte.* H emends to *a slaughte.*

2680   *Wecharde* (K). MS: *Wychere.*

2705   The four wells of Paradise (which were thought to be in the East) were cele-brated for their magical qualities (one was the Fountain of Youth) and thought to be the sources of the four great rivers of the East — the Nile, the Ganges, the Tigris, and the Euphrates.

2771   *breth* (Bj, Be, H). MS: *breste* (Br, K).

2797   *and* (Bj, Be, H). MS: *a* (Br, K).

2854   *Though* (Bj, Be). MS: *Thofe* (Br, K, H).

2868   *Unwine.* A legendary hero of the Goths, probably known to the poet from a lost English romance.

                Absolon. Absalom (2 Samuel 13-19), celebrated in medieval romance for his personal beauty.

2876   The adventure in the vale of Josephat, to which the *gestes* refer, is an episode in the *Fuerre de Gaderes*, a story of the Crusades.

2890   *Gerard* (Bj, Be, H). MS: *Ierante* (Br, K).

2891   He stabs him through a gyronny shield (a shield decorated with two colors divided into triangles).

2908   *Giauntes.* Bj and Be emend to *giauntes are*, but I have followed Br, K, and H in retaining MS.

2940   *duke dresses* (Bj, Be, H). MS: *duke* (Br, K).

2950   *Marches.* MS: *maches* (Br). Be emends to *matchless*, but I have followed K and H.

2951   *middle-erthe.* "The earth, as placed between heaven and hell, or as supposed to occupy the centre of the universe" (*OED*).

2977   *sleghte* (Bj, Be, K, H). MS: *elagere* (Br).

3013   *at heste* (Bj, Be, H). MS: *the beste* (Br, K).

3031   *in Hampton.* According to H, the phrase "indicates that the messenger's re-
ward is not simply a lump sum but an estate worth £100 a year – a princely
gift for a mere herald" (p. 351).

3057   *none* (GV, Be, H). MS: *no* (Br, K).

3061   *be deemed* (Bj, Be, K). MS: *idene the* (Br). H emends to *indeue the*, meaning
"endow you" or "provide you with a livelihood."

3064   *he.* Bj and Be emend to *sho*, but I have followed K and H in retaining MS.

3067   MS lines 3068-3083 are moved by Be to become lines 3112-3127. Although H
agrees with Be, I have followed K in leaving them in their MS position.

3074   *knighte.* GV, H, and Be emend to *king*, but I have followed Br and K in retain-
ing MS.

3101   He crosses over Lake Lucerne into Switzerland.

3117   *Slely.* MS: *slal* (Br). Bj and Be emend to *skathel*, but I have followed K.

3140   *for Pawnce and for* (Bj, Be, H, K). MS: *of Pawnce and of.* Br: *Plesaunce*
(Piacenza), *Pawnce* (Ponte), and *Pownte Tremble* (Pontremole) are towns in
Lombardy.

3150   *thus wele timed.* GV and Be emend to *him time semed*, but I have followed Br,
K, and H in retaining MS.

3186   *sceptre and swerde.* MS: *his ceptre (Br).* Be emends to *sceptre, for sooth,* but I
have followed K. H emends to *ceptre forsothe.*

3209   *honden.* Bj and Be emend to *holde*, but I have followed K in retaining MS. H
emends to *honouren.*

3212   *Cross-days*: Rogation Days, three special days of prayer preceding Ascension Day (forty days after Easter).

3220   *slakes his* (Bj, Be). MS: *slakes* (Br, H, K).

3241   *clerewort*. Bj and Be emend to *clevewort*, but I have followed Br, K, and H in retaining MS.

3251   Dame Fortune, with her Wheel of Fortune, is a familiar figure in late Medieval poetry, as are the Nine Worthies whom Arthur sees in his dream. The Nine Worthies first appear in fourteenth century works such as *The Parlement of Three Ages* and reappear as late as Shakespeare's *Midsummer Night's Dream*.

3256   *With brouches* (Bj, Be, H). MS: *bruches* (Br, K).

       besauntes are coins, originally from Byzantium, here coin-shaped golden discs.

3257   *Her back* (Bj, Be, H). MS: *With hir bake* (Br, K).

3263   *riches* (Bj, Be, K). MS: *reched* (Br), but K thinks MS may read *reches* anyway.

3272   *this* (Bj, Be). MS: *thir* (Br, K). H reads *thi*.

       roo (Bj, Be, K). MS: *rog* (Br, H).

3282   *tone eye* (Bj, Be, K, H). MS: *two eyne* (Br).

3308   *folded* (Bj, Be, K). MS: *fayled* (Br). H emends to *falded in*.

3345   Frollo was the ruler of France whom Arthur killed in single combat when he conquered that country as part of the conquests that immediately precede the action of this poem and that are summarized in the opening lines. The story is told in Geoffrey of Monmouth's *History of the Kings of Britain*, Book IX, chapter 11, where Arthur's adversary is called Flollo, and in Wace's *Brut* (which our poet may have known), where he is called Frolle or Frollo.

3352   *crispand* (Bj, Be, H). MS: *krispane* (Br, K).

3356   *Circled* (Bj, Be, K, H). MS: *Selkylde* (Br).

3408-10   Alexander the Great, Hector of Troy, and Julius Caesar are the three Pagan Worthies.

3412-16   Judas Maccabeus, Joshua, and King David are the three Jewish Worthies.

3422   *tone climand kyng* (Bj, Be, H). MS: *two clymbande kynges*.

3423   *Karolus* (Charlemagne) is the first of the three Christian Worthies. The second is Godfrey of Bouillon (line 3430), and the third is Arthur himself.

3427   *lifelich*. Bj and Be emend to *loveliche*, but I have followed Br, K, and H in retaining MS.

3434   He shall recover the cross when he conquers Jerusalem. Godfrey's deeds, like Charlemagne's (lines 3423-29), are prophesied, since Arthur historically precedes both.

3439   *ninde* (Bj, Be). Ms: *nynne* (Br, K, H).

3470   Be interprets *rowme* ("roomy, or full-cut") to be fashionable, as he does the *shreddes and shragges* ("scalloped edges") in line 3473, but I am inclined to agree with H that the stranger is dressed quite unfashionably.

3474   *slawin*. Bj and Be emend to *sclavin* ("pilgrim's garb"), but I have followed Br, K, and H in retaining MS.

        The scallop shells were the mark of a pilgrimage to St. James of Compostela in Spain, the palm branch of a pilgrimage to the Holy Land.

3480   *wathe* (Bj, Be, H). MS: *wawthe* (Br, K).

3505   Be reverses 3505 and 3506, but I have followed Br, K, and H in retaining MS.

3510   *I*. Bj and Be emend to *I was*, but I have followed K and H in retaining MS.

3530   *Of* (Bj, Be). MS: *To* (Br, K, H).

3541   From the Humber River (at the southern border of Yorkshire) to the town of Hawick (in southern Scotland), i.e., the whole North Country.

3545   Hengest and Horsa were traditionally the first Germanic (that is, Anglo-Saxon) invaders of Britain; Geoffrey of Monmouth (*History*, Book VI, chapter 11) gives the traditional account.

3592   *trome*. Bj, Be, and H emend to *trumpe*, but I have followed Br and K in retaining MS.

3605   Lines 3605 and 3606 appear in reverse order in the MS (Be).

3611   Apparently the painted cloths (sewn together and doubled) are meant to serve as a protection against arrows.

3648-49   The maiden on the *chef,* the upper third of the shield, is the Blessed Virgin, who is holding the Christ-child, the *Chef* or Lord of heaven. In 3650 the sense seems to be "noble."

3650   Arthur will not change his arms to disguise himself even when hard-pressed, as Mordred later does (lines 4181-85).

3662   *Wether* (Be). MS: *With hir* (Br, K, H).

        Ramming and boarding were the principal tactics in fourteenth century sea battles, since cannon had only recently been introduced.

3672   *bernes* (Bj, Be). MS: *braynes* (Br, K). H reads *berynes.*

3675   *Up ties* (Be, K, H). MS: *Vpcynes* (Br).

3678   *Many freke* (Bj, Be). MS: *ffreke* (Br, K, H).

3684   *englaimes* (Bj, Be, K, H). MS: *englaymous* (Br).

3709   *Galuth* is Gawain's sword, here personified as "a good gome."

3720   *in* (Be, K). MS: *and* (Br, H).

3743   *Engendure* may be a reference to Mordred's incestuous begetting (see Stanzaic *Morte Arthure*, lines 2955-56), though there is no direct reference to it in this poem.

3773   The Montagues were a famous Northern English family. The head of the family was a supporter of Richard II and a suspected heretic. He rebelled against Henry IV in 1400; he was beheaded and his head was displayed on London Bridge as a warning to other potential traitors.

3796   *help*. Be emends to *help me*, but I have followed Br, K, and H in retaining MS.

3797   *to see us* (Br, Be, K, H). MS: *to us*.

3864   *Fres*. Bj and Be emend to *Frisland*, but I have followed Br, K, and H in retaining MS.

3869   The golden griffin (a winged dragon) is Gawain's usual heraldic device.

3891   *sib-blood*. Mordred and Gawain are half brothers; their mother is Arthur's sister.

3911   *yeyes* (Bj, Be, H, K). MS: *?ee* (Br).

3924   *Swalters*. Bj and Be emend to *swafres*, but I have followed Br, K, and H in retaining MS.

3929   *trewth* (Bj, Be, H). MS: *trewghe* (Br, K).

3937   It is unclear whether the MS reads *Guthede* or *Guchede*. The former makes more sense.

3942   *encircled* (Bj, Be, K, H). MS: *enserchede* (Br).

3996   *kithe* (Bj, Be, H). MS: *kyghte* (Br, K).

4010   *Carried it* (Br, Be, H). MS: *Karyed* (Br, K).

4017   *Don for him* (Bj, Be). MS: *Done for* (Br, K, H).

4020   *erthe*. Bj, Be, and H emend to *bere*, but I have followed Br and K in retaining MS.

4095   The banners must be defended not only for the sake of honor but because signals made with the banners are the only means of communication during a battle.

4129   *sere*. Bj and Be emend to *fele*, but I have followed Br, K, and H in retaining MS.

4157   *Why then ne* (Be). MS: *Qwythen*. K explains that an emendation may not really be necessary since the *OED* glosses the MS word in the same words as the emendation.

4181   *churles*. OL and Be emend to *churlish*, but I have followed Br, K, and H in retaining MS. Mordred adopts the cowardly stratagem of changing his heraldic devices, which Arthur would never do (see note on line 3650).

4221   *and in* (Br, Be, K, H). MS: *and*.

4223   *he ne* (Br, Be, K, H). MS: *ne he*.

4237   *felettes*. Be glossed as "rib-plates," following Finlayson. K argues that it means "loins," from OF *filet*, while H suggests "bands of muscular tissue, especially the loins" (p. 444).

4303   Arthur is said to have been buried at Glastonbury.

4305   *day*. Be emends to *dayes*, but I have followed Br, K, and H in retaining MS.

4326   *In manus* is a common Medieval short form of *Pater, in manus tuas commendo spiritum meum:* "Father, into thy hands I commend my spirit," Christ's last words on the cross according to Luke 23:46.

4332   *Requiem*. Mass for the dead.

4343   *blude*. Bj and Be emend to *kin*, but I have followed Br, K, and H in retaining MS.

4346   *Brut*. The History of Britain, which begins with Brutus, who settled the country. *Brut* refers to any history of Britain, though the poet may have meant some specific work, such as the popular English prose *Brut*.

4347 This and the following lines are not by the original author of our poem. This line, which is the inscription on Arthur's tomb (dating from 1278), was added by a later reader of the manuscript. The next lines concern the scribe rather than the author of the poem. Robert Thornton, who lived in Yorkshire, about 1440, wrote out the manuscript that contains this and a number of other romances. The final Latin line, asking that Robert be blessed for his work, was written by a grateful reader in the later fifteenth century.

Glossary

Afrike *Africa*
again, againes *against*
Almaine *Germany*
als, also, as *as;* not an intensifier
and, and yif *if*
anon *immediately*
appert *open*
array *order, arrange(ment)*
as see *als*
ascrie *shout, cry*
at *from, at; to*
aunter *chance, adventure; risk, put in jeopardy*
austeren *bold, stern*
avauntward *forward guard*
avenaunt *seemly, noble*
avow *vow*
ay *ever, always*
ayer *go, proceed, march, wander, travel*

bachelor *young knight*
bale *evil, pain, sorrow*
banneret *senior knight, entitled to carry a banner*
batail *division of an army, battle*
bede *offer, proclaim*
beleve *leave, remain behind*
ben *to be; been; are*
bente *field, ground*
berde *beard*
bere *bear, carry*
berne *man*
bete *beat*

bide *abide, remain*
bird(e) *maiden*
blinn(e) *cease, stop*
blithe *glad, happy, calm*
blonk *horse*
borde *board, table*
(on)borde *aboard ship*
bore *wild boar*
bote *boat*
boun *prepare, go; ready*
bowr *bedroom, bower*
boy *knave, servant*
braid *hasten, go*
brand *sword*
braste *broke, burst*
brede *bread; roast, baked meat*
breme *fierce, wild*
bren(ne) *burn*
brent *burned*
breny *hauberk, mail corselet*
breste *breast*
brethe *anger*
brin(ne) *burn*
brint *burned*
brist *break, burst*
britten *beat down, broken*
broche *pierce, stab, spit*
brode *broad*
broder *brother*
brothely *fiercely, boldly*
brown *shining, brown*
burgh *town, fortress*
burlich, burly *stately, strong*

busk *go, hasten, prepare*
bustous *wild, strong*
but, but yif *unless, except*
by *by the time that, by*
bydene *together, as well*
(all) bydene *immediately*

capitain *captain*
carp *speak, say*
castel *castle*
certes *certainly*
charge *load, burden*
cheer *countenance, expression*
chef *chief*
cheftain *chieftain*
chese *choose, chose*
chevalry *chivalry*
cheve *achieve, attain, arrive at*
child *young man, child*
childer *children*
chis *make one's way*
cledde *clad*
clene *clean, bright, pure; completely*
clenlich, clenly *cleanly, completely*
clepes *calls, summons*
clere *bright, clean, pure; completely*
cleve *cut, cleave*
cog(ge) *ship*
comlich, comly *comely*
coronal *diadem*
corse *body*
cosin *relative*
cosin of kind *blood relative*
coste *coast*
coude *could, knew how*
courtais *courteous*
courtaisy *courtesy*
couthe *could, knew how*
cover *attain, recover, take*

cover up *get up on*
covered *armored*
curious *skillfully made*

dede *dead, death*
dele *deal out, give*
delt *dealt, gave*
dere *harm, injure*
dere *costly, dear*
derf *strong, dire*
destayn *destine*
deth(e) *death*
devise *divide*
dight *prepare(d), place(d), adorn(ed)*
do, don *cause, order*
douspeer *high nobleman*
doute *fear, doubt*
drayn *drawn, dragged*
dreche *delay, wait*
dredde *dreaded, doubted*
drede *dread, fear, doubt*
dreme *dream*
drerily *drearily, sadly*
drery *dreary*
drie *suffer, endure*
Drighten *God*
drive *go*
drow *drew, dragged*
duchery *duchy, dukedom*
durste *dare*
Dutch-men *Germans*

ech *each*
echon *each one, every*
eek *also*
eger *eager*
egle *eagle*
eier *heir*
elles *else*

286

encroche *invade, encroach*
enmy *enemy*
ere *before*
erl *earl*
erly *early*
erthe *earth*
escheve *achieve, obtain, get to*
este *east*
even *exactly, directly; even*
eves *edge of a wood*
eyen *eyes*

fader *father, sir*
fain *eager, glad*
fand(e) *found*
feld *field*
fele *many*
fell *fierce*
fend *fiend*
fer *far*
ferd *frightened, afeared*
fere *fear*
fere *companion*
(in) fere *together*
ferk *go, stride (forth), hasten*
ferly, ferlich *wonder; wondrously*
ferrom *distance*
(o)ferrom *from afar*
fers *fierce*
fersly, ferslich *fiercely*
feste *feast*
fewter *the spear-rest on saddle*
fey *dead, fated to die*
firth *wood, forest*
flamand *flaming, shining, gleaming*
flowr *flower*
fo *foe*
foine *duel, stab*
folde *earth, ground*

fomen *foemen*
fonde *try, prove*
fonge *take, seize*
for-thy *therefore*
forjousted *outjousted*
forray *plunder*
forset *besiege, attack*
found(e) *go, advance*
frain *ask*
fraist *try, seek, prove*
frap *company, troop*
free *noble*
freelich, freely *noble, nobly*
frek *bold*
freke *man*
freklich, frekly *boldly*
frend *friend, friends*
frendlich, frendly *friendly*
fresh *eager, strong*
freshliche, freskly *eagerly, strongly*
fro *from*
furth *ford, stream*

gab *tell lies, gossip*
gader *gather*
gain, gainest *quick, quickest*
(at the) gainest *by the quickest way*
galiard *jolly, bold*
game *pleasure, mirth*
gan *did*
gar(t) *cause(d), order(ed)*
gesseraunt *hauberk, corselet*
gird *go, go to; strike, attack*
give, gave *cause(d)*
glopin *be terrified, amazed*
gome *man*
gonfanoun *banner*
gonne *did*
gore *shirt*

Glossary

graith *go, prepare*
graithelich, grathely *readily, vigorously*
gree *victory, prize*
gref *grief*
gret *weep*
grete *great*
grette *wept*
greve *woods, grove*
greve *grieve*
gron *groan*
guerdons *rewards*
guie, guie(d), gui(de) *guide(ed)*

half *side, half*
harageous *bold, violent*
harlot *rascal, scoundrel*
hathel *noble, bold*
hautain *proud, pride*
hed *head*
hele *heal*
hele *hide, conceal*
hende *courteous, skillful, handy*
hendely *courteously, skillfully*
hent(e) *seized, took*
heraud *herald*
herberage *lodging*
here (herde) *hear(d)*
herken *hearken, listen*
herne-pan *brain-pan, skull*
herte *heart*
hertily, hertilich *heartily; mortally; cheerfully*
hest *command; promise*
hete (hette) *command(ed), promise(d)*
hethe *ground, heath*
heve *heave, lift up*
heved *head*
heven *heaven*
hew *hue, color*

hider *hither*
hie *hasten*
(on) hie *hastily*
hiely *quickly*
hight *called, promised*
hight *height*
(on) hight *on high*
hold, (held, holden) *consider(ed), regard(ed)*
hole *whole, sound*
hollich, holly *wholly*
holt *wood, forest*
hope *suppose, expect*
hove *wait, remain, stand, linger*
hundreth *hundred*

ich, ich a *each, every*
ichon *each one*
ilk(e), ilkon *each, every; same*
irous *angry, irate*
ivel *evil*
iwis *certainly*

jag *pierce, stab*
join *attack*
journee *day's work, day's fight, journey*

kaire *go*
keep *watch, heed, wait*
kidd *famous, well known*
kith *native land*
kithe *make known, declare*
know (knew) *acknowledge(d), recognize(d)*

laght *seized, took*
laine *conceal, hide*
large *distance*
late *expression, countenance*

leche *physician; to give medical attention*
lede *man, prince, nation*
lede *lead*
lees *lies, falsehood*
lef *dear, good*
lege-men *liege-men*
lele *loyal*
lely *loyally*
leman *lover, beloved*
lende (lente) *stay(ed), remain(ed)*
lende (lente) *grant(ed), give (gave)*
lene *lean*
lenge *stay, remain; live*
lenger *longer*
lenghe *length*
lepe *leap*
let *hinder, prevent, hindrance, delay*
leve *dear*
leve(d) *leave (left)*
lever *rather*
ligges *lies, reclines*
like *please*
liking *pleasure, desire; pleasing*
limm *limb*
limpe *befall, take place*
lithe *pleasant, graceful*
lithe *listen, hear*
long(es) *belong to; to long for, desire*
lordinges *lords*
lorn *lost*
lothly, lothliche *loathly, hateful*
lough *laughed*
Lumbardy *Lombardy*
Lyby *Lybia*

main *strong, important; strength*
mall *hit, hammer*
march *country, border, borderland*
may, *can, be able*

mede *meadow, mead*
mele *speak, say*
mene(d) *mean (meant), intend(ed)*
mene(d) *say (said), tell (told)*
mensk *courtesy, honor*
menskfully *honorably, courteously*
merk *go, march; proceed; allot, mete out*
mete *food, meal*
might *could*
mikel *much, large*
mo *more*
mod *mind, disposition*
moder *mother*
molde *earth, ground*
mon *must*
mone *moan, speak*
morne *mourn*
morrow *morning*
moste *must*
mot *may*
mot ye worthe *may you be*

ne *not*
ne . . . ne *not . . . nor, neither . . . nor*
needes *message, errand*
ner *near, nearer*
neven *name, tell*
nolde *would not, did not want to*
nomen *took, seized*
nones *occasion*
nother *neither*

of *by, from; of*
one *one, alone*
ones *once*
ought *owned, possessed*
outray *injure, outrage*
overling *overlord*
owe *own, possess*

owen *own*
ower *our*

palais *palace, castle*
paynim *pagan*
pece *piece*
persewed *pursued*
pight *adorned, placed, arranged*
pople *people*
press *go, hasten*
press *crowd, company*
prik *ride, spur*
priker *rider*
pris *excellent, choice*
proffer *offer oneself for battle, attack*
purpure *purple; purple cloth, dye*

quod *said*

raght *drew, pulled, took*
raik *go; proceed, set out; rush*
rank *strong, stout*
rathe *quick; quickly*
raunson *ransom, plunder*
real *royal; stately*
really *royally*
realtee *royalty*
reche *reach, offer, give*
reddour *fear*
rede (redde) *advise(d), read*
redily *readily, quickly*
redy *ready*
regn(e) *reign*
reme *realm*
renk *man*
rent *revenue, tax*
rere *rear*
rereward *rearguard*
rese *attack, rush*

resoun *reason*
reve *plunder, take*
rew *rue*
(him) rewes *it saddens him*
rewle *rule*
rewm *realm*
rewth *sorrow, pity, pain*
rich *strong, noble; wealthy; great*
right *adjust, set right*
right *straight, direct; directly*
riot *amuse oneself, plunder; amusement*
rit *tear, slash*
rive *rip, tear*
roo *peace, tranquility; wheel*
rout *company, troop*
roy *king*

sale *hall*
salue *greet, salute*
Sarazen *Saracen*
sayn *to say*
se *sea*
seek *go*
sege *siege, besiege*
segge *man*
seke *ill, sick*
seker *sure, certain; trust, swear*
sekerest *strongest, most dependable*
sekerly *certainly*
selcouthe *rare*
semble on *attack*
semble *assemble*
(him) seemes *he seems*
senn *since, then*
sere *various, many*
sese *cease, seize*
sesoun *season*
shalk *man*
sheer *shear, cut*

sheld *shield*

sheltron *troop, phalanx*

shend (shent) *shame(d), destroy(ed)*

shew *appear, show, to be seen*

shift *arrange, order, move about*

shire *bright, shining; fair, noble*

sho *she*

sholde *should, must*

shred *shredded, cut with scalloped edges*

sho *she*

sinne *since*

sithe *since, then, afterwards*

slee *slay, kill*

slo *slay, kill*

slogh *slew, killed*

so *as*

sodenly *suddenly*

solace *pleasure, rest*

somoun *summon*

sonder *apart, asunder; separate*

(in) sonder *asunder, in pieces*

soon *immediately*

sooth *truth*

soper, souper *dinner, meal*

sorte *company, troop*

soudeour *mercenary soldier*

sought *went*

sound *healthy; in safety*

sowdan *sultan*

spake *spoke*

speche *speech*

speed *succeed*

speke *speak*

spere *spear*

sprede, spredde *spread*

sprent *leaped*

sprong *sprung, broken*

squier *squire*

stale *troop, company*

steren *strong, stern*

sterte *leap, go*

steven *voice*

stiff *strong, stout*

stonay *astonish*

stounde *space of time, while*

stour *battle*

streme *stream*

strenghe *strength, stronghold*

stroy *destroy*

suite *group, company*

(in) suite *together*

sujourn *rest, sojourn*

surprised *captured, taken*

Surry *Syria*

swap *cut, slash*

swarth *grassy ground*

swelt *die, faint*

swilk *such*

swithe *fast, quick, very*

take *give, offer, take*

teen *sorrow, grief; grieve*

tere *tear*

there as *there*

there *where, there*

thider *thither*

thinkes *seems*

thir *these*

thirl *stab, pierce*

tho *then*

tho *those*

thole *allow, suffer*

thret *threaten*

thro *bold, strong; trouble*

throly *boldly, strongly*

tidandes *tidings, news*

tide *time; happen, betide*

til *to, until*

291

tinne, tint *lose; lost*
tite *quickly*
tithinges, tithandes *tidings, news*
togeder *together*
to-morn *tomorrow*
torfer *trouble, sorrow*
towr *tower*
traist *trust*
trechery *treachery*
tresoun *treason*
tresure *treasure*
trete *deal, treat with, bargain*
trew *true*
trewe, trewes *truce*
trewlich, trewly *truly*
trewth *truth, troth, pledged word*
trine *go move*
tristly *boldly, surely*
troufle *trifle*
trouth *pledged word, truth*
trow *suppose, expect*
trump *trumpet; blow on a trumpet*
Tuskane *Tuscany*

unsaught *hostile*
unsaughtly *with hostile intent*
unsound *injured, ill, not healthy*
unwinly *sadly, joylessly*

wandreth *trouble, sorrow*
ware *aware*
warlaw *warlock, wizard*
weed *garment, clothing; armor*
ween *expect, suppose; doubt*
weld *rule, control, wield*
wele *prosperity, joy*
welth *wealth*
wend *turn, go*
wend *supposed, thought*

wepen *weapon*
werily *wearily*
werray *make war on, attack*
wery *weary*
wex, wexed *grew, became*
widerwinne *enemy*
wight *strong; person*
(no) wight *not at all*
wightly *strongly*
wightness *strength, boldness*
wilne *want, desire*
wite *know*
with *by means of, with*
wo *woe*
wode *mad, crazy*
wolde *would, desired*
wonde *hesitate, doubt*
wonne *dwell*
work *do, make, effect*
worship *honor*
worthe *become, be*
wot *knew*
wrake *trouble, ruin*
wreken *avenge, wreak*
wroke *avenged, wreaked*
wrought *did, made, effected*
wye *man*

yare *ready*
yede *went*
yeld *yield*
yelden, yolden *yielded*
yeme *control, possess*
yere *year*
yerne *yearn, desire; eagerly*
yif *if*
ynow *many, enough*
yode *went*
yonge *young*